THE DOVECOTES OF HISTORICAL SOMERSET

by

John and Pamela McCann

with a Foreword by

Dr. R. W. Brunskill, OBE, FSA

S V B R G

SOMERSET VERNACULAR BUILDING RESEARCH GROUP

2003

Published in 2003
by the Somerset Vernacular Building Research Group
ISBN 0 9523824 31

The publication of this work has been made possible by generous financial
help from the following bodies:

THE COUNCIL FOR BRITISH ARCHAEOLOGY

THE MARC FITCH FUND

THE ROBERT KILN CHARITABLE TRUST

THE SCOULOUDI FOUNDATION

in association with

THE INSTITUTE OF HISTORICAL RESEARCH

THE COMMANDER DESMOND WILLIAMS BEQUEST

administered by

**THE SOMERSET ARCHAEOLOGICAL AND NATURAL HISTORY
SOCIETY**

Copies available from:

J. and P. McCann
Bristol Cottage, Greenhead, Sidbury, Devon EX10 0RH
Tel. and fax 01395 597428

Fergus Dowding
Yews Farm, East Street, Martock, Somerset TA12 6NF
Tel. 01935 822202

Printed in Great Britain by Direct Offset,
27c High Street, Glastonbury, Somerset BA6 9DR

This book is dedicated with gratitude to
Joanna Kinder, M.B., B.S., M.R.G.C.P., D.R.C.O.G.,
and her supporting team of National Health Service professionals,
without whose diligent care this study could not have been begun.

Foreword

by Dr. R. W. Brunskill, OBE, FSA

Dovecotes have always fascinated lovers of the countryside. In external appearance the tall, often cylindrical building with its unusual roof terminating in the neat cupola or louver, gives a sense of mystery. Internally the row upon row of nest-holes and the ingenious revolving ladder add a note of practicality. In the legends and literature of rural life the supposed importance of pigeons and their relationship to those whose social status was reflected in the possession and care of a dovecote provide a commentary on a part of the rural economy quite small in scale but quite large in significance.

Just over ten years ago John McCann published an article in which he set aside the legends and assumptions about pigeons and their accommodation, and examined afresh the whole story of the care of the pigeons, and the design in general and in detail of the dovecotes in which they were housed. The quite complicated story of the nurture of the pigeons and their protection from predators, whether winged or four-legged, was made simple – although some widely held, convincing, but incorrect theories were neatly demolished. In 1998 John McCann published a survey and commentary on the dovecotes of Suffolk, applying his general observations to the detailed study of such buildings in a county well known for its timber-frame, brick and clay lump.

Now John McCann and his wife, Pamela, have put forward the results of their research as represented in Somerset, a county in which stone predominates but in which brick and cob are also found. The design, construction and use of the dovecotes in the county have been carefully observed and recorded, and the general conclusions of study of dovecotes have been applied to the surviving examples in Somerset.

An appreciable number have survived to be recorded and explained, but such buildings are vulnerable. Charming they may appear, but they are difficult to use in modern farming or the domestic economy of houses of manorial or gentry status. It is good that the authors have prepared this study while the buildings do survive and it is heartening that they have provided the means whereby dovecotes everywhere can be understood and appreciated. Residents and visitors alike are very much in their debt.

R. W. BRUNSKILL

Contents

Illustrations

All photographs are by John McCann unless otherwise credited in the captions

Introduction

The dovecotes of Somerset have not been studied in depth before. In 1920 Arthur O. Cooke described eight of them in *A Book of Dovecotes* – all of which still exist. He lived at Edinburgh, and obtained his information by appealing for information in the press; then he re-wrote whatever came in from correspondents he had not met. So far as we know he did not visit any dovecotes in Somerset. More usefully, in 1921 the Right Reverend Ethelred Horne of Downside began to describe all the Somerset dovecotes which came to his notice. He wrote a five-page article about them for the *Somerset Year-Book 1923*, and continued to collect information. Hope Grange wrote a similar article for the *Somerset Year-Book 1937*.[1] Horne had many other archaeological interests, so his observations accumulated over the course of nineteen years. In 1940 he assembled his notes on the dovecotes he had observed with one or two photographs of each in a manuscript notebook, and deposited it with the Somerset Archaeological and Natural History Society.[2] Altogether he described thirty standing dovecotes, and briefly mentioned five others which had been demolished a few years earlier. The special value of his observations is that two of the dovecotes he described no longer exist; and about others he mentioned alterations which otherwise might be forgotten. Nevertheless, he did not find all there were, nor discuss any of them in depth. This survey describes and illustrates 49 dovecotes and pigeon-lofts in historical Somerset, assembles information about others which have gone, and identifies a few other buildings which have been mistaken for dovecotes.

ALTERED BUILDINGS
Anyone who looks at a dovecote today should be aware that large-scale pigeon-farming on the traditional pattern ceased some two centuries ago. The period of most rapid decline was during the French Revolutionary Wars of 1793–1815, as will be explained. Most dovecotes in Britain became redundant then or soon afterwards. Many were demolished or allowed to fall into decay. Others were adapted to small-scale production for household use, and others were converted to secondary purposes such as stables, cider houses and granaries. By interpreting these alterations, and seeing them against the background of changes in farming practice, we can sometimes see beyond their present condition to the dovecotes as they were designed and built.

Regrettably, the absence of this approach is the great weakness of most of the modern literature on dovecotes in Britain. Writers without experience of interpreting altered buildings describe dovecotes as they appear now, without trying to find out how they have changed since they passed out of economic use.

THE LOSS OF THE TRADITIONAL CULTURE
The keeping of pigeons for meat was formerly such a common practice in the countryside that it was not thought necessary to describe it in print. Some authors who were writing about the improved agriculture of their time included pigeon-

keeping for the sake of completeness, but it was only a minor theme, and most had little to say about it. They always arranged their material in hierarchies. Descriptions of livestock farming methods always began with horses and cattle, because they were regarded as proper subjects of study for gentlemen. Sheep were discussed next, pigs and goats briefly, and last came poultry. By the time the authors reached pigeons - if at all - they were running out of first-hand knowledge, so a few sentences copied from another book were usually all they could manage. The few exceptions, where a writer really had something to say about pigeon-keeping from first-hand experience are so important in this study that they will be quoted here where they are most relevant.

For five centuries large-scale pigeon-keeping was a prestigious activity of the nobility and gentry. When it ceased to be practised on that scale it almost ceased to be mentioned in print at all. Keeping pigeons for meat became a minor activity of tenant farmers and inn-keepers, and they had no reason to publish books about it. If any oral knowledge still existed by the late nineteenth century, it was this last phase of pigeon-keeping which was remembered. Dovecotes did not begin to interest historians and archaeologists until 1887, when R. S. Ferguson, Chancellor of the the Diocese of Carlisle, wrote an article about them in *The Archaeological Journal*.[3] By then the first-hand knowledge of how they had been used had been lost. For lack of better information he introduced some fallacies into the dovecote literature which have been copied from book to book, and article to article, ever since. They continue to appear in print to this day.

MODERN INTEREST

The twentieth century has seen a revival of interest in all traditional buildings; the study of dovecotes arises from this. Largely owing to the campaigning author and lecturer the Honourable Mildred Berkeley, who wrote and lectured about dovecotes from 1905, and Arthur O. Cooke, who extended her influence in 1920, they have come to be seen as valuable survivals from a past era.[4] Eventually most of them were given statutory protection as Ancient Monuments or Listed Buildings. Anyone who reads the modern literature on dovecotes will realise how often they are misunderstood – even by those who are actively engaged in protecting and preserving them. That is the situation we are in today.

BOUNDARY CHANGES

Since 1974 Somerset has been divided and re-assembled in different administrative areas. The historic county of Somerset consisted of what is now called Somerset, together with North Somerset, and Bath and North-East Somerset. When reporting on buildings which were built more than two centuries ago we need not concern ourselves with modern administrative areas.

Minor adjustments to parish boundaries have occurred over a long period. The dovecotes described here are identified by the civil parishes in which they are located today.

ACKNOWLEDGEMENTS

This study could not have been undertaken without the generous help and encouragement of people who are well-informed about Somerset's historic buildings – most of all John Dallimore and John and Jane Penoyre.[5] Mark McDermott kindly read the draft text and made many helpful suggestions. Other members of the Somerset Vernacular Building Research Group – Barbara Bowes, Jenefer Chesher, Stephen Croad, Penny Cudmore, Ann Heeley, and Tony Rodger – have made particular contributions. Others, some of whom we did not know earlier, have given valuable help – Mark Bailey, James Bond, Colin Brett, David Bromwich, Robert Croft, Fred Davis, David Dymond, Linda Hall, Pat Kington, Derek MacLaren, Michael McGarvie, Michael O'Connor, Frank Pexton, Mary Siraut, Klara Spandl, Bob Sutcliffe, Joan Thirsk and John Thorp. We would like to thank the Somerset Archaeological and Natural History Society, the Society for the the Protection of Ancient Buildings, and the staffs of the Somerset Studies Library, the Somerset Record Office and the National Monuments Record Centre for their help.

Above all we are grateful to the owners of these dovecotes, who have kindly allowed them to be examined, measured and photographed for this study. Readers can best express their appreciation by not intruding on their property without an invitation. Five dovecotes in Somerset are in public ownership – at Bruton, Dunster, Selworthy, Stoke-sub-Hamdon and West Bradley. Others are opened to the public occasionally.

A NOTE ABOUT WORDS

Doves are pigeons. 'Culver' is an old word for pigeon, once common in Somerset. In Somerset a building which housed pigeons was called a 'culver house', a 'dovehouse' or a 'pigeon-house' in the seventeenth century, as shown on pages 212-5. Shakespeare used the word 'dovecoat' in *Coriolanus*.[6] It occurs only once in the seventeenth-century documentary sources quoted, but by the eighteenth and nineteenth centuries the form 'dovecote' was becoming familiar. Nevertheless, 'dovehouse' and 'pigeon-house' continued to be the commonest terms used. Cooke greatly popularised the subject, using the word 'dovecote. Largely as a result of his work 'dovecote' has become the generally accepted modern term; it is convenient to use it here. (In Scotland a dove is a 'doo'; the building which housed them is correctly called a 'doocot').

In describing a building of two or more storeys in which only the upper cell housed pigeons the term 'pigeon-tower' is a more exact description. That cell is described as a 'pigeon-loft'. The less familiar terms used here are defined in the Glossary.

THE SCOPE OF THIS STUDY

This study is concerned primarily with historic dovecotes and with traditional pigeon-keeping, whose purpose was to produce young pigeons for food. Dovecotes are understood to be special-purpose buildings designed for that use. Small pigeon-lofts incorporated in other buildings such as houses and barns are covered only briefly, mainly because very little internal evidence survives to this day. Pigeon-lofts intended for ornamental or racing or courier pigeons are outside the scope of this study.

Glossary

Alighting ledge	A ledge below a tier of *nest-holes*, wide enough for pigeons to perch on, too narrow for a tree-nesting bird of prey.
Alighting step	A projecting slab below one nest-hole, serving the same purpose but not forming a continuous ledge.
Ashlar	Accurately squared hewn stone laid in regular courses with fine mortar joints.
Ashlar-pieces	Short vertical timbers rising from inner wall-plates or wooden pads on the head of a wall to the rafters.
Bath stone	An oolitic limestone of golden colour, quarried outside Bath. Used both in bulk and for dressings.
Beam-filling	Filling the spaces between rafters at the eaves with clay daub. This continued to be normal practice until the nineteenth century.
Blue lias	A blue-grey inferior limestone containing a variable proportion of clay – the commonest building material in central Somerset.
Butt-cogged	The simplest form of joint between a joist and a main beam. The end of the joist is sunk in a matching recess in the upper surface of the beam.
Cary stone	One of a highly variable series of yellow or buff fossiliferous limestones which underlie the south- eastern part of Somerset. Castle Cary is largely built of it.
Clay daub	Clay trodden with water and straw to make a plastic material which could be applied like plaster.
Chert	A hard stone consisting mainly of silica, found in the Blackdown Hills. It looks like flint but is more yellow in colour, and is extracted and used in large pieces, mostly as rubble.
Collar	A horizontal timber between two opposite rafters, above the tie-beam.
Columbarium	The Latin word for dovecote, favoured by churchmen.
Dendrochronology	The science by which timbers can be dated by measurement of their annual growth rings. For more detailed information see note 172.
Doulting stone	A fine-textured oolitic limestone, pale grey in colour, mainly used for quoins and dressings; it is quarried on the Mendips at Doulting.
Flight hole	A hole in the upper part of a dovecote through which pigeons could enter or leave. It can be of various shapes, but usually is just large enough for pigeons to pass through, too small to admit birds of prey.
Forelock	An unthreaded iron bolt with a slot through the end, secured by driving an iron wedge through the slot and bending it round over a washer.

Four-centred arch	A late medieval form – an arch formed of four arcs, two of short radius from centres on the springing line, and two of larger radius from centres below it.
Freestone	Stone which can be cut in any direction.
Glebe terrier	An account of the possessions of a rectory or vicarage, required at intervals by the Bishop.
Halved	Where two timbers cross, half the depth of each is cut out so that when they are jointed together the joint does not exceed the thickness of one timber.
Hamstone	An ocherous limestone from the Upper Lias quarried at Ham Hill, near Montacute, recognizable by its horizontal striations, and similar stone from the district.
Header	A brick laid at right angles to the wall, so that the end is exposed.
Inserted	Said of a feature such as a floor or window added after the original construction.
Joggled	Where two subsidiary timbers are jointed into the same main timber, not directly opposite each other.
Kneeler	A short piece of the coping to a gable, bonded into the wall.
Louver	A turret on the roof of a dovecote which allowed the pigeons to enter but which was designed to keep out birds of prey. Also spelled 'lover' and 'lovre' in contemporary sources. The spelling 'louvre' is a modern corruption, erroneously influenced by the Louvre in Paris.[7]
Medieval	In academic history the Middle Ages are assumed to have ended in 1485, but buildings changed more rapidly from about 1540 owing to major economic developments of the time. They are described as medieval if they were built before 1540.
Nest-box	A cavity for pigeons to nest in, constructed separately from the structural fabric.
Nest-hole	A cavity for pigeons to nest in, incorporated in the structural fabric of the building.
Ovolo	A moulding consisting of a quarter-round or quarter-ellipse, bounded by fillets. Of classical origin, introduced to English architecture in the late sixteenth century, common in the seventeenth century.
Perching ledge	A ledge on the outside of a dovecote provided for pigeons to perch on, where they could shelter from strong winds.
Pintle hinge	An L-shaped iron fitting driven into the jamb of a doorway, on which the door was hung.
Pipe	The contemporary word for a vertical funnel (usually of wood, occasionally of sheet metal) through which pigeons descended into the interior of a dovecote (see pages 171–2).
Pitching hole	An aperture in a wall at loft level, made to pitch hay or straw through from the deck of a wagon.

Potence	The modern name for a revolving frame which supported a ladder, which allowed the pigeon-keeper to search the nest-holes without descending. The word was not in contemporary use, but was introduced into English in 1887 by R. S. Ferguson, quoting from a description of dovecotes in France by E. E. Viollet-le-Duc.[8] Strictly, it means the bracketed arm of a gallows.
Putlog holes	Square holes at regular vertical intervals in a stone wall, used for scaffolding during construction, and later for maintenance. Loosely filled at other times.
Scarf	A joint by which two timbers are joined end to end.
Soffit	The under-surface of any architectural feature or component.
Splayed	When referring to a building, at the sides of a window aperture the fabric may be cut back at an angle to allow daylight to spread to all parts of the interior. Some doorways were splayed too. In connection with early carpentry, where two in-line timbers are *scarfed* together at an acute angle.
Squab	A young pigeon two to four weeks old, still unable to fly.
Stock-lock	A hand-made lock formed within a solid block of wood.
Stop	The end of a chamfer, often finished ornamentally.
Stretcher	A brick laid parallel to the wall, so that the long side is exposed.
Sub-medieval	A building is described as sub-medieval if it was built after 1540, but retaining medieval characteristics.
Tree-ring dating	See *Dendrochronology*.
Two-centred arch	An arch which can be drawn with two curved lines of the same radius from opposite centres.
Undersquinted	In carpentry, where two timbers meet at a *splay* (see above) which reverses at the ends to form a wide Z-shape.
Wall-plate	The horizontal timber along the top of a wall, on which the roof timbers are mounted.

Chapter 1
How dovecotes were used

WHAT WAS A DOVECOTE FOR?

All domesticated pigeons are descendants of wild blue rock doves, *Columba livia*, which in nature inhabit high cliffs, and nest in recesses in caves; they feed mainly on seeds. (They should not be confused with wood pigeons, *Columba palumbus*, a tree-nesting species which exhibits quite different behaviour). They breed five or six times a year, producing a clutch of two eggs. Both parents incubate them for seventeen days, and each clutch produces a male and female (hence the expression 'a pigeon pair'). The parents feed the young with partly-digested food ('pigeons' milk') until they are able to fly at the age of about thirty days. Then – in nature – the parents drive the young off the nest. The unfledged young birds are called squabs. As they approached the age at which they would fly the pigeon-keeper collected them from the nest-holes and wrung their necks. Squabs were the main product of the dovecote. There is no evidence that the eggs were consumed, except occasionally for medicinal purposes.

The young became ready to breed when they were four months old. Therefore the first pairs of the year, hatched in March or April, produced young the same year.

The practice of pigeon-keeping is extremely ancient, originating in the eastern Mediterranean region some 5,000 to 10,000 years ago. One may surmise that early hunter-gatherers collected the helpless squabs from caves. Domestication of pigeons can be traced back to the introduction of grain farming; it spread from region to region as grain farming spread.[9] The art of pigeon-keeping was to provide a building which pigeons would inhabit as in nature they inhabited a cave, to stock it with birds, and to collect the squabs just before they were ready to fledge. This was called *searching* the dovecote. The squabs were almost as large as adult birds, but as their flying muscles had never been used the meat was exceptionally tender. The purpose of a dovecote was to produce a supply of this succulent meat as a luxury for the rich. Contrary to some widely held beliefs the rich already had sufficient supplies of fresh meat *throughout the year*. (Modern studies show that in the Middle Ages members of the nobility and upper classes ate 2–3 pounds of fresh meat every day of the year, except on days when for religious reasons meat was forbidden. Seventeenth-century household accounts in Devon specifically state that sheep or cattle were slaughtered for the table in every month of the year).[10]

THE SEASONAL NATURE OF THE SUPPLY

It has often been stated that dovecotes produced fresh meat in winter, when otherwise their owners were dependent on salt meat. This is a double fallacy introduced by Ferguson in 1887, which has been copied from book to book by authors who have not studied the contemporary evidence. It continues to appear in popular articles. All later research has shown that there is no substance in it.[11] At all periods fresh meat was to be had throughout the year – by the wealthy. The meat of pigeon squabs was just a luxurious supplement. *It is impossible to appreciate the social significance of dovecotes unless their association with a luxurious way of life is understood.*

By comparison with other birds dovecote pigeons have an exceptionally long breeding season. The first young of the year were produced in March and April, and young continued to be hatched at intervals until October. Una Robertson has studied household accounts in Scotland in the eighteenth century, and has identified two periods of the year when the most squabs were produced, April to May and August to October – the periods when other kinds of fresh meat were easily available.[12] Two other studies of English household accounts from the thirteenth century to the eighteenth century confirm this seasonal pattern.[13] For instance, in 1412-3 Dame Alice de Bryene's large household at Acton, Suffolk, consumed 100 pigeons in April, 238 in May, 54 in June, 54 in July, 336 in August, 340 in September, 275 in October, and 147 in November – but none in December, January or February, and only 4 in March.[14] In the first century B.C. Varro wrote that (in the Mediterranean climate) pigeons do not breed between the winter solstice and the spring equinox.[15]

Occasionally some pigeons produced squabs in winter, but as a food supply the quantity was negligible. A wealthy household like that of the Earl of Salisbury in 1634 could buy in small numbers of winter squabs, and so could enjoy this delicacy out of season. Their rarity was expressed by the price paid, *four times* as much in February as in October.[16] Most gentry households relied on the squabs produced by their own dovecote. Effectively pigeons disappeared from the table before the end of November, and became available again after Lent the following year.

STOCKING THE DOVECOTE

In 1415 King's Hall, Cambridge, built a new dovecote. The building accounts have not survived, but one of the first 'expenses of the dovehouse' recorded was the purchase of four dozen live pigeons to stock it.[17] When a dovecote was stocked from another dovecote it was useless to buy mature pigeons and release them immediately – they would simply fly home again! In 1581 Leonard Mascall described how it was accomplished. Young pigeons which had not yet flown were introduced to the new dovecote: 'To make them tame ye shall give them first mil wheate, and then fetches [vetches], then Comine [cumin], for these graynes will make them love the house much, and sometimes to give them the gurgions [coarse residue] of sifted wheat. Let them not go forthe of the house fifteen dayes after ye have taken them and when ye give them leave to go forth, let it be towardes the evening, or in a troublesome or raynie time, to the end that they may return, and not tarry long forth of the dovehouse'. An eighteenth-century writer gave similar advice, saying that pigeons confined to the dovecote and fed well for twelve days would not fly away.[18]

In 1846 the naturalist Charles Waterton built a new dovecote to replace an old one at Walton Hall, Yorkshire. On a March day while the pigeons were out feeding he blocked the entrance to the old building and opened the new one. The pigeons took to it the same day, and by November of that year had produced several hundred squabs.[19]

FEEDING THE PIGEONS

In nature pigeons feed mainly on the seeds of wild plants. In traditional practice dovecote pigeons were left to find their own food from the surrounding land for most of the year. On meadow, pasture and heath this caused no harm to anyone. If permitted to they would also feed on cultivated crops, but these were not as vulnerable as might be supposed. Pigeons cannot alight and feed on standing corn. In 1726 Richard Bradley wrote about seeding: 'It is my opinion that they eat none of the grain but what happens not to be cover'd and consequently would never grow; for they do not dig as Rooks do, but peck as they walk from place to place; and then it is rather advantageous to the Farmer to give them Freedom of the Field'.[20] At periods when crops were vulnerable children were employed to drive away all birds; pigeons did not constitute a separate hazard. Ferguson and those who copied him drew a false analogy with social conditions in France, asserting that English peasants were oppressed by their lords' pigeons feeding on their crops. On the contrary, throughout history Englishmen of all classes have had the right to drive pigeons off their crops.[21]

In the depth of winter pigeons were fed with grain and pulses, and also for a short period after mid-summer when there was little food for them on the ground. This was called the 'benting time', because otherwise they would have had to subsist on bents, wild grasses.[22] Pigeons will eat green vegetation and small snails, but primarily they are seed-eaters. In farmyards and on cultivated land they could often find spilled or wasted grain. As Richard Bradley wrote in 1726, 'The farms which consist chiefly of Arable Land feed Fowls with little Expence: they will live upon the Offals of the Barn Door, which without them would be lost'.[23]

At Baltonborough in the 1450s manorial accounts record that beans for the pigeons were being grown on the demesne (see pages 216 and 218).[24] In traditional practice the pigeons were fed on the ground near the dovecote. By the early nineteenth century a change in the law and changes in farming practice made it necessary to confine them to the dovecote at certain times of year, and to feed them inside.[25] Special feeding platforms were installed which had not been necessary earlier, as illustrated at Dunster and Fairfield, Stogursey (figures 1 and 161). In 1807 Thomas Rudge estimated that one thousand pigeons ate a bushel (36 litres) of corn a day.[26]

MAINTAINING THE BREEDING STOCK

The pigeon-keeper 'allowed one flight to fly' – that is, he allowed one month's batch of squabs to grow to maturity to become breeding stock. Some retained the first flight of the year; others 'let the harvest flight fly'. The decision on which batch to retain for breeding depended mainly on the local food supply, but like

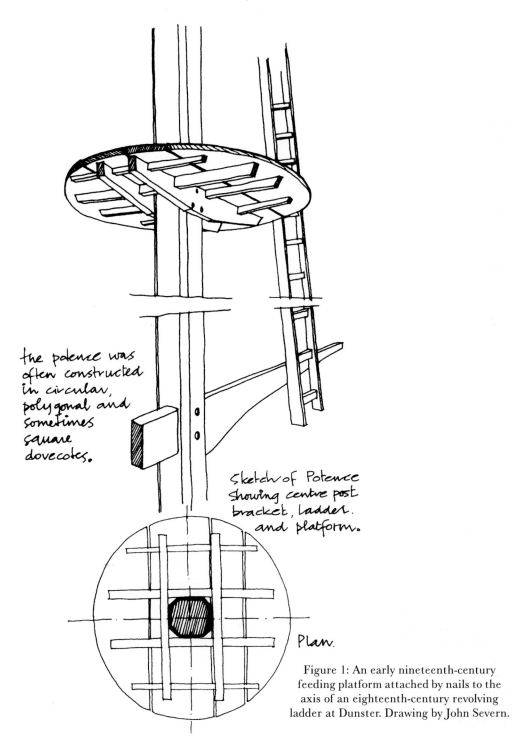

the potence was often constructed in circular, polygonal and sometimes square dovecotes.

Sketch of Potence showing centre post bracket, ladder. and platform.

Plan.

Figure 1: An early nineteenth-century feeding platform attached by nails to the axis of an eighteenth-century revolving ladder at Dunster. Drawing by John Severn.

everything else in livestock management it was a personal choice based on experience and judgement. The objective was always the same, to maintain a young and healthy breeding stock which would produce a sufficient supply of squabs for the kitchen or the market.

At the end of the breeding season the surplus males and the old birds which had ceased to breed frequently were culled. This operation was described by Leonard Mascall in 1581. A net was spread over the *louver* at night while the pigeons were inside. One man drove the pigeons out while another on a ladder examined the birds caught in the net, and either released them or wrung their necks.[18] The culled birds were not thrown away but their meat was tough, and could be made palatable only by prolonged stewing. Una Robertson has shown that they were given to servants.[27] Only the squabs were considered to be of any value.[28]

MINERAL SUPPLEMENTS

Like dairy cows, pigeons need a mineral supplement. By the eighteenth century pigeon-keepers had worked out that the main requirements were salt, calcium and grit, but their less scientific predecessors prepared what was called a 'salt-cat' from ingredients which sound disgusting to modern readers. The salt-cat or mineral supplement was hung in the dovecote for pigeons to peck from. If it was not provided they would peck lime mortar from buildings. Early descriptions indicate that much superstitious ritual went into preparing the salt-cat, and also into charms intended to drive away predators.

USES OF THE MANURE

The pigeon droppings were a valuable by-product. The traditional practice was to allow the dung to accumulate on the floor of the dovecote, and to remove it in winter to avoid disturbing breeding birds. In 1577 Thomas Tusser set out in verse the tasks for each month of the farming year. Under January he wrote:

> *Feed dove (no more killing), old Dove house repaire,*
> *Save dove dong for hopyard, when house ye make faire.*

Eighteenth-century and later writers, more aware of the virtues of cleanliness, advised removing the dung at frequent intervals. In 1669 John Worlidge claimed that one load of pigeon manure was worth ten loads of animal manure; it was economical to cart it to wheat and barley in the most distant fields. (This statement was much plagiarised by later writers who had not much of their own to write).[29] Also, it was sold to tanners for treating hides.

From 1560 pigeon dung was collected to make saltpetre for gunpowder. Until then England had been wholly dependent on imported gunpowder. Queen Elizabeth's Privy Council paid a Friesian immigrant, Gerhard Honrick, to reveal the method by which saltpetre was produced on the Continent. Agents of the Crown were given compulsory powers to collect pigeon manure from private dovecotes, and to dig up the earth floors, to be used in the production of saltpetre. In 1625 a Crown order forbade owners of dovecotes from paving the floors; nothing but 'good and mellow earth' was to be used. The abuse of these powers by a private monopoly appointed by Charles I caused much resentment, and became one of the matters in contention between Parliament and Crown. The orders were revoked in 1641.[30] In 1735 John Moore wrote 'The Salt-petre Men produce it after this Manner to this very Day'.[31]

WHITENING THE DOVECOTE

In all countries and at all periods the interiors and parts of the exteriors of dovecotes have been whitened. Ovid wrote (in Waterton's translation):

> *See, to the whitewash'd cot what birds have flown*
> *While that unwhitewash'd, not a bird will own.*[32]

Different reasons have been given for this practice – to guide the birds home in poor light, because it repels insects, or simply because pigeons like it. An eighteenth-century writer advised that the dovecote should be 'whitewashed within and without, that being the colour most pleasing to the pigeons'.[33] No one knows why pigeons are attracted by white surfaces, but it seems possible that in nature roosts which have been occupied for a long time were coated with guano, so rock doves came to associate a whitened area with security from predators. Practical pigeon-keepers knew only what their predecessors had told them, confirmed by their own observation and experience.

Early nineteenth-century writers such as St. John Priest advocated lime-washing the interiors of the nesting places to control infestation by insect parasites.[34] Today we often find traces of lime-wash inside dovecotes, and occasionally on the outside, but mostly it has been washed away by weather.

Chapter 2
Who could own a dovecote

Whether the Romans built special-purpose buildings for pigeons in Britain has not been established with certainty. Effectively pigeon-keeping was introduced – or re-introduced – by powerful Norman lords in the twelfth century. In this period to build and and stock a dovecote was an expensive operation which only the wealthy could undertake, so by common law pigeon-keeping became a prerogative of lords of manors, comparable with the right to build and operate a mill. Corporate landlords such as monasteries and colleges exercised the same rights within their manors. An informal relationship between the size of the manor and the number of pigeons became established. Only the most powerful lords with the largest estates built a dovecote with more than one thousand nesting places.

Some parish priests were permitted to keep pigeons too – at first in the upper parts of churches, later in freestanding buildings. In 1587 the limitation to lords of manors and parish priests was re-asserted in the Court of Exchequer.[35] Following the dissolution of the monasteries and chantries (1536 - 1548) about one-fifth of the land of England passed into secular hands. Many of the new owners built dovecotes on their estates to assert their position, irrespective of whether the religious houses or chantries had exercised the privilege earlier.

C. Northcote Parkinson observed that organizations erect their most resplendent buildings when their status is already in decline.[36] His argument might well be applied to the lords who built dovecotes. In the twelfth and thirteenth centuries feudal magnates exercised real power, but their dovecotes were plain, functional buildings. As the powers and privileges of landlords declined their dovecotes became grander. Dovecotes became symbols of high social status – or of asserted status. Increasingly, they were built of the best materials in the most fashionable style of the day. Effectively they encapsulate the history of British architecture in microcosm.

From 1619 a re-interpretation of common law allowed any freeholder to build and stock a dovecote.[37] The number of dovecotes increased – and wealthy landlords emphasized their status by building larger and more impressive ones. Despite some criticism that the numerous dovecotes already constituted a nuisance more continued to be built.[38] In 1655 one observer estimated that on average there were three dovecotes in every parish. (That is the only basis for the much-quoted – but very dubious – statistic that by then there were 26,000 dovecotes in England).[39]

By the early nineteenth century many tenant farmers had become pigeon-keepers, inserting pigeon-lofts in the roofs of barns, stables, and other buildings. Some erected what was called a 'standard box' (i.e. a box on a standard) in the middle of the farmyard (figure 5). By then the dovecote had ceased to be a symbol of high socio-economic status. Keeping pigeons for meat became a minor activity of farming households, like keeping poultry, and a convenient source of instant supplies for inn-keepers.[55]

Chapter 3
How dovecotes were designed

Unlike other domesticated creatures pigeons were free to fly away at any time. Sometimes they left en masse to join the flock from another dovecote, or to join a wild flock, for reasons which were not always apparent to the owner.[40] Consequently they acquired a reputation for being fickle birds which had to be wooed by providing favourable conditions. The difference between one dovecote and another in the same region often derives from the different opinions of their owners about what conditions were most congenial to pigeons.

PIGEONS' INSTINCTIVE RESPONSES TO BIRDS OF PREY

In level flight pigeons fly at more than 60 miles (100 kg) an hour, fast enough to elude all birds of prey except the peregrine falcon, but they are vulnerable to attack when perching, or when taking off and gaining height. Much of their behaviour is an instinctive response to this hazard. They choose high places on which to perch so that they can see birds of prey approaching, and they stay together in a flock because the more eyes there are, the sooner a predator will be seen. By diving from a high point they can pick up speed rapidly and get away.

THE PERCHING BEHAVIOUR OF PIGEONS

Like the wild rock doves from which they are descended they are well adapted to perching on sloping surfaces and narrow ledges; they have no difficulty in perching on pitched roofs. When not out feeding, and particularly in the early morning and evening, they warm themselves in the sun. In strong winds they find a sheltered place to perch – on the lee side of the roof, or on a string course or ledge on the lee side of the building. Near the coast and at other exposed sites the owner provided special ledges for that purpose.

SELECTING THE SITE FOR A DOVECOTE

Those who built dovecotes were guided by observation and a body of experience about the pigeons' requirements. They observed that pigeons instinctively avoid woodland and tall trees, where hawks can approach them unseen, so they selected an open site. They observed that pigeons naturally choose to perch on the roofs of tall buildings, so they built dovecotes high. In 1698 Roger North wrote 'the lovre should not be lower than the ajoyning buildings, and neerest trees; for the hauks will have an advantage to descend upon them, that cannot strike so well rising'.[41] They noted that pigeons were alarmed by sudden noise, so they sited them some way away from buildings which might generate noise. In a period when most manors had a water-mill, that was the place which generated the loudest noise, so the dovecote was always sited well away from it. Pigeons can become accustomed to a high level of ambient noise – as one may see with feral pigeons in a city centre –

but a sudden loud noise will put them all to flight. The loud roar when a mill sluice was opened was sufficient to scatter the pigeons.

PROTECTION FROM BIRDS OF PREY

The predators which pigeon-keepers were most concerned about were birds of prey. Contemporary authors described eagles, buzzards, kites, hawks, crows and owls as 'winged vermin' (together with other creatures which the more scientific naturalists of our day believe cannot predate on pigeons). The pigeons entered and left the dovecote at its highest point, the apex of the roof. This aperture was protected from predators by a turret called a louver. In many the sides consisted of parallel sloping boards six inches apart. Pigeons could alight easily on the boards and pass between them, but the larger birds of prey could not. Very few early louvers have survived to the present day, but there is a good example at Kelston (figure 2, opposite page 42). On other dovecotes the louver consisted of a stone cap raised sufficiently above the flight hole to admit the pigeons, while preventing other predators from entering (figure 176).

From the eighteenth century gamekeepers were employed on large estates to systematically destroy birds of prey with guns, traps and poison. Winged predators became less of a problem to the pigeon-keeper. From this period we notice that dovecotes in large estates have louvers of more architectural design, canopies designed as much for appearance as to exclude predators (figures 42, 146, 163 and 168). Some of these were fitted on much older dovecotes (figure 16).

PROTECTION FROM FOUR-LEGGED PREDATORS

In Britain until the eighteenth century the only land animals which harmed pigeons were polecats, martens, and domestic (or feral) cats. In 1347 at Standon in Hertfordshire the annual yield of a dovecote fell from seven shillings to two shillings; the auditors accepted the explanation that 'it was destroyed for most of the year by polecats which were caught afterwards and the doves re-stocked'.[42]

Little evidence remains of the devices which were used against them. Some dovecotes were surrounded by water-filled moats, now only identifiable (if at all) as dry earthworks. Polecats could sometimes climb the corners of a rectangular dovecote and enter at the eaves. At

Figure 3: This ledge at Charlton Mackrell was to prevent predatory polecats and martens from climbing the corners of a stone dovecote and entering at the eaves.

Charlton Mackrell the square dovecote has projecting stone slabs high on the corners to prevent polecats and martens from climbing (figure 3). Surviving examples are rare in Britain, but similar corner ledges are still quite common in France, where stone martens continued to be a hazard much later.

DESIGNING THE INTERIOR

When the owner or master builder took decisions about the design of a dovecote he was not consciously setting out to reproduce a natural cave, but observation and experience told him that pigeons instinctively choose to nest in dark places. Many dovecotes were built without windows, deriving sufficient light from the aperture through which the pigeons entered. If a window was provided it was small, usually only a narrow loop high in the wall.

Most early dovecotes had nest-holes of bulb-shape – a narrow entrance passage leading to a wider chamber within the wall. Arranging the chamber to one side of the entrance passage had the merit of making it darker, providing the pigeons with a greater sense of security. Other plan shapes were used – reversed wedge, L-shaped, simple rectangular box-shapes and others (figure 188). A pigeon-keeper would notice that some nest-holes were always left unoccupied, and would develop ideas about why some were less attractive to the pigeons than others.

Builders of early dovecotes provided as many nest-holes as the building would accommodate – from a foot or so above ground level (just high enough to be clear of rising damp) to the roof. By the eighteenth and nineteenth centuries other factors had to be taken into account, and fewer nest-holes were provided, as will be reported. It was desirable to leave no projections or horizontal surfaces inside which were wide enough for a bird of prey to perch on. Therefore any internal ledges were deliberately made too narrow to be used by tree-nesting birds of prey. Any which managed to get inside would eventually fall to the ground, where they could be despatched by the pigeon-keeper.

In 1682 the Rector of Clayworth in Nottinghamshire built a brick dovecote, and wrote about the design in his diary.[43] In 1698 Roger North discussed in detail how he designed his new dovecote at Rougham, Norfolk.[44] In 1726 the Reverend John Laurence described how he built a dovecote of cob in Northamptonshire.[45] Otherwise, few pigeon-keepers committed their thoughts to paper. The buildings themselves, where they survive in sufficiently unaltered condition, provide the best evidence of how they were designed.

THE INTRODUCTION OF BROWN RATS

Rats had been present in Britain since the Roman occupation, but these were black rats, *Rattus rattus* – a different species from the destructive rats with which we are more familiar, and entirely different in behaviour.[46] They were indigenous in south India, and could not survive in a temperate climate except as parasites in man's heated buildings. Black rats ate fruit and grain; they did not predate upon livestock, and they could not gnaw through building materials or hard containers. They were a nuisance in the towns but they were never widespread in the countryside. Early farming literature shows that they were not regarded as significant pests on farms.[47] Throughout the early part of the eighteenth century the churchwardens of Horsington paid a bounty for the destruction of all creatures which were then held to be vermin, including polecats, stoats, otters, foxes, hedgehogs, and all kinds of birds, but rats were not mentioned.[48]

Figure 4: The two species of rats which have had an impact on Britain, to the same scale. From G. E. H. Barrett-Hamilton and M. A. C. Hinton, *A History of British Mammals*, London, 1910-21. By permission of the British Library.

That changed entirely with the introduction of a new species, brown rats, *Rattus norvegicus* (figure 4). They were burrowing animals indigenous in eastern Asia, at the same latitudes as Britain. In the eighteenth century they spread overland to Russia, and were carried to Britain by ships from Baltic ports. The evidence has been discussed in detail elsewhere, but in brief it indicates that brown rats entered Britain at the port of London in the period 1720 - 1730, and first spread up the River Thames and its tributaries.[49] They were carried from port to port by coastal shipping, and from there spread up other waterways and drainage channels. We do not know exactly when they reached Somerset. Horsington is in the extreme south-eastern part of the county, thirty miles inland; the churchwardens' accounts there continued to record frequent payment of bounties for the destruction of vermin until 1761, but still rats were not mentioned.

To most pigeon-keepers the arrival of brown rats in a district was a disaster. Brown rats could get into most dovecotes by penetrating the gaps in walls of stone rubble, or by burrowing under them, or by gnawing the edges of the door. Where one rat found its way in it left traces which others followed; the building soon became completely infested. Rats ate the eggs and attacked the helpless young pigeons; within a short time the whole breeding stock would be destroyed. Some dovecotes fell out of use at this time and were never used again. There was a period of confusion before the behaviour of the new pests was understood, but eventually pigeon-keepers found that an effective defence was to block the lower tiers of nest-holes with stone, often plastering over them to form a smooth surface which brown rats could not climb. Blocked nest-holes may be seen clearly in figures 29, 45 and 69; they are present but less conspicuous elsewhere. Other dovecotes were altered in major ways to rebuild the nest-holes above the reach of rats (as at Norton-sub-Hamdon and Montacute). Dovecotes built after this time were designed from the outset to be rat-proof, either by arranging all the nest-holes at a safe height or by setting the whole pigeon-loft at first-floor level.

Figure 5: The type of small dovecote on a standard which was erected in farm-yards and inn-yards, known to contemporaries as a standard box, i.e. a box on a standard. The man is taking the squabs, wringing their necks, and handing them down to the women, who collect them in their aprons. From W. H. Pyne, <u>Microcosm</u>, London, 1805. By permission of the British Library.

Chapter 4
The decline of dovecotes

Existing dovecotes continued in use, and new ones continued to be built, until the French Revolutionary Wars began in 1793. The immediate effect on agriculture was that the price of wheat rose sharply. Average prices rose to nearly twice peace-time levels, eventually peaking at three times in 1812. The newly-formed Board of Agriculture issued a series of county reports; all the authors condemned pigeons as wasteful, arguing that they consumed more value in corn than their meat and manure were worth. In corn-growing districts dovecotes were closed or demolished. By 1798 John Billingsley, reporting on Somerset farming to the Board, could write '[Pigeons] are considered so ravenous and mischievous, that few are kept'.[50]

The trend continued. The remaining dovecotes fell into disrepair, or were converted to other purposes, particularly as stables, cider houses and granaries. In 1825 J. C. Loudon wrote that pigeons were 'scarcely admissible in professional agriculture, except in grazing districts, where the birds have not so direct an opportunity of injuring corn . . . Pigeons are now much less cultivated than formerly, being found injurious to corn fields, and especially to fields of peas. They are, however, very ornamental; a few may be kept by most farmers, and fed with the common poultry'.[51]

This was the great period of change. In districts where pastoral farming predominated dovecotes continued in use longer, but the scale of pigeon-keeping was reduced. A change in the law in 1827 clarified every farmer's right to shoot pigeons which were damaging his crops.[52] From that time every pigeon-keeper had to reduce his flock to the small number he could feed in the yard with other poultry. He had to feed them adequately at sowing and harvest times, or shut them in, to ensure that they would not raid his neighbours' crops. Feral pigeons and pigeons from other dovecotes tended to join the flock, and would occupy any vacant nest-holes. The only way to reduce the number of pigeons in a flock was to reduce the number of nest-holes. In some dovecotes a floor was inserted at mid-height, retaining the upper part as a pigeon-loft while allowing the lower part to be used for other agricultural purposes. (It was easily done, for the joists could be inserted in the nest-holes). In 1851 William Trotter expressed the attitude of many farmers when he wrote: 'I keep pigeons, and I have no hesitation in pronouncing them unprofitable; they, however, display so much character that I delight to see them'.[53]

Meanwhile at gentry houses the practice was growing of keeping ornamental pigeons for pleasure. For this purpose it was not necessary to provide a special-purpose building. A set of nest-boxes bracketed to a wall, or a 'standard box' (i.e. a box on a standard) was usually sufficient (figure 6). From this period the traditional open louver was replaced by groups of small flight holes, usually of inverted-U shape (figures 124 and 176, opposite p.187). These constricted entrances effectively

Figure 6: Small structures which were used to accommodate pigeons in the nineteenth century. Left: From J. C. Loudon, *An Encyclopaedia of Agriculture*, London, 1825. Right: From *Cassell's Household Guide*, London, 1869.

excluded birds of prey, but as they allowed pigeons to enter only one at a time they would not have been of much use earlier when hundreds of birds sought refuge from a predator simultaneously.

TRAP SHOOTING

The modern sport of clay pigeon shooting is a humane substitute for the earlier practice of shooting at live pigeons released from cages. This was a new development from about 1800. Shooting clubs were formed, and expanded rapidly, creating a large demand for live pigeons. Unscrupulous suppliers supplied it by stealing all the adult pigeons from dovecotes at night, leaving the young birds to starve. Charles Waterton's isolated dovecote was robbed repeatedly, so he demolished it and built a pigeon-tower close to the house, carefully designed to be thief-proof; the pigeon-loft was twenty feet above ground. He described the thieves' methods in 1839.[54] From that period isolated dovecotes were found to be too vulnerable to theft; many were demolished. New pigeon-lofts were built in protected positions, often within enclosed courtyards.

By the middle of the nineteenth century the traditional practice of keeping pigeons for meat was all but dead. When R. S. Ferguson became interested in dovecotes in 1886 all the examples he could find in Cumberland were disused or derelict. He could not find anyone who could tell him about the practice of pigeon-keeping from first-hand experience, so he took most of his information from less relevant historical works. He quoted at length from Viollet-le-Duc, a French architect who had written in the 1850s.[8] He assumed wrongly that what applied in France applied equally in England. English social structure and English law were entirely different from those of France. Ferguson retained a personal memory of coaching inns on the great north road which had kept pigeons as 'a ready viand for the sudden traveller' – but this was just the final stage of pigeon-keeping for meat. The coaching inns had gone into decline with the construction of railways in the 1830s and 1840s.[55]

We should be grateful to Ferguson for initiating the modern study of dovecotes and for undertaking the first county survey, but we should be aware too that he originated some of the persistent fallacies which have distorted English dovecote studies ever since.[56]

Chapter 5
The survey of Somerset dovecotes

The dovecotes described here have been arranged in approximate chronological order. The earliest ones are six or seven centuries old, they are all incomplete or much altered, and the surviving evidence is often difficult to interpret. Readers who dislike grappling with ambiguous evidence may prefer to start reading the survey at a later point, where more complete buildings are described. Norton St. Philip, on page 77, or Shapwick House, on page 118, are good points at which to start reading – returning to the earliest dovecotes later as familiarity with the problems of interpretation grows.

DIMENSIONS, DISTANCES AND ORIENTATIONS

Dimensions are given in the traditional English units in which the dovecotes were built. For consistency distances are expressed in yards and miles.

> 1 inch = 25.4 mm
> 1 foot = 12 inches = 0.305 metre
> 1 yard = 3 feet = 0.91 metre
> 1 mile = 1,760 yards = 1.61 km

The orientation of each building is stated exactly in the opening paragraph about each, and in the captions of exterior photographs. After that it is considered sufficient to describe each feature in terms of the nearest cardinal point.

STATUTORY LISTING

Unless otherwise stated all the buildings described here are Listed as Buildings of Special Architectural or Historic Interest, Grade II - the category in which 92 per cent of all Listed Buildings fall. Grade II* indicates a particularly good example, and often that the building has been preserved in unaltered condition. Grade I indicates buildings of national importance. In addition some of the earliest are Scheduled as Ancient Monuments.

A NOTE ABOUT GROUND LEVELS

Ground levels tend to rise over a long period owing to the formation of humus and the deposition of waste material. In ancient buildings the original floor level is often well below the surrounding ground. In this survey it has not always been possible to determine the original ground level, so heights are stated from present ground level.

A HEALTH WARNING

Anyone who investigates the interior of a dovecote should be aware of the danger of psitticosis. It is a serious lung disease, though fortunately quite rare, more often attributable to cage birds than to pigeons. The main danger is of inhaling the dust where an infected bird has died. Using a suitable protective mask is recommended.

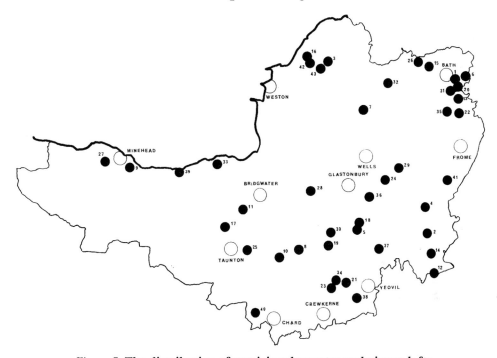

Figure 7: **The distribution of surviving dovecotes and pigeon-lofts**
by the parishes or towns in which they occur (in a few cases there are two in one parish)

1 Bath (Widcombe House)	17 Kingston St. Mary (King's Lood and Hill Farm)	29 Shepton Mallet
2 Bratton Seymour		30 Somerton
3 Brockley (Chelvey)	18 Kingweston	31 Southstoke
4 Bruton	19 Long Sutton (The Court House and Sutton Hosey Manor)	32 Stanton Drew
5 Charlton Mackrell		33 Stogursey (Fairfield)
6 Claverton		34 Stoke-sub-Hamdon
7 Compton Martin church	20 Monkton Combe	35 Wellow
8 Curry Rivel	21 Montacute	36 West Bradley
9 Dunster	22 Norton St. Philip	37 West Camel (The Old Rectory)
10 Fivehead (Cathanger Manor)	23 Norton-sub-Hamdon	
11 Goathurst (Halswell House)	24 Pilton	38 West Coker
12 Henstridge	25 Ruishton	39 West Quantoxhead
13 Hinton Charterhouse	26 Saltford	40 Whitestaunton
14 Horsington	27 Selworthy	41 Witham Friary
15 Kelston	28 Shapwick (Manor and House)	42 Yatton (Ham Farm)
16 Kenn		43 Yatton (Claverham)

WITHAM FRIARY (ST 744 410)

Witham Friary is near the source of the River Frome, within two miles of the Wiltshire border. The former dovecote was part of a Carthusian grange where the lay brothers lived. It is 60 yards south-east of the twelfth-century church, on land declining gently to the south. It is a rectangular stone building aligned east-west, 26 feet long by 19 feet wide, and 14 feet high to the eaves. It has passed through several uses since it ceased to be a dovecote, and has been comprehensively converted into a village hall. There is a door to the west, and large windows to west and north, all modern (figure 8). It is Scheduled as an Ancient Monument and Listed Grade II*.

Figure 8: The medieval dovecote at Witham Friary from the north-east. The window was inserted when it was converted to a village hall.

The fabric

It is built of coursed Forest Marble rubble, a mid-Jurassic limestone, with quoins of Doulting stone. It has modern pointing outside and lime mortar inside. There are two-stage diagonal buttressses at all four corners (figures 8 and 10). The west wall has been wholly rebuilt. A small extension has been added to the south.

The nest-holes

Only five nest-holes in the south-east corner remain open, but blocked nest-holes are visible elsewhere in the north, south and east walls (figure 9). (About fifteen were still open when Horne visited in 1939). They are arranged in regular chequer pattern one foot apart, and are 6 inches square at the entrance. In plan they are of asymmetrical bulb-shape, up to 10 inches wide and 18 inches from front to back. They were lined from the outset with lime mortar, of which substantial amounts survive. It is possible to trace 12 tiers of nest-holes, the lowest 3 inches above the present wood-block floor. So many have been destroyed in later alterations that the original number of nest-holes can be determined only by calculation, but this indicates that there were about 60 in a complete tier.

Figure 9: Witham: nest-holes in the south-east corner, some blocked, others still open. Most of the freestone ledge has been renewed, but part of the original ledge is shown at right.

Wallace Gill, the architect of the conversion in 1900, wrote that the original floor level was four feet below the present floor, so probably there were two or three tiers below those which are visible now. On this assumption it is likely that there were at least 840 nest-holes up to eaves level, and about 50 more in diminishing tiers in the gables, less those omitted for the doorway and window (if there was one), making a minimum of about 870. (Gill estimated that originally there were about one thousand nest-holes).

There is a single ledge of freestone round the inside of the three original walls, 4 feet 3 inches above the present floor and projecting 6 inches, with a chamfered soffit. Most of it is modern, but sufficient of the original ledge remains to indicate that Gill merely re-made as much of it as had been damaged in later uses of the building (figure 9). Allowing for the raised level of the present floor this would have been over 8 feet above ground originally. This is not an alighting ledge for the pigeons, as it serves only one tier of nest-holes. Comparable ledges have been found elsewhere.

The roof

This is mainly modern, set on rebuilt masonry well above the highest tier of nest-holes; it is clad with red clay tiles. Cooke reported in 1920 that 'it still retains its ancient timber-work', but as there is no evidence that he went there, this may be due to a misunderstanding. Some of the present roof timbers are old but not original.[57]

Origin and later uses

The schedule of Ancient Monuments states that this dovecote dates from *circa* 1300, and is a copy of the one at the Charterhouse of Mount Grace in Yorkshire. In 1544 it was included with Manor Farm (to the west) in a grant of monastic property to Sir Ralph Hopton. In 1747 it was mentioned in the deeds of Manor Farm as 'the stable, stall and garden lying on the other side of the street which hath been for many years held in severalty'. By 1812 the building was being used as a silk manufactory, but by 1846 it had been converted to a pair of cottages.[58] In 1900 it belonged to the Duke of Somerset; Wallace Gill converted it into a parish hall. He wrote that the building had not been previously recognized as a dovecote (figure 10), but that 'on clearing out a lot of modern cross walls and floors we found that this building was one large room, and that the whole of the walls had been originally lined with pigeon cots, formed in the main structure of the building, not added subsequently . . . The place had been very much pulled about several times in the last two hundred years, and no traces could be found of the original doors or of any windows. All the original work we found has been carefully preserved, but the west wall was in such a dilapidated state that we had to rebuild it . . . We were obliged to form new doors and windows, and these we managed to put in without disturbing any original work . . . The roof was about three feet below the present roof; traces of the line of this old roof can still be seen. All the existing pigeon holes were found walled up and plastered over; this was probably done a century or so ago when the place was turned into two cottages. I had all the plaster knocked off so that the cots can now be traced, and a few of them are opened so that their construction can be seen. Traces of grain were found in all the pigeon holes that were opened'.[59]

Gill suggested that the original door was in the west wall; in accordance with medieval practice it would have been small. The windows, if any, would have been small too, placed high in the gables. The pigeons entered by one or two louvers on the ridge of the roof.

The grain which Gill found in the nest-holes was not left by pigeons, for it is never found in undisturbed nest-holes elsewhere. It may have remained from use as a stable with loft above; or at some time the building may have been used as a granary.

We should be grateful to Wallace Gill for preserving so carefully all that was original in the building, and for describing what he did in converting it to modern

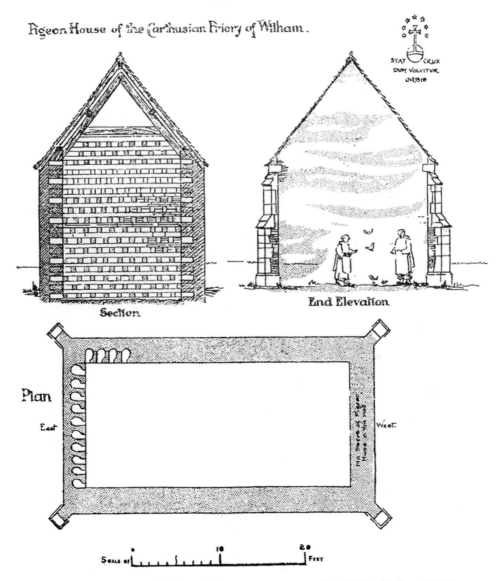

Figure 10: The dovecote of Witham Friary, as reconstructed in 1901 by Wallace Gill. From
Proceedings of the Bath Natural History and Field Club, volume 10, 1905.

use. (One might wish that modern conversions of dovecotes were equally scrupulous
of original features, and so well documented). Since then it has been used as a
photographer's studio, and at the time of writing a proposal to use it as a studio for
artists is being considered.

We are grateful to Michael McGarvie and Roger Powley for information about
this building.

PRIORY GREEN, DUNSTER (SS 990 437)

This round stone dovecote is at the foot of a steep hill to the north, now in a small garden approached from a modern road (figure 11), but formerly it was in the farmyard of Dunster Priory. The nearest contemporary building is the Priory barn 30 yards to the east. The dovecote is 24 feet in external diameter, and 19½ feet high to the eaves, reducing slightly towards the top in barrel-like form. The doorway faces east, and a high window faces south. Later tall stone walls abut to north and south. It is Scheduled as an Ancient Monument and is Listed Grade II*. It belongs to Dunster Parochial Church Council, and is open to the public at the usual times.

The fabric

It is built of roughly squared blocks and rubble of Devonian sandstone with clay mortar, with modern pointing. The wall is 3 feet 10 inches thick at the base. The outside exhibits traces of early lime render.

Figure 12: Dunster. The medieval door-frame appears to have been re-set at a higher level.

The doorway

The door-frame is deeply recessed within an aperture in the masonry 5½ feet high by 3½ feet wide (figure 12). It forms a two-centred arch made in three sections, and is undoubtedly medieval, both from the shape and the quality of the carpentry; it has survived so well because it is sheltered from the weather. It is 4 feet 5 inches high to the apex of the arch, and 1 foot 8 inches wide, deeply rebated on the inside for a door one inch thick opening inwards. The ledged oak door is old too, though not of comparable antiquity, probably of the eighteenth century. Over it are three old oak lintels 6 inches deep, respectively 10, 9 and 9 inches wide, the inner one shaped to the curvature of the wall, and one modern lintel outside. The jointed and pegged wooden threshold is 3 feet

Figure 2: A typical louver of the sixteenth and seventeenth centuries. The inclined boards allowed the pigeons to alight and pass through, but were so spaced as to prevent the larger birds of prey from penetrating to the interior. This is at Manor Farm, Kelston.

Figure 11: The medieval dovecote at Dunster from the south-east.

Figure 18: Wellow, the upper part. The nest-holes have been neatly filled with bricks, and the alighting ledges have been cut back flush to form a cool store for foodstuffs, with a new entrance to the north-west.

Figure 19: Wellow, looking up into the ancient roof. Nothing is visible of the structure outside the ring-purlin at mid-height, as it is masked by modern bituminous felt.

above ground level outside, and is 10 inches above the modern stone floor inside. From outside it is approached by three stone steps recessed within the aperture in the masonry.

The window

The unglazed window is 2 feet 4 inches high by 1 foot 11 inches wide, splayed inside, with a restored oak frame and one vertical oak bar. The sill is 15 feet above outside ground level, deeply splayed inside. Over it are four oak lintels 4 inches deep, respectively 7, 7, 7 and 11 inches wide; the inner one (which is of re-used timber) is shaped to the curvature of the wall. A single tier of nest-holes continues above the lintels.

Figure 13: Dunster: the upper part of the revolving ladder, and the upper feeding platform attached to its axis, with a splayed window at left.

The nest-holes

In the wall are tiers of nest-holes arranged in irregular chequer pattern. 15 tiers are visible, the lowest 3 feet 4 inches above the modern stone floor (figures 13 and 14). They are 6 inches square at the entrance, and of asymmetrical bulb-shape in plan, mostly turning to the left within the wall. They are irregular in

Figure 14: Dunster. Are there lower tiers of nest-holes, blocked and covered by plaster? Because it is Scheduled as an Ancient Monument it has not been possible to investigate.

width, with an average depth from front to back of 16 inches. 501 nest-holes are visible; there is reason to believe that others are blocked and concealed by plaster. The interior has been newly whitewashed.

Protective measures against brown rats

Below the visible nest-holes the wall is coated with old lime plaster. It is likely that other nest-holes are present under the plaster (figure 14). They would have been blocked and plastered over in the eighteenth century, when it became necessary to protect the stock against what was then a new hazard, brown rats. There is sufficient height for three concealed tiers above the modern floor, and there *may* be more below that level. Because this building is Scheduled as an Ancient Monument it has not been possible to remove plaster to investigate the possibility.

The revolving ladder and feeding platforms

This dovecote retains a revolving ladder (or *potence*), comprising a tapering axis of chamfered square section and two tapering horizontal arms which support a steeply inclined ladder. The arms pass through mortices in the axis and are

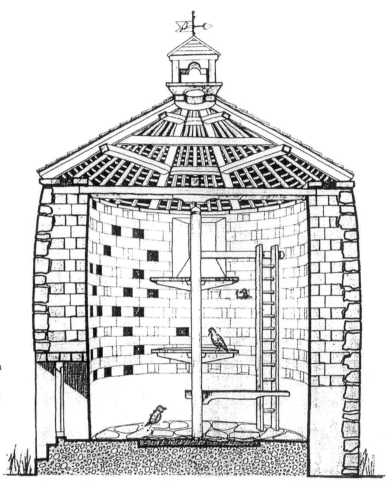

Figure 15: Dunster, a vertical section. By courtesy of Somerset County Council.

haunched and pegged (figure 15). A ladder of the type in common use in the early twentieth century is attached to the ends of the arms by hand-threaded wrought iron hook-bolts. Both bearings have been replaced since 1936, for Horne described the axis as 'having an iron pin at each end. The one at the base works in a hole in a stone in the floor, and the top one in a hole in an iron plate fixed to a cross beam' – i.e. it was pivoted in the same way as all other revolving ladders which survive in British dovecotes. Now there is a metal cone recessed eccentrically in the lower end of the axis, revolving on an iron pin mounted in a wooden beam sunk in the floor. The upper pivot is enclosed in a modern block of wood mounted under the cross-beam.

On the axis are two feeding platforms, the lower one 6 feet 3 inches in diameter and 6½ feet from the floor, the upper one 5 feet 2 inches in diameter and 12 feet from the floor, both fastened to the axis with nails. Their construction is illustrated in figure 1.

The roof and louver

On the head of the wall are two circular wall-plates or ring-beams of 4 x 7-inch horizontal section. The inner one has been partly renewed, but it includes undersquinted splayed scarfs characteristic of fourteenth-century carpentry.[60] The outer ring-beam is inaccessible. There are eight principal rafters, and a circular purlin or ring-beam spiked to the soffits of the principals (figure 15); some sections of it have been renewed with machine-sawn timber. The common rafters are modern. The present cladding is of blue slates (evidently replacing old stone tiles), with a modern louver and weather-vane.

Dating and development

There is no documentary evidence concerning the origin of this dovecote, but the carpentry of the door-frame and the ring-beams on the wall-head suggest that it is of fourteenth-century construction. This would associate it with the Benedictine priory, a cell of Bath Abbey, of which the barn oppsite is the only remaining building. It was dissolved in 1539, and the property then passed to the Luttrell family of Dunster Castle. The revolving ladder (apart from the altered bearings and ladder) is typical of eighteenth-century carpentry, and the feeding platforms mounted on it are typical of the early nineteenth century. The small doorway and revolving ladder show that this dovecote has never been adapted to a secondary use.

This dovecote and its revolving ladder have been the subject of much misinformation. Unaware of Horne's description of the original pivots, the Reverend M. McCormick, vicar of St. George's Church in the 1960s, arranged to have the lower pivot X-rayed by portable apparatus operated by Maple Ltd. for Shell's Thornton Research Centre. In an article he claimed that 'the Dunster dovecote is the only ancient one in the world which still has its revolving ladder in full working order on a 400 year-old bearing'! He also claimed that the dovecote 'was probably first built by the Norman baron de Bohun put into the Castle by William the Conqueror'. (There is no evidence to support this either). In 1989 a limited investigation of the ground below the lower pivot was undertaken by R. A. Croft, Field Archaeologist of Somerset County Council. He confirmed that the revolving structure had been re-set no earlier than the last quarter of the nineteenth century.[61] McCormick's misleading article was printed as a leaflet, which has been reprinted many times, and has been sold to visitors ever since.[62] A revised edition is being prepared.

The dovecote is illustrated in a painting of 1830 by S. G. Tovey, depicted among other farm buildings (figure 16); the high abutting walls were not present. It belonged to Dunster Castle estate until 1951-2, when much of the estate was sold off, and it was then acquired by Dunster Parochial Church Council. Evidently it was repaired and altered (while still in private ownership) after Horne's visit in 1936; it was re-roofed, a new louver was built, following the form of the decayed louver then still in place (as illustrated in 1830), and the revolving ladder was re-set on new bearings.

Major repairs were undertaken by St. Cuthberts in 1989, with the aid of grants

Figure 16: Dunster dovecote in 1830, with a pig-house abutting at left. A picture by S. G. Tovey in the Braikenridge Collection, by courtesy of the Somerset Archaeological and Natural History Society.

from Somerset County Council, Exmoor National Park Authority and English Heritage. The present weather-vane was erected, created to a new design.

There is a problem about the high doorway and floor. In ancient dovecotes it is common to find that the deposition of humus – particularly at the foot of a hill – has left the floor level inside well below the ground level outside. This effect may be seen at Cotehele and Anthony House in Cornwall, at Wellow, Stoke-sub-Hamdon and Shapwick Manor in Somerset, and at many other early dovecotes. Here the paved floor of the dovecote is substantially *above* outside ground level. Apparently in eighteenth-century alterations the wooden door-frame was raised. The lintels over it appear to have been re-set 1 foot 10 inches above their original positions. By this means the access has been raised above the level which brown rats could reach. The solid floor may have been built up too, using earth indistinguishable from the natural earth.

THE MANOR HOUSE, FARM LANE, WELLOW (ST 741 584)

Wellow is two miles south of Bath, on the north slope of the valley of the Wellow Brook. The cylindrical dovecote is 60 yards north of The Manor House, on land rising steeply to the north-west. Farm Lane passes a few yards to the south-east, beyond a thick hedge. The dovecote is 21½ feet in external diameter and 12 feet high to the eaves (see front cover). The original doorway faces south, and there is an inserted high doorway to the north-west. It is Listed Grade II*.

The fabric

It is built of roughly squared blocks of oolitic limestone rubble outside, and lime mortar. On the inside it is all of freestone, above a plinth of rubble 1½ feet high. The wall is 2½ feet thick. There are no windows; some small vents have been made later.

Figure 17: Wellow, the lower part. An alighting ledge was provided to every tier of nest-holes. The joists of the floor inserted in the eighteenth century are fitted in the seventh tier. As in many ancient dovecotes, the earth floor is well below the level of the ground outside.

The doorways

The doorway to the dovecote part is 4½ feet high by 2 feet wide, with a jointed and pegged hardwood frame and timber lintels (front cover and and figure 17).

Wrought iron pintle hinges are still present in the left jamb. As is often found in ancient buildings, the earth floor inside is 1½ feet below ground level outside. There is evidence that originally the doorway was set lower, before the ground level outside built up. The lintels have been raised about one foot; inside, two tiers of nest-holes have been cut away to gain the extra height.

The inserted doorway is 5 feet 11 inches high by 3 feet 3 inches wide, and is approached by three stone steps. Both doorways have nineteenth-century ledged and boarded doors.

The nest-holes

These are best seen in the lower part of the building; the upper part has been converted to a food store (figure 17). They are arranged in regular chequer pattern, formed in dressed freestone. The entrances are 5½ inches high by 4½ inches wide. Inside they are of asymmetrical bulb-shape in plan, 10 inches wide and 11 inches from front to back. All those in one tier turn to the left inside, all those in the next tier turn to the right. There are seven tiers up to joist level, with 37 - 39 nest-holes in a tier, lined originally with lime mortar. Below each tier is an alighting ledge 2 inches wide and 4½ inches thick.

The inserted floor and upper room

Timbers have been inserted in the seventh tier of nest-holes to form a floor 7 feet high, consisting of an elm beam 13½ x 11½ inches of horizontal section to which hand-sawn joists of 5½ x 2-inch vertical section are butt-cogged. Above this are 9 more tiers of nest-holes: nearly all of them have been filled with brick. The alighting ledges have been cut back very neatly to form a smooth vertical surface, and the surface has been whitewashed (figure 18, opposite p.43). This room is entered by the north-west doorway. Three splayed vents have been cut high in the wall, each 6 inches square.

The roof

On the wall-head are sections of an incomplete oak ring-beam 3½ inches deep by 14 inches wide, now much decayed. Four principal rafters rise from it to a round wooden frame in the apex of the roof, which at the time of inspection was obscured by modern timbers and a dense mat of cobwebs (figure 19, opposite p.43); later collars cross below it. At half-height a ring-beam in four sections is jointed and pegged to the principals. Below this the rafters are concealed by modern bituminous sarking; above it one can see eight substantial common rafters of oak in each quadrant, plus some modern timber. Two tie-beams of re-used timber are halved together, the joint strengthened with a wrought iron strap. This roof is almost complete. It is rare to find the roof of a medieval dovecote in such good order. It has been thatched, but originally it was built to support stone tiles.

Dating and use

This is a well-preserved medieval dovecote, very well built, so of high status. It is difficult to assign a period of origin to it, but the most prominent owner of the manor was Sir Thomas Hungerford, steward of John of Gaunt, who became the first Speaker of Parliament in 1377. He purchased Wellow and Farleigh in 1369, built Farleigh Hungerford Castle, and died in 1397. It seems not unreasonable to associate this fine dovecote with him.[63]

In the eighteenth century a floor was inserted and the internal wall surface above was made smooth to adapt it to a superior use, at considerable cost in skilled stonemasonry. As there is very little lighting, some cross-ventilation, and a wide door on the cool north-west side it was evidently intended for cool storage – whether of game, cheese or other foodstuffs cannot be determined now.

Including the blocked nest-holes above the inserted floor, originally there were 16 tiers of 43 nest-holes each, less some omitted for the door, about 680 in all. The lower tiers of nest-holes would have been vulnerable to brown rats, but they have not been blocked. This suggests that here the keeping of pigeons ceased when brown rats reached Somerset in the eighteenth century. There is no indication that the lower storey has been used since then, except perhaps for minor storage.

The small size of the nest-holes, the smallest found in this survey, suggests that this dovecote was not particularly successful in retaining its flock. That must remain a matter of speculation; but as dovecotes became more common later, mostly with more commodious nest-holes, the pigeons would have been tempted to desert.

Horne visited this dovecote in 1920, and described it much as it is now, except that 'a natural trunk of an oak supports the floor in the centre'. The wooden pads which located it below the beam are still present. The building was empty when examined.

THE PRIORY, STOKE-SUB-HAMDON (ST 471 174)

Stoke-sub-Hamdon is immediately north-west of Ham Hill, where the famous Hamstone comes from, and one mile south-west of the ancient Fosse Way (now the road A.303). The roofless cylindrical dovecote is situated 50 yards west-south-west of the hall of 'The Priory', and 4 feet west of an eighteenth-century stone barn which was gutted by fire in 1969 (figure 20). The site declines gently from west to east. It is 22½ feet in external diameter, and 13 feet high. The doorway is to the north, and there is a high window to the south. It is Scheduled as an Ancient Monument and is Listed Grade I. 'The Priory' belongs to the National Trust, and (with all the ancillary buildings) is open to the public at the usual times.

The fabric

It is built entirely of dressed Hamstone with lime mortar, re-pointed with modern mortar on the outside only. The masonry is in excellent condition on the north and east sides, deeply weathered on the west and south-west where it is exposed to driving rain. The wall is 3 feet thick, and has been repaired at the head; the hollow-moulded cornice is a modern replacement. There are four equidistant stepped buttresses of ashlar projecting 2½ feet at ground level, 2 feet 1 inch wide. On the west side of the south-west buttress is an inscription FT 1867 five inches high, deeply cut.

Figure 20: The dovecote of the National Trust complex at Stoke-sub-Hamdon called 'The Priory', from the south-south-east.

Figure 24: The dovecote of The Manor House, Pilton, from the south. The original entrance is nine feet above ground level. Note the original buttresses at left.

Figure 25: Pilton: the original doorway, blocked on the inside, showing the original lintels.

Figure 26: Pilton dovecote from the west, showing the inserted stable door and pitching doors.

Figure 21: Stoke-sub-Hamdon: the doorway from outside.

The doorway

The doorway has a two-centred arch formed from two large pieces of Hamstone which meet at the apex (figure 21). The crown of the arch is 4 feet 3 inches above the stone threshold; it is 2 feet 1 inch wide. There is a rebate 3½ x 3½ inches all round for a heavy door opening outwards, which had one hinge on the left when Horne visited in 1921. The present door opens inwards. The earth floor is well below the level outside.

The window

The window aperture is 2 feet square on the outside, slightly splayed to the inside. The sill is 10½ feet above the floor. There is no frame.

Figure 22: Stoke-sub-Hamdon: the northern part of the interior.

The nest-holes

There are 13 tiers of nest-holes in regular grid pattern, the lowest tier 1½ feet above the earth floor (figure 22). The entrances are 6 - 6½ inches high by 7 - 9 inches wide. They recede at a slight angle to the left, maintaining the same height, but opening out inside the wall to form a space 9 inches wide by 15 - 18 inches from front to back (figure 188). They were lined with lime plaster originally, of which substantial remains survive where it is protected from rain. There are 46 nest-holes in a complete tier; 20 are omitted for the door, and 9 for the window, making a total of 569. Apart from some in the topmost tier which have been blocked by modern repairs they are mostly in good order. On the west side there is a discontinuity in the tiers which may indicate a major repair (figure 23).

Figure 23: Stoke-sub-Hamdon: a discontinuity in the tiers of nest-holes on the west side.

The former roof

The former roof is reported to have been conical, but no evidence of it remains. Horne reported that the dovecote had been described as 'in a ruinous condition' in 1888, but in 1921 he found it in good order (though roofless).

Dating and origin

The two-centred doorway is undoubtedly medieval. This was never a priory - the name 'Priory Farm' dates only from 1902. It was part of the manor of Stoke Beauchamp. The Beauchamp chantry was established here in 1304. It consisted of a provost and four priests; it was in decay by 1444. It is unlikely that five celibates could consume the produce of so large a dovecote, so it was probably built for a wealthy secular lord with a substantial retinue. The manor has passed through many hands, and it can only be a matter of guesswork to attribute the dovecote to a particular lord. Some of the medieval lords of the manor had grants only for life, or otherwise had insecure tenure. Five lords who could have been its builders are

(1) Sir Matthew de Gournay, who held the manor from 1389; he died in 1406, (2) Sir John Tiptoft, who died in 1443, (3) Edmund Beaufort, Duke of Somerset, who held the manor from 1452, and died in 1455, (4) his son Henry, Duke of Somerset, who held it from then until his death in 1464, (5) George, Duke of Clarence, who held it from Henry's death.[64]

There is no indication that the building has been altered to protect it from brown rats. The wall is deeply founded and has tight joints, so it is inherently resistant to rat penetration, the only vulnerable point being the door. If the bottom of the door were covered by an iron plate, or if a dog were kennelled nearby this dovecote would be fully protected from brown rats. The small doorway (which was probably 4½ feet high when in use) shows that this dovecote has never been adapted to a secondary use - unless the discontinuity noted above indicates that a larger doorway has been inserted on the west side, and carefully closed again later. In the absence of information about repairs since the late nineteenth century this possibility cannot be explored. The National Trust purchased Priory Farm in 1946.

THE MANOR HOUSE, PILTON (ST 590 409)

Pilton is 2½ miles south-west of Shepton Mallet. The manor house, despite its eighteenth-century appearance, is of thirteenth-century origin and was formerly a house of the Abbot of Glastonbury. Alterations and improvements in the fourteenth century are well documented.[65] The dovecote is 19 yards west of the nearest part of the medieval house (now an outhouse), and originally stood isolated; a later range of outbuildings abuts to the east. It is 25 feet long by 22 feet wide; the original doorway faces south-south-east. The dovecote has been converted to a stable with hay-loft above; the present doorway and pitching hole face north. An inserted window faces west. It is situated on land declining steeply to the south, so that on the north side the height to the eaves is 15½ feet, but on the south the height is 24 feet (figures 24, opposite p.50, and 27).

The fabric

It is built of coursed blue and white lias rubble in lime mortar, with quoins of Doulting stone, with modern pointing. The walls are 3 feet thick. A pair of two-stage angle buttresses of Doulting ashlar 2 feet wide and projecting 2½ feet at the base extend 16 feet up the south-west corner and are fully integrated with the fabric. Scars in the masonry and the absence of quoins below that height show that similar pairs of buttresses at the other three corners have been removed. Two relieving arches low in the east wall (shown in pecked lines in figure 27), one containing a fragment of a doorhead, formerly led to an undercroft, to which there is no access now.

The original doorway

This is 4½ feet high by 2 feet 3 inches wide with a segmental arch, and is situated at the east end of the south elevation (figure 25, opposite p.51). The gradient of the site is so steep that although it is at floor level inside it is 9 feet above ground level outside. Inside the arch are two original oak lintels 5½ inches

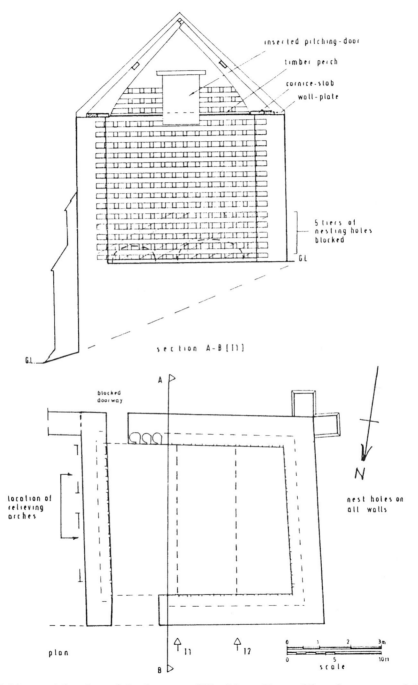

Figure 27: Measured drawings of the dovecote of The Manor House, Pilton, by courtesy of the Somerset Vernacular Building Research Group.

deep by 13 inches wide, still in good condition. It is blocked with rubble on the inside but exposed on the outside.

The inserted features

A floor was inserted to convert the dovecote into a stable with hay-loft above, which has been removed since. A doorway 7 feet 4 inches high by 4 feet 9 inches wide was made at the east end of the north wall, and at the other end of this wall a pitching hole 4 feet high by 2½ feet wide (figure 26, opposite p.51). A window 3½ feet square was inserted centrally in the south wall, which has been blocked later (figure 24, opposite p.50). An aperture for a window or pitching door 5 feet high by 4 feet wide has been inserted in the west gable, now louvred. A stone feeding trough has been built against the north wall, and another at the south-east corner, against the blocked doorway.

The nest-holes

Tiers of nest-holes in regular chequer pattern occupy the walls from floor to roof. The entrances are 6½ inches high by 5 to 7½ inches wide, separated at the sides by blocks of Doulting freestone 10 inches wide. Between the tiers are two courses of blue lias. The plan shape is unusual and is best illustrated by a drawing (figure 28). All the nest-holes in one tier turn to the left inside, all those in the

DETAILS

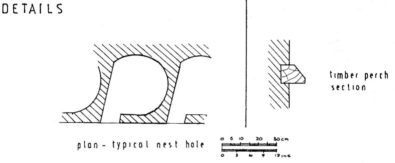

plan - typical nest hole

timber perch section

Figure 28: Details of Pilton: the plan of the nest-holes, and a vertical section of the wooden perching ledges originally fitted inside both gable walls. By courtesy of the Somerset Vernacular Building Research Group.

next tier turn to the right. 14 tiers are visible to eaves level, with 54 in a complete tier. Three more incomplete tiers are visible in each gable, of which 23 nest-holes survive in the east gable and 12 in the west. Above and on each side of these there were more nest-holes earlier, but they have been lost in later repairs. If there was an original window in the gable that has been lost too. The two gables would have contained about 70 nest-holes in diminishing tiers. 15 nest-holes were omitted for the original door, so originally there were about 811 nest-holes.

A square-edged cornice of white lias projects 4 inches at the head of each long wall. A chamfered ledge of timber formerly continued the same line across the gable walls (figures 28 and 29). A fragment of it remains *in situ* in the west wall, but elsewhere there is only the trench in the masonry in which it was set.

Figure 29: Pilton, the west gable wall. Note the tiers of blocked nest-holes at the bottom, and the fragment of wooden perching ledge at top right.

Protection against brown rats: the blocked nest-holes

The lowest nest-holes are set marginally below the present floor, which is paved with stone. All the nest-holes in the five lowest tiers have been blocked with stone to a height of five feet for protection against brown rats (figure 29). Others were blocked later when the building was converted to a stable. Above the inserted window in the south wall some of the nest-holes are distorted and blocked by repairs where the lintels subsided. Apart from these, and the incomplete tiers in the gables, most of the nest-holes are in good order.

The roof and former louver

The roof is in three bays. The main structure is original, with two pairs of principal rafters with short curved feet set on wide wall-plates and the cornice of white lias, with a short spur butting against it (figure 27). One principal has a jointed section at the base, chase-mortised into the principal and pegged through in much the same way as an arch-brace, evidently to form the same shape as the others. Apparently this was done because the available timber was not wide enough to form the spur. There is one trenched purlin in each pitch, and smaller extra purlins have been added later. The roof has been crudely tied against expanding forces with rough timber nailed to the principals, and more effectively by stainless steel rods. It is clad with nineteenth-century red clay corrugated tiles.

The louver was formerly mounted in the central bay. Its position can be deduced from later alterations, but is not sufficiently clear to be worth illustrating.

Dating and use

This is a medieval building of high quality, built for the Abbot of Glastonbury. Two comparable roofs within four miles had already been tree-ring dated to 1441 and 1466 respectively, so we thought it likely that this dovecote was built about the same time. In January 2003 the building was tree-ring dated; one core was taken from a lintel over the original (south) doorway, and eight cores from various roof timbers. The felling date was determined as 1441-6.[66]

The laying of a concrete floor in the ancillary building to the east has blocked access to the former undercroft. The conversion of the dovecote into a stable with a paved stone floor probably indicates that the undercroft has been filled in.

The inserted floor of the hay-loft was still present when the building was Listed in 1985; it has been removed since. It has left no evidence, because the joists were supported in the nest-holes. Horne visited the building in 1920, at which time the south and west walls were largely covered by ivy. He noted the south window still open at that date, and wrote 'the nest holes are in a bad state of repair and are difficult to count'. This building has been carefully repaired and conserved in recent years, and is now in much better order than it was then. It is used only for minor storage.

WEST BRADLEY COURT BARN, WEST BRADLEY (National Trust)
(ST 547 370)

This is 3 miles east-south-east of Glastonbury, on flat land. The dovecote was built early in the fifteenth century with a great barn of Glastonbury Abbey, as one construction. The barn continued in use, but the dovecote was allowed to fall into decay and collapse. The surviving part was eventually reconstructed as a cow-shed. In 1936 both were extensively repaired in that form.

The barn is orientated north-west to south-east. The dovecote was a square building against the south-east gable end, narrower in span and with a lower ridge. Its shape is still clearly outlined on the gable wall (figure 30). It is Listed Grade I with the barn, belongs to the National Trust, and is open to the public by written application.

Figure 30: West Bradley Court barn, West Bradley, from the south-south-east. The cowshed in the foreground has been formed from what remained of the dovecote.

The fabric

The barn and remaining parts of the dovecote/cowshed are built of blue lias rubble laid in clay mortar. The sides of the nest-holes are formed of freestone. Many of these have been replaced by modern freestone quarried at Doulting, laid in lime mortar. By the 1930s nothing remained of the south-west wall of the dovecote: it has been rebuilt as a plain wall without nest-holes.

The nest-holes

In the gable wall of the barn tiers of nest-holes are formed in chequer pattern. The nest-holes are 8 inches high by 5 inches wide, separated at the sides by freestone blocks cut to an approximate T-shape; they enclose a plan area 9 inches wide by 16 - 18 inches from front to back (figure 188). The tiers are separated by two courses of rubble 2½ inches deep. There are 9 nest-holes in each tier, the lowest 1½ feet above the earth floor. 11 tiers are visible within the roof of the cowshed, and another 4 tiers above it. Above that there is visible evidence of another tier, cut off horizontally by modern stonework. Originally there would have been 3 more tiers above that, diminishing in length as they rose into the roof, but they have been lost in modern repairs.

Figure 31: West Bradley. The nest-holes on the left have been restored. Those above the roof are more authentic.

The nest-holes which can be examined inside the cow-shed are mostly reconstructions executed in 1936, but their form was derived from the original nest-holes, as may be seen above (figure 31). The north-east wall includes a doorway 6 feet 4 inches high by 2 feet 11 inches wide, and is built up solid, without nest-holes, 3 feet 2 inches thick. The south-east wall is of coursed rubble to a height of 4 feet; above that nest-holes are formed much as in the wall opposite (although partly in chequer pattern, partly in grid pattern). There are 7 tiers, with 9 nest-holes in a complete tier, diminishing in length as they rise into the roof. The south-west wall is only 1 foot 5 inches thick, not sufficient to include nest-holes; it has an unglazed window.

The roof
The present roof was built in 1936, following the form of the cowshed which was present then. Most of the timber is modern, but three collars of hand-sawn hardwood have been re-used in it. It is clad with corrugated red clay tiles.

The origin – and twentieth-century restoration
The barn has been studied extensively, and has been dated to the early fifteenth century by scholars with expert knowledge of Somerset buildings.[67] The dovecote was structurally integrated with it, and so is of the same date. By the twentieth century little remained of the dovecote except a 'ghost' in the south-east gable wall of the barn, and some tiers of nest-holes in the south-east wall of the cow-shed.

John Macgregor, representing the Society for the Preservation of Ancient Buildings, found the barn semi-derelict in September 1932, and drew the Society's attention to it. The Society began a long campaign to have it repaired and preserved for future generations. Prolonged negotiations with the absentee landlords and their agent, the tenant, H.M. Office of Works, the National Trust, the Somerset Archaeological and Natural History Society and others continued for four years. Early in 1935 the roof collapsed. A public appeal was launched, and by May 1936 the restoration had been completed at a cost of £350. A major contributor who guaranteed the cost from the outset was Roger Clark of Street, Quaker and shoe manufacturer.

In the winter of 1937–8 the restored roof was damaged by a storm. By September 1939 it had been restored to the condition in which it was in October 1936. Throughout, most attention was concentrated on the barn; the dovecote/cowshed was barely mentioned. Finally it was presented to the National Trust.

Figure 32 may clarify what was present earlier. The side walls would have had nest-holes from 1½ feet above ground to the eaves – 14 tiers of 9 holes each. The gable walls would have had as many again, plus 30 - 35 in each gable. If there was a window at all it would have been small, probably a narrow loop in the south-east gable. Allowing for the nest-holes omitted for that and a low doorway there would have been about 550 in all.

The lower tiers of nest-holes may have been blocked for protection against brown rats, but twentieth-century rebuilding has confused the evidence. In the

Figure 32: Imaginative reconstructions of the former dovecote attached to West Bradley Court barn, by Pamela McCann.

south-east wall the lowest tier of nest-holes has been re-constructed 4 feet above ground, untypical of medieval dovecotes, and unlike the wall opposite (where the lowest tier is 1½ feet above ground). The north-east wall is thick enough to contain nest-holes, but has been re-constructed without any. Some of the rebuilt masonry appears to imitate the pattern of blocked nest-holes. If this interpretation of the limited evidence is correct the dovecote continued in use for its original purpose after the mid-eighteenth century.

THE MANOR HOUSE, WEST COKER (ST 520 135)

West Coker is three miles south-west of Yeovil. Pevsner wrote that this is 'an exquisitely beautiful small manor house'.[68] It is of irregular half-H plan (figure 33), fully described in the Listed Building report of 1984. It is of fifteenth-century origin, sensitively restored early in the twentieth century. The fabric is wholly of Hamstone, with lime mortar. There were two pigeon-lofts, widely separated. The main loft is at the south side of the house, partly in an attached tower and partly within the main building. There was a subsidiary pigeon-loft at the east end of the north wing.

The main pigeon-loft

The original entrance to the main pigeon-loft was a doorway (now blocked) in the east side of the tower 13 feet above ground, 5 feet high and 2 feet wide with an arched head, accessible only by ladder (figure 34). From it a stair leads to a small room on the second floor of the main house, lined from floor to roof with nest-

Figure 33: The Manor House, West Coker, from the east. The subsidiary pigeon-loft is indicated by a pointer. The larger pigeon-loft is out of sight to the left of the south wing.

Figure 34: West Coker, from the south-south-east. The original entrance to the main pigeon-loft is the arched doorway on the right side of the attached tower, behind a rainwater down-pipe. The positions of former flight holes are indicated by pointers.

holes. From there four steps lead up to the gable room of the tower, also lined with nest-holes. It has been adapted in the twentieth century, first as a study, later as a spare bedroom for grandchildren.

The nest-holes

Every vertical surface of this complex interior is occupied by nest-holes, simple box-shaped recesses arranged in a regular grid pattern (figures 35 and 36). All are 8½ inches high and most are 8½ inches wide or wider. The depths from front to back vary from 11 to 14 inches; they are painted white with modern paint. 287 nest-holes are still visible; others have been lost by the insertion of windows and other twentieth-century alterations. In 1936 Sir Matthew Nathan, the then owner, wrote in a letter to Horne that originally there had been about 400 nest-holes.

The flight holes

The pigeons entered by two or three round flight holes one foot in diameter. One is high in the south-facing gable of the tower, now glazed, with a wide stone perching ledge below (figures 34 and 36). A similar hole further west in the south elevation of the main building has been blocked with stone, but retains a stone

Figure 35: West Coker, inside the main pigeon-loft. Looking east: nest-holes above the internal stair.

Figure 36: West Coker, the main pigeon-loft. Looking south-east into the gable of the tower, showing a round flight hole and the nest-holes remaining after early twentieth-century conversion.

perching ledge. Below an early twentieth-century window in the east elevation of the tower is another wide stone ledge, possibly surviving from a third flight hole destroyed when the window was inserted. All are visible in figure 34.

The north-eastern pigeon-loft

Similar nest-holes remain in the east gable of the north wing, in an extension which was built about 1600 (figure 33). All are 8 inches high and 15 inches from front to back; the widths are about 8 inches, varying slightly. Only 25 are left; they too are painted white. A large window has been inserted in the gable, destroying some of them. It is not clear how many more there were earlier, but probably not more than a dozen. At the other end of the three-bay garret is a stone wall in which blocked nest-holes are visible, making a total of *about* 70. As this is in the roof there are no side walls, but it would have been possible to provide one or two tiers of nest-boxes made of wood or wattle and daub on the long sides of the loft, at the base of the roof.

This pigeon-loft is entered by a trap at the inner (western) end, with a stone stair. No evidence survives of the access for the pigeons.

Dating and use

The southern pigeon-loft was built with the oldest part of the house, conveniently near what was then the kitchen. The shape of its doorway is typical of the fifteenth century. In the east gable of the north wing the nest-holes are similar in size and shape, although this part of the house was built more than a century later. One can only speculate why it was necessary to have two pigeon-lofts so far apart. Was the smaller pigeon-loft part of a separate household? At the time common law required that when an owner died one-third of the house was to be allocated to his widow for the remainder of her life. Was the north wing extended about 1600 to provide a widow's dower? If so, the small pigeon-loft was intended to supply her with enough squabs to maintain the standard of living she had enjoyed earlier as mistress of the house.

The owner has kindly supplied a transcript of a steward's account concerning an earlier dovecote on the same manor for the year beginning Michaelmas 1308. He answers for 61 doves 'from issues of the dovecote without tally or witness', from which six were deducted for tithes. He records receiving 13¾d from their sale, at four doves for a penny. This indicates that most of the squabs produced were consumed within the household, and that the small surplus was sold.[69]

THE CHURCH OF ST. MICHAEL THE ARCHANGEL, COMPTON MARTIN (ST 555 570)

This is the only parish church in Somerset which includes a columbarium or pigeon-loft, although a few others are known elsewhere in England.[70] Compton Martin is on the northern slope of the Mendips. Pevsner described the church as 'Perhaps the best Norman church in Somerset'.[71] The chancel is Norman, of two rib-vaulted bays, with a fifteenth-century chancel arch. Above the vault the outer walls have been built up to form a pigeon-loft (figure 37). Inside it is 22 feet from east to west and 16 feet from north to south. The floor is irregular, composed mainly of the vaulting below; the height to the almost flat roof is 6 feet.

The fabric

This is of Pennant sandstone rubble in clay mortar, with dressings of Dundry stone. The outside has been much repaired, and pointed with lime mortar. The quoins of the columbarium are perceptibly different from those of the chancel below. The walls are 2 feet thick.

The doorway

In the north wall, at the west end of the loft, is a doorway 14 feet above ground, accessible only by ladder (figure 37). It is 4 feet 8 inches high by 2 feet 2 inches wide, with a four-centred arch. The head and jambs are chamfered on the outside, and are deeply rebated inside for a door. The door itself consists of three hand-sawn boards of irregular shape with strap hinges of wrought iron. It appears to be of eighteenth-century construction, but the hinges may be original.

The former flight holes

About 11 feet east of the doorway is the frame of a rectangular aperture 2 feet high by 10 inches wide, chamfered outside and splayed to the inside. It has been blocked with later masonry and plastered. An exactly similar aperture is present in the south wall, blocked and plastered in the same way; it is now enclosed by the roof of the south chapel (figure 38). Probably the flight holes were blocked during alterations recorded in 1858. (For comparison, in the fifteenth-century tower of Collingbourne Ducis church, Wiltshire, there is a flight hole of similar size leading to a pigeon-loft inside).[72]

Figure 38: A blocked aperture in the south wall, identical with that in the north wall (now enclosed by the lean-to roof of the south chapel).

Figure 37: The chancel of Compton Martin church from north-north-east, with the columbarium above. The doorway is at top right. To the left of it, above the buttress, is a blocked window or flight hole.

Figure 39: Compton Martin: nest-holes in the north wall. Photograph by Frank Pexton.

Figure 40: Compton Martin: nest-holes in the south wall. Photograph by Frank Pexton.

Figure 41: The dovecote in the churchyard of Norton-sub-Hamdon, from the north-north-east.

Figure 42: Norton-sub-Hamdon:
inside the doorway. Note the
inscribed date at lower right.

Figure 43: Norton-sub-Hamdon: the nest-holes re-built in the eighteenth century.

Figure 44: Norton-sub-Hamdon: the eighteenth-century roof, restored *circa* 1958. The metal collar at the apex is too small to be used for access by pigeons. Probably it replaced a larger one, of the same diameter as the upper ring-beam.

Figure 45: Norton-sub-Hamdon: the eighteenth-century louver.

The quatrefoil window

Centrally placed in the east wall is a quatrefoil aperture which with its surround is 2 feet square. It was not shown in a drawing of 1835 by J. Buckler.[73] An area of disturbed masonry in the south wall suggests that it was there originally, and was moved to its present position in the alterations of 1858.

The nest-holes

Integral in the north and south walls are nest-holes arranged in irregular chequer pattern. They vary in size and shape, but mostly the entrances are 6½ to 7½ inches high by 6½ inches wide. Inside the same height is maintained, but in plan most of them form a symmetrical bulb-shape 10 inches wide. From front to back they are about 13 inches deep, although in some the depth has been reduced by repairs to the outside. Blocks of Dundry freestone between the nest-holes form concave curves at the sides. The lowest tiers are level with the crown of the vault. In the south wall there are 39 nest-holes in four tiers (figure 39, opposite p.66). In the north wall there are 31 nest-holes in five shorter tiers (figure 40). The pattern is confused by later repairs, but probably there were 80 nest-holes or more in these two walls when built. It is possible that earlier there were nest-holes in the east and west walls too, but if so they have been lost in later alterations.

Origin and use

From the thirteenth century some parish churches have had pigeon-lofts. In the common law of England pigeon-keeping was restricted to lords of manors and parish priests, until this limitation was eventually ended by a change in the law in 1619.[37] The architectural details suggest that this pigeon-loft dates from the fifteenth century. It was described in a glebe terrier of 1606 as 'a pigeon house over the chauncell', but another of 1639 makes no reference to it, which may indicate that by that date it had fallen out of use.[74]

The number of nest-holes is small compared with manorial dovecotes. Even if originally there were nest-holes in all four walls there would not have been more than 140; but a celibate priest, who would have lived alone or with one colleague, could not have consumed as many squabs as a manorial household.

This loft has never been converted to other uses, and to this day it remains unused except for minor storage.

A more detailed article about this pigeon-loft, with more illustrations, was written jointly with Mark McDermott and Frank Pexton, and published in *Somerset Archaeology and Natural History* volume 143 of 2001. We are grateful to them, and to the Reverend Heather Matthews and Alan Thomas, architect, for their help.

THE CHURCHYARD OF NORTON-SUB-HAMDON (ST 470 160)

Norton-sub-Hamdon is half a mile west of Ham Hill. The dovecote stands 14 yards south-west of the church tower, just inside the western boundary of the churchyard (figure 41). It is 18 feet in diameter and 13 feet high to the eaves, with a doorway to the north. It is Listed Grade II*.

The fabric

It is built wholly of Hamstone. The outer face is of coursed quarry-faced blocks, the courses diminishing in depth towards the top and battering slightly, with a simple freestone cornice. The wall is 3 feet 2 inches thick. Putlog holes are visible on the north side – one open, others filled. There are four equally-spaced buttresses of ashlar, each 1 foot 11 inches wide and projecting 2 feet 1 inch at the base. The date 1762 is faintly inscribed on the north face of the south-western buttress.

The doorway

The doorway is square-headed, 4 feet high by 2 feet 2 inches wide, chamfered all round and rebated 2½ inches inside for a door, with wrought iron pintle hinges in the right splay. The door itself is modern. The threshold is of stone; inside, three stone steps descend to a concrete floor 1½ feet below ground level outside (figure 42).

The interior and nest-holes

The inside has been wholly rebuilt; it is dated by the inscription 1785, finely carved in the left splay of the doorway (figure 42, between pp. 66 and 67). Ashlar rises unbroken from the floor to a height of 5 feet 1 inch. Above that is a regular grid pattern of nest-holes formed of rectangular blocks, without alighting ledges (figure 43). Each nest-hole is a simple box-shaped recess 8 inches square and 15 inches from front to back. There are 11 tiers of nest-holes with 42 in a complete tier. Allowing for interrupted tiers above the doorway this makes a total of 444 nest-holes.

There is old whitewash inside and outside the nest-holes, but not on the ashlar below them.

The roof

The roof was rebuilt in the eighteenth century, and has been restored since. It retains its eighteenth-century form, although most of the present timber is machine-sawn oak (figure 44, opposite p.67). It comprises ring-beams on the wall-head and at the apex, a ring-purlin at mid-height, sixteen full-length common rafters and sixteen common rafters rising to two-thirds height, all pegged. It is clad with stone tiles with small flat-topped dormer windows to south-east and north-west, each formed by three ashlar blocks. One has a pegged oak frame with one vertical iron bar; they are unglazed.

The louver

At the head of the common rafters is a modern metal cylinder a little over one foot in diameter, too high to be examined. Over it is a round stone cap supported on four stone legs turned to an elegant urn profile (figure 45, opposite p.67).

Dating and development

The Somerset Archaeological and Natural History Society visited in 1921. 'Lieut.-Colonel Quantock Shuldham wrote to say that the dovecote was not included in the churchyard, though adjoining it. It remained part of the manor, the churchwardens paying him a yearly rent for its use. The court-house of the manor, long since pulled down, was not far away, which no doubt accounted for the position of the dovecote'.[76] The dovecote was given to the church in 1957, and repaired soon afterwards.

This is a late medieval dovecote which, unusually, is mentioned in an early document. A terrier of the copyhold tenants of the manor recorded in 1555 begins: 'Nicholas Newcourte holds there in right of Alice, his wife, late the wife of Robert Phillippeson, deceased, all the capital messuage, 13s. 4d., and site of the manor aforesaid, **situate and built by the parish church there** together with one close of land and pasture annexed to the same messuage, containing 3 acres and a half, called the Court Close, **one dovecote 6s. 8d., next the messuage aforesaid**, one water mill,' etc.[75]

The building was substantially altered in the eighteenth century. Originally it was built with slightly battered walls of quarry-faced Hamstone outside and rubble inside, in which the nest-holes were sunk. By analogy with other medieval dovecotes the nest-holes would have risen from just above ground level. When brown rats reached this district the lower tiers evidently proved to be vulnerable to them. In 1762 the buttresses were added for additional support, and the rubble masonry was re-pointed to provide better protection. Evidently this proved insufficient, for in 1785 the inner lining of stone rubble was stripped out and replaced by ashlar to a height of over 5 feet, with new nest-holes above. A simple freestone cornice was built at the wall-head, and a new roof was built. The small dormers and louver date from the same operation.

Horne reported that a trap-door closing off the exit for the pigeons was still present when he was there. It has gone now. The metal collar at the apex which now forms the entrance (figure 44, opposite p.67) is of too small a diameter to be used easily by pigeons. This seems to be a modern aberration; probably it replaces a larger 'pipe' of the same diameter as the ring-beam on which it was mounted, already in a decayed condition when found.

The dovecote is used now only for minor storage. Interested visitors may usually obtain the key at a cottage nearby.

In 1613 a glebe terrier of Norton-sub-Hamdon mentioned 'one little rounde dove house standing in the middest of the upper orchard'. Evidently this was another dovecote, as it went with the parsonage.[77]

CRANE FARM, PESTERS LANE, SOMERTON (ST 480 283)

The farm is on the southern edge of Somerton, on the south-west side of a small valley through which a tributary of the River Cary flows. The dovecote is on ground rising steeply to the south-west, 10 yards south-west of the medieval manor house. In its present form it is a cider house. It is rectangular, 28 feet by 19 feet, facing north-east towards the house (figure 46). There is a central doorway, two windows and a high loading door in the front elevation, and another loading aperture to the rear, all of which were made when it was converted to a cider house. It is now 17 feet high to the eaves, with a mono-pitch roof descending towards the rear, but earlier it was taller, and had a gabled roof.

Figure 46: The former dovecote at Crane Farm, Somerton, converted to a cider house. From the
north-north-east.

The fabric

It is built of coursed blue lias hammer-dressed to form exactly rectangular
blocks, with clay mortar. The high quality of the masonry can be seen best at the
north-west end, where it is protected by an extension built in the nineteenth century.
Elsewhere it has been pointed with cement mortar. The wall is 2 feet 8 inches
thick.

The original height

A low-level oblique aerial photograph taken from the east in 1924 shows the
cider house (as it was then) with a steep double-pitch roof standing above the barn
immediately to the east.[78] When it was designed as a dovecote it was desirable to
build it as high as possible, for pigeons are instinctively attracted to tall buildings.
It was converted into a cider house in the same form, but the great height was no
longer useful. In the 1950s the original roof and gables were demolished, the walls
were cut down, and the present asbestos lean-to roof was built. A mass of tumbled
masonry at the back and south-east end are all that remain of the parts cut off.

The present doorway, windows and high loading doors

The present square-headed doorway is 6 feet 10 inches high by 3 feet wide,
the lintel and jambs formed in Hamstone, with a rebate for a door opening inwards.

This was made for the cider house; doorways of early dovecotes were much smaller. Its insertion has destroyed any evidence of the original doorway. The existing windows and high loading door have nothing to do with its use as a dovecote, so there is no need to describe them here, except to say that all remaining detail is typical of the early nineteenth century.

The nest-holes

From 1 foot 8 inches above the earth floor the walls are occupied by a regular grid pattern of nest-holes (figure 47). The entrances are 6 - 6½ inches square; inside they are of reversed-wedge plan, 11 inches wide and 15 - 16 inches from front to back. 14 tiers are visible, and part of a fifteenth where the top of the front wall has been cut off. There are 60 nest-holes in a complete tier, making at least 900 nest-holes, less a small number omitted for the original doorway. Another tier may be missing above those which are visible. The nest-holes would have continued up the gables in diminishing tiers, so originally there were about 1,000 nest-holes.

The blocked nest-holes and inserted floor

The three lowest tiers of nest-holes have been neatly blocked with blue lias rubble dressed to size, with lime mortar, to a height of 4 feet 8 inches (figure 47). As discussed in Chapter 3, this was done in the eighteenth century to protect the stock from brown rats. Above that four tiers are still open in the long walls, three

Figure 47: Somerton. The south-east wall. Note the blocked nest-holes.

tiers in the end walls. A floor has been inserted 8 feet from the ground, consisting of two transverse beams and longitudinal joists of vertical section; only the north-western bay is still present, partly collapsed. Many nest-holes at this level have been used to support the floor timbers, and are partly blocked to fit the joists. Above floor level five more tiers have been blocked to prevent apples from rolling in, except above the cider press (still present against the rear wall). The surface has been lime-plastered. 14 feet above ground (or 6 feet above the inserted floor) the nest-holes are left open, because apples would not have been stacked above that level.

Dating and use

An eighteenth-century document refers to 'lands hereafter called and known by the name of Somerton Erleigh ... but now called Crane Farm'. John de Erleigh (the fifth) succeeded to Somerton Erleigh in 1337 as a minor, at which time it was first described as a manor. His lands were held by his mother Elizabeth until 1361. The manor house has been tree-ring dated to 1338, so it was built soon after she obtained possession.[79] The dovecote may not be contemporary with the house.

It is difficult to identify a later owner who could have built the dovecote, but two possible owners were William Neville, Earl of Kent, who died in 1463, and George, Duke of Clarence, lord of the principal manor, who held it from then until his death in 1478. (No original timber has survived in the dovecote, so there can be no confirmation from tree-ring dating). Soon after 1597 the estate was broken up and leased, and Crane Farm ceased to be a manor.[80]

The blocked nest-holes near the base show that it continued in use as a dovecote after the mid-eighteenth century. It was converted to a cider-house early in the nineteenth century, and remains essentially in that form. It is used now as a log-store.

THE TITHE BARN, STANTON DREW (ST 596 633)

Stanton Drew is in the north of the county, on the River Chew. The dovecote stands on level ground just south of

Figure 48: The former dovecote of The Tithe Barn, Stanton Drew, converted to a stable, from the west-north-west.

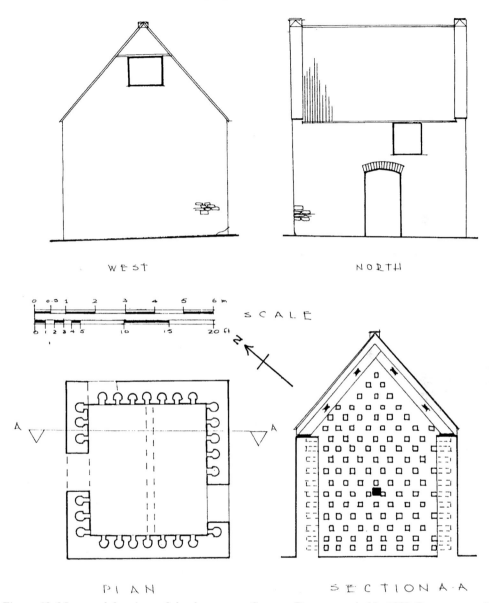

WEST   NORTH

SCALE

PLAN   SECTION A·A

Figure 49: Measured drawings of the dovecote at Stanton Drew, recorded in 1989. By courtesy of the Somerset Vernacular Building Research Group.

the Chew, and 8 yards south-west of the nearest contemporary building, the tithe barn of Rectory Farm, which has been converted into a dwelling. The dovecote is 19½ by 18½ feet, and 13 feet high to the eaves, with a doorway facing north-west, and windows facing north-west, south-west and north-east (figures 48 and 49).

The fabric

It is built of Triassic red sandstone rubble with dressings of oolitic limestone from the nearby Dundry quarry, with lime mortar, re-pointed with cement mortar. The walls are 2 feet 5 inches thick.

The doorway

This is 7 feet 4 inches high by 4 feet wide, with a segmental arch of blue engineering bricks, suitable for a stable. The original doorway is assumed to have been in the same position, but substantially smaller.

The inserted windows

Obliquely above the door is a pitching hole 3 feet square which has been converted into a modern window. There are apertures 3 feet square high in the south-west gable, and low in the north-east elevation, which also are now converted to modern windows.

Figure 50: Stanton Drew: nest-holes in the north-east gable wall.

The nest-holes

All internal wall surfaces are occupied by an irregular chequer pattern of nest-holes (figure 50). The entrances are 6 inches square. Inside they open out to form symmetrical bulb-shapes in plan, 10 inches wide and 13 inches from front to back. They are lined with lime mortar. The lowest tier is 1½ feet above the floor of stable bricks. There are 11 tiers of nest-holes to eaves level, with 32 in a complete tier, and 6 diminishing tiers in the gables. Of about 475 nest-holes originally, 440 are still present and open. There are no alighting ledges. The whole interior has been whitewashed, including the insides of the nest-holes.

The roof

The ridge of the pitched roof is aligned north-east to south-west. The gables retain raised coped verges, but the roof itself has been rebuilt in softwood, clad with double Roman clay tiles. When examined for Listing in 1985 it was clad with corrugated iron.

Dating and use

There is little evidence on which to date this building. When it was Listed, before modernization, it was reported to be in poor condition, and considered to be 'probably mid-fifteenth century'. In the nineteenth century it was converted for use as a stable with a hay-loft over. A floor was inserted, of which an axial beam and about half the joists remain *in situ*. It is used only for minor storage.

BLACKFORD HOUSE FARM, SELWORTHY (SS 925 453)

This cylindrical stone dovecote is delightfully situated on the floor of a wide valley, surrounded by wooded hills, on the northern fringe of Exmoor. The ground declines gently from east to west. The manor house of Blackford stood on the opposite side of the road to the south, but was destroyed by fire in 1875. The nearest farm buildings are to the east, themselves gutted by fire later; the present farmhouse is beyond them. The dovecote is 23½ feet in external diameter, and 15 feet high to the eaves (figure 51, opposite p.78). There is a large doorway to the south-west. It is Scheduled as an Ancient Monument and is Listed Grade II*. It belongs to the National Trust and is always accessible.

The fabric

It is built of coursed Devonian sandstone rubble with lime mortar. There are substantial remains of an external coat of lime render. The wall is 4 feet thick.

The doorway

The present doorway was made in the nineteenth century to adapt the building as housing for cattle when it had ceased to be used as a dovecote. It has destroyed all trace of the original doorway, which would have been small. It is 6 feet 3 inches high by 3 feet 6 inches wide, with a chamfered oak frame rebated for a door opening inwards. Over it are a shallow segmental arch of hand-made bricks and two oak lintels nearly a foot square, the inner one shaped to the curvature of the wall, the outer one modern. The earth floor slopes with the ground outside. The door is modern; it is fitted with an early nineteenth-century stock-lock removed from the door which it replaced.

The nest-holes

In the wall are 11 tiers of nest-holes in irregular chequer pattern, the lowest tier 2½ feet above the earth floor (figures 52 and 53). Each has an entrance 6 - 6½ inches square; inside the same height is maintained but the sides open out to form irregular bulb-shapes in plan, 10 - 11 inches wide and 18 - 22 inches from front to back. There are 28 to 32 holes in a tier; allowing for those omitted for the doorway

Figure 52: Selworthy: tiers of nest-holes and the flight hole. The holes in the conical roof are putlog holes.

there were about 320 nest-holes originally, of which 302 remain. The surface has been lime-washed to the base of the roof.

The roof

The roof is in the form of a truncated cone both outside and inside. It is built of diminishing courses of limestone rubble, with a round hole at the apex about 2½ feet in diameter through which the pigeons flew in and out (figure 52). Structurally it functions as a dome. This is a more stable construction than the corbelled roofs found in other early dovecotes in the south-west; probably that is why it has survived so well. The flight hole has been glazed to keep out the rain and to light the interior. Two tiers of rectangular holes are visible in the roof, but these are putlog holes. They have been left unfilled, and it is possible that some have been occupied by pigeons, but that was not their main purpose. (In French the same word, *boulins*, is used for putlog holes and nest-holes, which illustrates their similarity).

Dating and use

There are no datable features, but the general type and the thickness of the wall suggest that it was built in the fifteenth century – or earlier. Horne wrote that the manor belonged to the Cluniac priory of Montacute. The English Heritage re-assessment undertaken for the Monuments Protection Programme suggests an earlier origin, and states that the manor belonged to the Lovel family in the thirteenth century.

When Horne visited in 1936 the flight hole was covered by a flat stone and the roof was overgrown with grass. The adjacent field was called Culver Close. In 1944 Sir Richard Acland presented the dovecote to the National Trust. It was repaired in 1993.

The inclined site accounts for the height of the lowest tier of nest-holes; the plinth was built to a level above which they would not be affected by rising damp even at the highest part of the site. When brown rats became a hazard to other dovecotes in the eighteenth century these nest-holes were just high enough to be beyond their reach, so there was no need to alter them.

POND BARTON, NORTON ST. PHILIP (ST 771 559)

This large rectangular dovecote is situated on the crest of a hill (figure 54, between pp. 78 and 79). Formerly part of Manor Farm, it is now included in the garden of a modern house, Pond Barton (figure 55). It is aligned east-west, 24½ feet long by 19 feet wide, and 16 feet high to the eaves. The original entrance is in the middle of the south side. A later entrance has been inserted in the north side, near the east end. There is a window high in the east gable. It is Scheduled as an Ancient Monument and Listed Grade II*. It is open to visitors at the convenience of the owner.

The fabric

It is built of coursed oolitic limestone rubble with lime mortar, with dressings of Bath stone. The walls are 2 feet 5 inches thick.

Figure 56: Norton St. Philip: the original south doorway.　　　Figure 57: The original south doorway from inside.

The doorways

The original doorway is formed of eight massive blocks of Bath stone, below a relieving arch of rubble with a triangular keystone (figure 56). The arch is of a shape which Pevsner defined as Tudor, consisting of two short-radius curves and two straight lines.[81] It is 4 feet 10 inches high by 2 feet 8 inches wide, deeply chamfered all round, with a 2½-inch rebate inside for a door. The original pintle hinges are still present in the right jamb. Inside the arch is a massive timber lintel one foot square (figure 57). The threshold is of stone; the internal floor level is 1½ feet below that outside. The inserted doorway to the north is 6½ feet high by 3 feet wide.

The window

The gable window is 16½ feet above ground, estimated to be 3 feet high by 1½ feet wide. It has a four-centred arch with recessed spandrels (figure 58, between pp. 78 and 79). On the outside the stone has been cut away later to fit a rectangular grid, with holes for fixings above and below. Inside there are wide splays and timber lintels (figure 59).

The nest-holes

The whole interior is occupied by a regular chequer pattern of nest-holes from the earth floor to the roof (figure 59 and 60). The entrances are 7 inches square;

Figure 51: The National Trust dovecote at Blackford Farm, Selworthy, from the west.

Figure 53: Selworthy, facing south-east. Note the irregular spacing of the nest-holes, and the height of the lowest tier above the earth floor.

Figure 54: The dovecote at Pond Barton, Norton St. Philip, from the west-north-west.

Figure 55: The dovecote from the garden of Pond Barton, Norton St. Philip.

Figure 58: Norton St. Philip: the window in the east gable.

Figure 65: The dovecote at Shapwick Manor School, from the north-west.

Figure 70: The dovecote at Ham Farm, Yatton, from the north. Photograph by Pamela McCann.

Figure 72: The dovecote of Cathanger Manor, Fivehead, known as the North Barn, from the south-east.

Figure 59: Norton St. Philip: the east gable wall.

inside they are of asymmetrical bulb-shape, 12 inches wide and 18 inches from front to back. All the nest-holes in one tier turn to the left, all those in the next tier turn to the right. They have been originally lined with lime mortar. Up to eaves level there are 15 tiers each of 43 nest-holes, and in the gables there are 66 more nest-holes in diminishing tiers. Of the 698 nest-holes which were present originally, 633 are still open and in good order.

There are two ledges 2 inches wide all round the interior, 3½ inches deep with chamfered soffits, at heights 6 feet and 11½ feet (figure 60).

Figure 60: Norton St. Philip: detail of nest-holes and a ledge.

The roof and former louver

Below the eaves is a concave coving of freestone. The gables are coped, with moulded kneelers and cruciform ornaments. The roof structure is almost wholly original, of butt-purlin construction in three bays, with ashlar-pieces to the rafters. Slightly cambered collars span between the principals. In the middle bay there are two additional purlins which formerly supported the louver (figure 61). Above these purlins the upper parts of some rafters are omitted for the louver. It is clad with stone tiles.

Dating and use

This handsome dovecote was built about 1500 by the Carthusian Priory of Hinton Charterhouse. In 1523 the last Prior but one, John Batmanson, leased the grange to the Flower family, who continued to occupy it after the Priory was confiscated by the Crown in 1539. A survey of 'the Graunge or Farme of Norton' in 1638 records that it was owned by the Right Honourable Lord Craven, and occupied by Jeffery Flower. It lists 'A well built house with the site thereof with gardens, orchards, courts, yards, very faire barns, stables, granaries, malt houses . . . **with a very profitable pigeon house**'. This is the earliest documentary evidence of the dovecote.[82]

Figure 61: Norton St. Philip: the roof, showing the extra purlins in the middle bay which formerly supported the louver.

When Horne visited in 1921 it was in use as a pigsty. He wrote: 'Inside, the place has been much destroyed in fitting it up as a pigsty and it has evidently been put to other uses previously'. Either he was being unreasonably dismissive, or the superficial conversion to a pigsty has been carefully reversed since then. Now, apart from the loss of the louver and the insertion of the north doorway it appears to be original and unaltered. It is rare to find such a perfect example of a major monastic dovecote. The owner has installed a wooden floor about a foot above the original earth floor, clear of the walls, to preserve the building against modern use. It is used now for minor storage.

HOME FARM, KINGWESTON (ST 528 308)

Kingweston is 2½ miles north-east of Somerton. The dovecote is a roofless cylindrical building 10 yards west of the late eighteenth-century farmhouse, on the boundary between the garden and the farmyard. It is 20½ feet in external diameter, and stands 14 feet high (figure 62). The most visible entrance is a low doorway to the east but this is an insertion; the original entrance to the north-east has been blocked. There are windows to the south-south-east and east. The adjacent ground level has risen about a foot, so measured heights are unreliable.

Figure 62: The former dovecote of Home Farm, Kingweston, from the south-south-east, showing the inserted doorway and windows.

The fabric

It is built of coursed blue lias rubble with lime mortar, and is 3 feet 3 inches thick, with a plain coping. A substantial growth of golden lichen gives the stone a warm grey appearance when seen from a distance.

The doorways

The original doorway to the north-east was blocked on the outside when it was obstructed by the building of a stone garden wall, leaving a recess inside (figures 62 and 63). It is 3½ feet high by 2½ feet wide, slightly splayed towards the outside. Two original oak lintels 8 inches wide by 6 inches deep remain exposed, the inner one accurately curved to match the curvature of the wall. Another doorway of similar size was made facing east into the garden. It has straight timber lintels 3 inches deep, respectively 9, 8 and 5 inches wide, of which one is re-used. A jointed hardwood door-frame remains *in situ*, rebated for a door opening outwards, with one wrought iron pintle hinge visible in the right jamb, and a large wrought iron square staple for a draw-bar or bolt on the left. Old lime plaster survives inside the doorway where it is sheltered from rain.

Figure 63: Kingweston: the interior. The original doorway, now blocked, is at the left, the inserted doorway is at the centre.

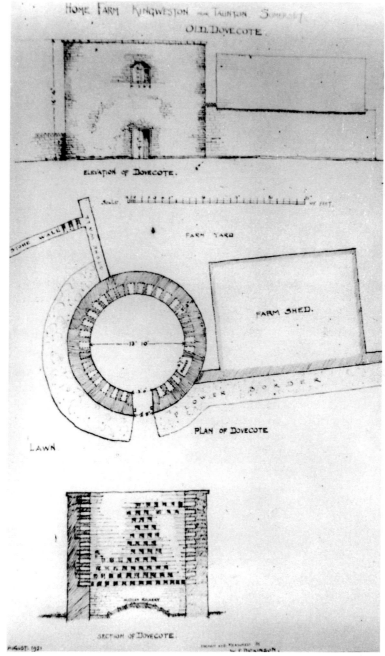

Figure 64: Kingweston: measured drawings prepared by W. F. Dickinson, F.R.I.B.A., for Ethelred Horne in August 1921. Enlarged from Horne's photograph. By courtesy of the Somerset Archaeological and Natural History Society.

Windows

The original window faces south-south-east, and is 9½ feet above ground. It is 3 feet wide by 2 feet high; the lintel and masonry above have been renewed. Horne's photograph of 1921 shows the lintel collapsing, and two courses of rubble and a plain coping above; since then it has been repaired. A later window has been formed above the inserted doorway, 3 feet wide by 2½ feet high, 8 feet above ground.

The nest-holes

From one foot above the earth floor tiers of nest-holes rise in chequer pattern. The entrances are 6 to 6½ inches square; inside, they are of the same height but vary greatly in plan. Most are of reversed-wedge shape, 9 to 11 inches wide at the back and 14 - 16 inches from front to back, but some are more bulbous in shape. There are 15 tiers, with 35 in a complete tier. 9 nest-holes were omitted for the door and 6 for the first window, so there were about 510 nest-holes, of which over 490 remain.

The blocked nest-holes

The three lowest tiers of nest-holes have been neatly blocked with hammer-dressed blue lias and lime mortar, to a present height above ground of 3½ feet, but probably 4½ feet when it was done (figure 63; they are not shown in Dickinson's drawings, figure 64). This part of the wall has been smoothly lime-plastered, but much of the plaster has weathered away.

Dating, use and modern repairs

The wall thickness and the horizontal section of the original timber lintels show that this building is unlikely to be later than the sixteenth century in origin. As some original intels remain *in situ* there is a possibility that it could be dendro-dated. Horne described it in 1921 as ruinous; stones were coming out round the windows and the original render was falling off. Inside it was in better condition; he reported that it had been repaired recently. The internal plaster, extending just inside the nest-holes, is of that time. The dovecote has been kept in good repair since.

While it was still in economic use the construction of a new garden wall obstructed the entrance, so a second doorway was made, of the same size as the original, and a second window above it. This dovecote was still in use for its original purpose after the middle of the eighteenth century, for the lower tiers of nest-holes were blocked to protect the stock against brown rats. As the doorway has not been enlarged this dovecote has never been converted to a secondary use. Since the roof collapsed a small garden has been made inside.

SHAPWICK MANOR SCHOOL, SHAPWICK (ST 418 386)

Shapwick is immediately north of the Polden Hills. This dovecote is situated 33 yards south-east of the manor house, now part of Shapwick Manor School, on land declining gently to the north-west. It is approximately circular, 22½ feet in external diameter, and 15 to 16 feet high to the eaves (figures 65, between pp. 78 and 79,

Figure 73: The North Barn, Fivehead, from the west.

Figure 76: The dovecote described as Central Somerset A, from the south-east.

Figure 80: The dovecote of Toomer's Farm, Henstridge, from the east-south-east.

Figure 81: Henstridge, showing nest-holes from floor to roof formed in the brick lining, the blocked west window, and the roof of stone rubble.

Figure 66: Shapwick Manor dovecote, from the east, with part of the house beyond.

66 and 67). The doorway and a high inserted window face west. It is Scheduled as an Ancient Monument and Listed Grade II*.

The fabric

It was built originally of roughly coursed blue lias rubble. In the least altered section a solid plinth stands 2 feet 3 inches high, with a moulded capping of Doulting stone. This is best seen on the west side (figure 65). The wall is 3 feet 8 inches thick. Three two-stage buttresses are irregularly disposed round the east side. Large sections of wall have been rebuilt in various phases, as shown in C. J. Bond's measured drawings (figure 67). The first phase of rebuilding, to the south, was executed in regular courses of squared blocks of blue lias; in this part the moulded plinth has been reconstructed. A later phase extends from 6 feet north of the doorway to the south-east buttress; this part has no external plinth (see back cover). Bond suggests that there may have been other phases of repair or rebuilding which are not easily distinguished now. Horne visited the building in 1920, and reported: 'A considerable portion fell down some years ago, and has been carefully replaced'.

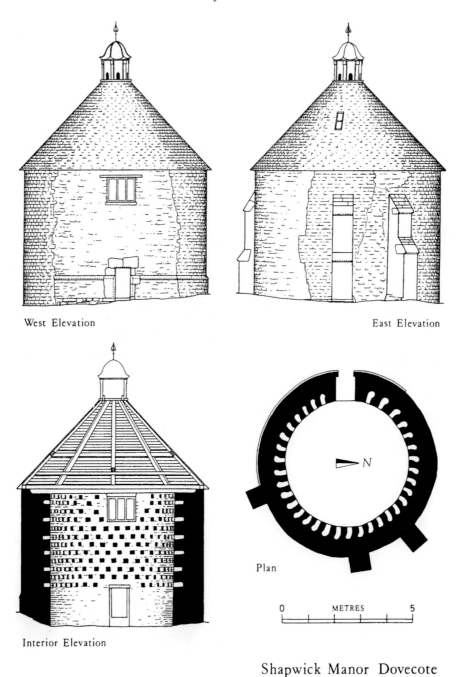

West Elevation

East Elevation

Interior Elevation

Plan

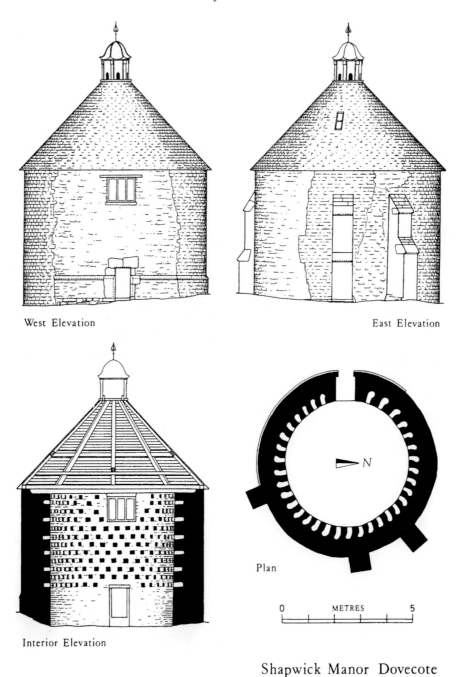

0   METRES   5

Shapwick Manor Dovecote
Somerset

C J Bond, 1989

Figure 67: Shapwick Manor dovecote, measured drawings by J. C. Bond, from *Proceedings of the Somerset Archaeological and Natural History Society*, volume 133, by courtesy of the Society.

Figure 68: Shapwick Manor, the doorway (and Pamela McCann for scale, height 5' 7½") with a two-metre rule.

The doorway

The rectangular doorway is 3 feet 7 inches high by 1 foot 11 inches wide, formed by large blocks of Doulting stone, and is chamfered all round (figure 68). The nineteenth-century ledged and boarded door is hinged on the left to open inwards, mounted on original wrought iron pintle hinges. The earth floor inside is one foot below the level outside.

The inserted window

This is 2½ feet high by 3 feet wide, situated not quite vertically above the doorway. The wooden frame and glazing date only from the 1930s.

The nest-holes

The interior is of solid rubble to a height of 2 feet 8 inches; above that is an irregular chequer pattern of nest-holes (figure 69). They are irregular in size and shape but, as shown in Bond's drawing, most are about 6 inches square and of an asymmetrial bulb-shape. All those in one tier turn to the left, all those in the next tier turn to the right. The depth from front to back ranges from 21 inches to 10 inches where they have been reduced by repairs to the outside. There are 14 tiers, with 37 nest-holes in a complete tier. 426 nest-holes are visible and open. Probably there were about 500 nest-holes originally. There are no alighting ledges.

Figure 69: Shapwick Manor, the interior. Blocked nest-holes are just visible at bottom left.

Protection from brown rats

The nest-holes in the two lowest tiers have been blocked with stone rubble to protect the stock from brown rats. In one section the two lowest tiers are omitted, the lowest nest-holes being at a height of 4 feet 7 inches - that is, aligned with the lowest *unblocked* tier in the older masonry. Therefore this part was re-built after brown rats reached the area.

The roof and cupola

Horne obtained a memorandum by a former owner, H. B. T. Strangways: 'On September 15th 1893 I went over the old Pigeon House with Andrew Stevens of Meare with the view to having the roof made water-tight for the winter . . . Stevens came on October 26th 1893 and took the slates off, and we then found that the roof was so rotten that it must all be renewed. On the dome of the house, inside, we found the date 1836 painted, and the dome was evidently made about that time. On the lead covering the dome the letters W.W. and H.+ A. with a cross between the latter were scratched with a point.

The old roof had four principal rafters, that is, two pair of couples, these were fastened to the wall plate at the bottom and to a round ring at the top, and again by circular side timbers; there were four secondary principals which did not reach the top, and the intermediate spaces were filled up with ordinary rafters which decreased in number towards the top. The slates were of a light grey colour, and had been hung on pegs in the old fashion.

Ivy had been allowed to overgrow the roof, and the water flowing down this had caused a great deal of the damage. I had the ivy killed three years ago, but the damage had been done.

The letters R.M. were painted in two places inside the dome'.[83]

The present conical roof is modern, clad with slate. The octagonal cupola has been reconstructed, with eight flight holes of inverted-U shape and a weather-vane.

Dating and use

It is impossible to suggest a date of construction except to say that this dovecote is medieval in origin. Bond concluded that many of the repairs had been only to the outer face of the walls, leaving the inner masonry intact. Strangways found that the dome was dated 1836. The fact that by 1890 'the old Pigeon House' was overgrown with ivy implies that it was already disused for its original purpose, although the care and expense he devoted to having the roof repaired indicates that he still took a pride in it. In 1937 Hope Grange reported: 'The owner told us, her predecessor had had all the ivy removed and the stones repointed and a new window inserted'.[84] The small doorway indicates that it has never been converted to a secondary use. Some pigeons are still in residence.

HAM FARM, NORTH END, YATTON (ST 419 673)

North End is in the plain between the Congresbury Yeo and the River Kenn, within 2½ miles of the Bristol Channel. The cylindrical dovecote stands on level ground 25 yards south of the early nineteenth-century farmhouse, close to the public road. It is 19½ feet in diameter, 11 feet high to the eaves (figure 70, opposite p.79). The doorway faces west. There are no windows.

The fabric

It is built of coursed blue lias rubble with clay mortar, completely covered by ivy. The wall is 3 feet thick.

The doorway

This has been enlarged for secondary use, and is now 6 feet high by 3 feet 1 inch wide, with timber lintels and a jointed and pegged oak frame. The door itself is early nineteenth-century, ledged and boarded with fine roll-mouldings.

The nest-holes

The whole interior is occupied by a regular chequer pattern of nest-holes from 1½ feet above the floor (which is of an early form of concrete) to the roof (figure 71). The entrances are 6 to 6½ inches high by 7 inches wide. Inside they are of the same height, forming asymmetrical bulb-shapes in plan, typically 11 inches wide and 19 inches from front to back. All those in one tier turn to the left, all those in the next tier turn to the right. There are 14 tiers of nest-holes, with 29 in a complete tier. Allowing for those omitted for the door there are 374 nest-holes in all. Before the doorway was enlarged there were nearly 400. There is a plain ledge 6½ feet above the floor, 4 inches wide and 1 inch thick.

Figure 71: The dovecote of Ham Farm, Yatton, the interior. Note the nest-holes blocked with rubble and lime mortar at the bottom.

Protection from brown rats

The four lowest tiers have been blocked with rubble and lime mortar to a height of nearly 5 feet, as a response to the introduction of brown rats in the eighteenth century. This alteration is clearly visible in figure 71.

The roof

The roof has been rebuilt in machine-sawn softwood, and is thatched, with a weather-vane.

Dating and use

Horne visited this dovecote in 1926, and described it as 'rather a poor specimen'. It is difficult to see why, for his photograph shows it much as it is now, covered in ivy. Even more curiously, it is Listed as 'late seventeenth/early eighteenth century'. The round plan, the 3-foot-thick walls, and the nest-holes of asymmetrical bulb-shape all suggest a medieval origin. It is similar to the dovecote at Home Farm, Kingweston, but less altered and in better condition. There is no original timber from which it could be tree-ring dated.

The lower tiers of blocked nest-holes show that it continued in use as a dovecote after brown rats reached Somerset in the eighteenth century. The present doorway has been enlarged from a smaller original doorway, but there are no other alterations to adapt it for secondary use. It has been used as a potato store, and is used now for storage of garden accessories.

NORTH BARN, CATHANGER, FIVEHEAD (ST 342 228)

This is the largest dovecote in Somerset, and perhaps in the West Country. It is as large as a great barn, and for a long time was used as one. It was formerly part of the major manor of Cathanger, above the scarp facing north over West Sedge Moor. Division of the property has included it with the garden of a small house converted from another farm building. It is situated on ground declining gently to the north, 30 yards west of the manor house, aligned east-north-east to west-south-west. It is 52 feet long by 22½ feet wide, and 16 feet high to the eaves (figures 72, opposite p.79, 73, opposite p.84, and 74). There are inserted wagon entrances in both long sides, and an inserted pitching hole in the south side.

The fabric

Most of it is built of coursed white lias rubble with lime mortar. On the east gable end there are alternate courses of squared blocks of North Curry stone and narrower courses of white lias, producing a striking banded appearance when seen from the manor house. The upper part of the west gable end has been rebuilt, and is clad with corrugated metal. At the top of the long walls several courses of squared blocks are visible, evidently rebuilt. Putlog holes at regular intervals are clearly apparent in the north long wall, less visible elsewhere. The walls are 2 feet 10 inches thick.

The original doorway, inserted wagon entrances and floor

The original doorway is lost, blocked when this building was converted for use as a corn barn. An area of newer masonry in the south side just west of centre indicates where it was. Near the middle of the south side a large entrance has been inserted, 9 feet wide and extending to the roof, splayed to the inside; the upper part is now closed with boarding (figure 73). Opposite it another entrance has been inserted, 5 feet 11 inches wide by 7 feet 7 inches high, unsplayed, with rebuilt masonry above. Between them is an intact threshing floor of timber, itself a rare survival. The remainder of the floor is finely paved with stone flags.

DOVECOTE,
CATHANGER, FIVEHEAD.

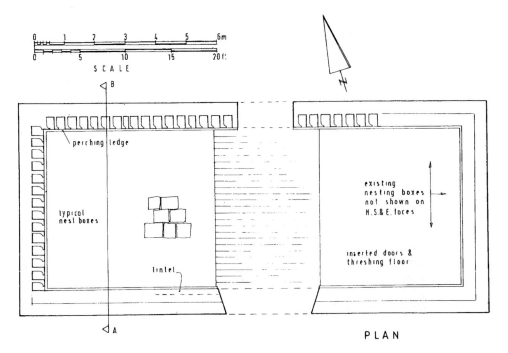

SCALE

perching ledge

typical
nest boxes

lintel

existing
nesting boxes
not shown on
N.S.& E. faces

inserted doors &
threshing floor

PLAN

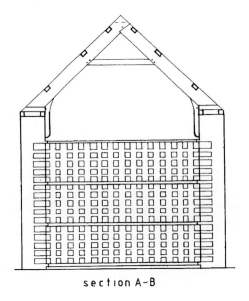

section A-B

Figure 74: Plan and vertical section of the dovecote of Cathanger Manor, Fivehead. By courtesy of the Somerset Vernacular Building Research Group.

The inserted pitching hole

A high pitching hole 4½ feet square has been made in the south side, between the inserted wagon entrance and the west end, and later blocked with boarding. No evidence remains of original windows.

The nest-holes

A grid pattern of nest-holes formed in hammer-dressed white lias occupies the whole interior from 1 foot above the floor to a height of 13½ feet (figure 75). The entrances are 6½ inches high by 7 inches wide, varying slightly. Inside, the height is the same; each hole forms an almost rectangular plan 11 - 12 inches wide and 13 - 16 inches from front to back (figure 74). All the entrances in one tier are offset to the left, all those in the next tier are offset to the right. There are plain ledges below the lowest tier of nest-holes, and above the fifth, tenth and fifteenth tiers (at heights 4½ feet, 9 feet, and 13 feet). They project 3 inches and are 3 inches thick.

There are 15 tiers of nest-holes, with 13 in each tier in the east gable end, making 195 nest-holes, and 14 in each tier in the west gable end, making 210. In the long walls the pattern of nest-holes is interrupted by the large inserted entrances,

Figure 75: The dovecote at Cathanger Manor, Fivehead, towards the north end.

but there is sufficient length for 36 nest-holes in each tier, making 540 in each long side. Some nest-holes would have been omitted for the original door to the south, say about 15. Therefore originally there were at least 1,470 nest-holes.

Other dovecotes of this size were divided into two cells by a cross-wall, with separate doorways and louvers, and were operated as twin dovecotes. There are examples at Newton-in-the-Willows, Northamptonshire, and Eriswell, Suffolk.[85] The partition wall across the middle provided extra nest-holes in each side, greatly increasing the total capacity. If Cathanger was originally in the form of two cells there would have been two additional sets of nest-holes in the internal gables, but 60 less in each long wall. Calculation indicates that there would have been at least 1,800 nest-holes.

However, the upper courses of masonry have been rebuilt. Within the existing building there is sufficient height for two additional tiers of nest-holes above the fourth ledge, providing another 198 nest-holes. The four gables would provide space for many more. Therefore the total may have been 2,000 or more! This is not improbable. At Newton-in-the-Willows there are 2,000 nest-holes, and at Eriswell there were about 1,800.

The roof

The parapet of the east gable has a plain coping, and an eroded ornamental finial. The roof has been rebuilt in the seventeenth century. The structure is in six bays, the principal rafters numbered with scribed assembly marks from east to west. There are three butt-purlins in each pitch, a square-set ridge-piece, and straight collars between the principals. All the common rafters and some main timbers have been replaced, and steel reinforcements have been fitted. It is clad with red clay double Roman tiles.

Dating and use

This dovecote was formerly part of the manorial complex of Cathanger. The manor house has a medieval core, but in its present form it was built in 1559 by John Walsh, Serjeant-at-law (equivalent to a Queen's Counsel today), who recorded the fact in an inscribed plaque in the south wall. (Later he became Chief Justice of the Common Pleas; he died in 1572).

The dovecote forms part of a symmetrical group west of the manor house, with a gatehouse in the middle and a barn to the south. The characteristic banded masonry occurs in all three and the manor house, suggesting that the whole complex was carried out by the same owner. It was mentioned in the *inquisition post mortem* of Walsh's grandson, Edward Seymour, in 1613: 'the capital mansion of Cathanger, **a dovecote**, garden, orchard and 390 acres of land in Cathanger, Fivehead and Curry Mallet'.[86]

The position of one original door is identifiable, and is off-centre. If there was a cross-wall there would have been another small door where the south wagon entrance is now. As the roof has been rebuilt no evidence remains of the former louvers.

In its present form this dovecote retains over 1,200 nest-holes (in 1939 Horne counted 1,236). Originally it had at least 1,470 nest-holes, and probably 1,815 - 2,000 or more. Thus it is the largest dovecote in Somerset. The dovecote which most nearly approaches it in size is at The Court House, Long Sutton, also much altered, which had about 1,087 nest-holes originally.

The building eventually fell out of use as a dovecote and was comprehensively converted into a corn barn. Wagons loaded high with sheaves of corn were drawn in from the south side, and could be drawn out empty to the north. The sheaves were stacked almost to the roof on the stone floors to each side of the threshing floor. During the following few months the corn was threshed with flails, and winnowed in the draught between the opposite entrances.

The owner reports that a major snowfall in 1964 caused part of the roof over the south entrance to collapse. It was found that the gables were tending to topple inwards, so major repairs were executed, including the insertion of modern timbers and steel reinforcing structures.

CENTRAL SOMERSET A

By request of the owner this dovecote is not identified. It is situated in the garden of a manor house of fifteenth-century origin, 25 yards east-north-east of the main entrance, on land declining steeply to the south-east. It is aligned north-south, 30½ feet long by 21½ feet wide, and is 17 feet high to the eaves (figure 76, opposite p.84). The original entrance is in the south end, with a later window above. It has been comprehensively converted into a coach-house with a hay-loft or granary above. Some two-thirds of the floor has been built up to align with the higher ground level at the north end, and double doors have been inserted there, with a loading door over (figure 77).

The fabric

It is built of coursed blue lias rubble with dressings of Hamstone, with modern cement pointing. At the south-east corner there is a two-stage diagonal buttress. Up to the level of the sill of the south window the wall is 2 feet 6 inches thick, and is largely original, with modern repairs. Above that the wall rises at reduced thickness, and is later in date.

The original doorway

The doorway is a little east of centre, 5½ feet high by 2½ feet wide, with plain-chamfered jambs (figure 78). The chamfered four-centred arched head has been renewed in modern freestone but is assumed to follow the original pattern. Inside it are two hardwood lintels of horizontal section, 4½ x 11 inches and 8 x 11 inches; one of these may be original. The door itself is ribbed and dates from the early twentieth century.

A re-set original window?

A loop of dressed Hamstone which appears to be original has been re-set at the north-east corner, beside the vehicle entrance (figure 77). It is 20 inches high by 3 inches wide, with 9-inch chamfers outside. Its original position is unknown,

Figure 77: Central Somerset A, from the north-north-east.

but it may have been moved from the south gable when the present window was inserted.

The inserted apertures and false flight holes

The south window is 3 feet 8 inches square, splayed internally, with a modern casement. The loading doorway at the north end is 6 feet 7 inches high by 3 feet 7 inches wide; the door itself is ledged and boarded. To each side of it are five imitation nest-holes in chequer pattern, and two more above it (figure 77). In height they vary from 7 to 8 inches, and in width from 5 to 6 inches. They do not penetrate the wall, and are more symbolic than functional, evidently intended to indicate that the building has been a dovecote. There are two similar imitation nest-holes in the south gable, with a narrow stone ledge below (figure 76). A curious piece of worked stone has been re-set in this wall.

The nest-holes

Inside, the original walls are wholly occupied by nest-holes in regular grid pattern. The sides are formed of blocks of tufa, with two courses of blue lias between tiers (figure 79). The entrances are 7 inches square; inside they are of the same height but in plan they are of reversed-wedge shape, 9 - 10 inches wide at the

Figure 78: Central Somerset A – the south doorway.

back. Where unaltered they are 16 inches from front to back, but in the east wall many have been reduced in depth by modern repairs to the outside. The lowest tier is 1 foot 7 inches above the concrete floor at the south end. A few feet to the north of this the floor rises 2 feet 8 inches, with four steps, covering the lower tiers of nest-holes. Eight tiers are visible up to the inserted floor, and one (partly blocked) at that level. Before the conversion there were 20 nest-holes in each long wall and 12 in each short wall. Therefore originally there were at least 576 nest-holes, less about a dozen omitted for the south door, of which some 500 are still visible.

However, it is clear that the upper part of the building was taken down and rebuilt in the nineteenth century when the dovecote was converted to a coach-house. By comparison with other dovecotes it would have had at least two more tiers, so probably there were 700 - 800 nest-holes originally.

Above the fourth tier, 5 feet above lower floor level, there is a plain ledge 4½ inches thick which projects 2 inches; there are no other internal ledges.

The conversion

A floor has been inserted 11 feet above the original floor level by supporting transverse joists in the ninth tier of nest-holes. (This was done in the nineteenth century, but the present joists are machine-sawn, so evidently they have been renewed since then). The loading door at the north end has a round cat-hole, which indicates that it must have been approached by a walkway earlier. The south window was formed then, and the upper parts of the original walls were rebuilt in plain masonry without nest-holes to the present height. The roof is modern, and is clad with red clay triple Roman tiles.

Figure 79: Central Somerset A: the south-east corner, showing the top of the modern door.

Access

Despite the owner's diligent efforts it proved impossible to gain access to the upper storey, so this was inspected only from the cat-hole to the north and from outside the glazed south window. Examination inside may provide further information.

Dating and use

There can be no certainty about the period of origin, but this dovecote does not appear to be contemporary with the earliest part of the manor house. Probably it was erected by one of the post-Dissolution secular owners (the Listed Building entry suggests Sir John Sydenham in 1578). The only original timbers which might be tree-ring dated are the lintels over the south doorway.

Substantial repairs were carried out in the first years of the twentieth century, and the the head of the south doorway was replaced. The building is now used for miscellaneous storage.

Figure 84: The dovecote at Monkton Combe, from the south-south-east.

Figure 86: Monkton Combe: the window in the south-west gable.

Figure 88: The dovecote of The Grange, Horsington, from the south-south-west. It extends as far as the first white rainwater pipe.

Figure 93: The dovecote of Manor Farm, Kelston, from the east-north-east. Note the perching ledge at the base of the gable, and the putlog holes above.

Figure 94: Kelston: the original doorway remains unaltered.

Figure 97: Kelston: the roof, facing east.

TOOMER'S FARM, HENSTRIDGE (ST 708 190)

This site is in the south-eastern extremity of the county. The round stone dovecote stands isolated in a level paddock, 50 yards south-west of the present farmhouse, but 80 yards from an older manor house (now used as a barn). It is 21 feet in external diameter and 12 feet 9 inches high to the eaves (figure 80, between pp. 84 and 85). The doorway faces east-north-east, and there are high windows to east and west.

The fabric

The outer part of the structure is of coursed oolite rubble with clay mortar. The conical roof is of similar stone, formed by corbelling stone tiles in from the outside until they meet at a flight hole 2 feet in diameter. There is one stepped buttress to the north-east. Inside, the fabric is of finely-made bricks, $9^{1}/_{8}$ x $4^{1}/_{4}$ x $2^{1}/_{4}$ inches in lime mortar. Four courses rise $10^{1}/_{4}$ inches. In some places one can still see the 'penny joint' – a decorative finish which the bricklayer formed by drawing a coin along a straight edge while the mortar was still soft. This finish is often seen on the outside of Georgian houses but it has not been seen before inside a dovecote. The composite wall is 3 feet 4 inches thick.

The doorway

The original small doorway has been enlarged for use as a cider house. It is 6 feet high by 4 feet 3 inches wide.

The windows

The windows are immediately below the eaves, 3 feet high by $1^{1}/_{2}$ feet wide, both blocked with rubble outside. In the east window the internal splays are visible. The west window is blocked inside with modern brickwork.

The nest-holes

The wall is occupied from the earth floor to eaves level by a regular chequer pattern of nest-holes formed in brickwork (figure 81). The entrances are $5^{1}/_{2}$ inches high by 5 inches wide. Inside they are of L-plan, 11 inches wide by 14 inches from front to back, and $8^{1}/_{2}$ inches high. In one tier all the nest-holes turn to the left inside, in the next tier they all turn to the right. There are 13 tiers, with 25 nest-holes in each tier, making 325 in all. Some nest-holes were lost when the doorway was enlarged, so probably there were nearly 350 when this brick lining was built. In a small section north of the doorway the bricks at the front have fallen away, revealing the insides of some nest-holes, but otherwise most are in good order.

Evidence of a former revolving ladder

Two decayed stubs of timber are built into the top of the brickwork, indicating that formerly there was a beam across from north-north-east to south-south-west. The present farmer, who has been there since 1954, remembers the beam *in situ*. It would have been installed to support the upper pivot of a revolving ladder.

The roof and louver

The interior is shaped like a dome; it has been repaired with lime mortar round the flight hole (figure 82). The stone cap above the flight hole survives, but

Figure 82: Henstridge, showing the blocked east window and the roof of stone rubble.

the space through which the pigeons flew in and out has been filled with stone rubble. Above the cap is a rough stone obelisk.

Dating and use

Toomer's Farm takes its name from Richard of Toomer, who bought land in Henstridge in 1307. By 1574 the Toomer estate had become a manor. The manor house was mentioned in 1565, and by 1584 a pigeon house was associated with it. There is no reason to doubt that this is the building which is now present, although it has been altered since. From the late 1690s Toomer's became a tenant farm.[87] In 1839 the farm belonged to Sir William Medlycott, baronet, and was occupied by Sarah Coombs. The dovecote passed out of use as such about that time. The field in which the dovecote stands was described as Pasture, and had the interesting name Cunniger, a version of coney-garth, i.e. rabbit warren.[88]

Seen from the outside this is a typical West Country vernacular dovecote, probably dating from the sixteenth century. It may be compared with the one at Selworthy (figure 51), or with examples in Devon at Pridhamsleigh and Bigbury, and others in Cornwall. It is the most easterly example of the type.

When Horne visited in 1937 he wrote: 'The stone roof is badly overgrown with bushes and trees. The dovecote is now used as a cider cellar and is in a poor state of repair'. Now it is disused and empty apart from some rotted timbers on the floor. The Listed Building description wrongly attributes it to the eighteenth century, evidently taking the inserted brick nest-holes as part of the original construction.

In the first half of the eighteenth century the stone structure of the dovecote was lined with brickwork; the windows and revolving ladder were probably inserted at the same time. Of the present wall thickness the inner 1½ feet consists of brickwork, leaving only 1 foot 10 inches of stone rubble. This is too thin for a stone wall containing nest-holes, so evidently the inner face of stone rubble was cut away as the brick lining replaced it. Perhaps a new owner was dissatisfied with the irregular nest-holes sunk in the stone rubble, or perhaps by then it was beginning to fail structurally. The fact that nest-holes were constructed from floor level suggests that this was done before brown rats became a hazard later in the eighteenth century.

MONKS' RETREAT, MONKTON COMBE (ST 772 619)

The village of Monkton Combe is 2 miles south-east of central Bath. The dovecote is situated 60 yards south-west of Monks' Retreat private residential home (formerly part of Church Farm), on land decling to the east. It is 23 feet square and 18 feet high to the eaves (figures 83 and 84, opposite p.98). A doorway and

Figure 83: The dovecote at Monks' Retreat, Monkton Combe, from the north.

two apertures face south-east; each gable has an unglazed window. A smaller stone farm building abuts to the north-east, and a shed to the south-west.

The fabric

It is built of coursed squared blocks of Bath stone and rubble, with quoins and dressings of freestone, in lime mortar. The walls are 3 feet thick.

The doorway

The present doorway is 7 feet high by 3½ feet wide, suitable for a stable, with an arched head of unusual shape (figure 85). It is chamfered on the outside, and has a 2-inch rebate inside for a door opening inwards. Examination shows that it has been altered from a much smaller doorway, re-using some of the dressed stones. Originally it was shorter and narrower, as in other dovecotes of the period, with a four-centred arch. A new straight-edged stone was inserted in the head to create the present wide arch.

The original windows

The windows in the gables are each of three rectangular lights with hollow-chamfered mullions and surrounds under a moulded dripstone, too high to measure. In the south-west window the two outer lights are blocked with stone (figure 86); in the north-east window all the lights are blocked (figure 83). The frames exhibit holes for a central bar in each light to support a lattice or grid to keep out birds of prey. Inside the jambs are splayed, with four original lintels.

Figure 85: Monkton Combe: the doorway, enlarged for use as a stable, and inserted apertures related to that secondary use.

The inserted floor

A floor has been inserted at a quite early date, consisting of a chamfered beam aligned north-west to south-east, and joists of square section inserted in the nest-holes, with a stair trap in the east corner. A decayed vertical ladder remains *in situ*.

The inserted apertures

A small unglazed window has been formed beside the door, and a square pitching hole not quite symmetrically above it, to adapt the building as a stable with hay-loft above. Another pitching hole has been inserted in the rear (north-west) wall, and has been blocked later. A third pitching hole has been made in the north-east gable wall, connecting it to an adjacent (later) farm building. These alterations derive from divisions of the property. Originally the whole complex of buildings was associated with Church Farm. Later the part containing Monks' Retreat and the former dovecote was divided from Church Farm, necessitating the blocking of the rear pitching hole and the formation of another. Even today there is no access to the small stone building north-east of the dovecote.

The nest-holes

All internal wall surfaces are occupied by a regular grid pattern of nest-holes from 2 feet above the stone floor to the roof, formed in dressed limestone (figure 87). The entrances are 6½ inches square; inside they form symmetrical bulb-shapes in plan, 12 inches wide and 16 - 17 inches from front to back. There are seven tiers of nest-holes below the inserted floor, many of which are blocked with stone, eleven more tiers up to eaves level, and six diminishing tiers in each gable. Each complete tier comprises 44 nest-holes. Many have been lost by the insertion of apertures, but of about 880 nest-holes originally some 400 or more are still open. There is a plain ledge all round the interior 5 inches wide and 2½ inches thick, 8½ feet above the floor.

Figure 87: Monkton Combe: the upper part of the interior facing south, showing nest-holes and an inserted pitching door.

The roof

The ridge is parallel with the entrance elevation. The gables retain moulded copings and finials but the roof itself has been rebuilt in softwood, destroying the evidence of the former louver. It is now clad with double Roman clay tiles, but a building of this status and high quality would have been roofed with stone tiles originally.

Dating and secondary uses

The building is best dated by the gable windows, which are typical of the late sixteenth century (figures 83 and 86). Later the dovecote was converted to a stable with hay-loft above; the inserted floor and the numerous inserted apertures represent this phase. A blocked low aperture near the south corner shows that it has been used as a pig-sty also. The owner reports that within living memory it has been used for cattle. Despite the various alterations it remains in excellent condition. When visited about forty white fantail doves were in residence.

THE GRANGE, HORSINGTON (ST 701 237)

Horsington village lies on the western slope of the wide valley of the River Cale, a tributary of the Stour. The Grange is the present name of the former Rectory, a large house whose front elevation is dated 1686, but incorporating an earlier core in the rear wing. The dovecote is 25 yards north-west of the earliest part of the house. It is now part of a long service range aligned east-north-east to west-south-west, parallel with the older house, 72 feet long by 24 feet wide, and 13 feet high to the eaves (figure 88, between pp. 98 and 99). A stream runs close to the north side. The dovecote is the earliest part, at the west end of the range. The east end was built as a coach-house in the eighteenth century, and between that and the dovecote are stables. Lofts above the coach-house and stables have been converted into a modern flat. In the east elevation of the coach-house are two groups of external nest-holes (figure 89).

The fabric of the dovecote

The dovecote is built of coursed cornbrash limestone rubble in clay mortar, later pointed with lime mortar. Inside, it is 16 feet 3 inches by 15 feet 8 inches. The walls are 3 feet 8 inches thick. At the east end, where it abuts on the stables, a large area of wall near the north-east corner has been rebuilt without nest-holes; also a large section of the north wall near the north-west corner, both mortared with lime (figure 90). The former was probably for a large inserted doorway for horses, later blocked. The latter may be due to a collapse towards the stream.

The doorways

The original doorway was in the west end against the north wall (figure 91). It has been blocked with masonry on the outside, leaving a recess inside 5 feet 8 inches high by 3 feet 8 inches wide. Over it are two original oak lintels 15 inches wide by 11 inches deep.

A larger doorway has been inserted centrally in the west end (figures 88 and

Figure 89: Horsington: the coach-house at the other end of the same range, from the east.

91). It has a re-set hollow-moulded two-centred arched head, and is 6 feet 7 inches high by 3 feet 5 inches wide. The moulding reaches only to two rectangular blocks at the springs of the arch; the plain jambs are splayed to the inside. The door is ledged and boarded.

A third doorway (now in use) is in the south elevation, at the south-west corner. It is 6 feet high by 2 feet 11 inches wide, with a square head.

The window

A large window has been inserted centrally in the west end, 6½ feet high by 3 feet 5 inches wide; the sill is over 9 feet above ground (figures 88 and 91). Above it an area of disturbed masonry indicates the position of a smaller original window, of which the lintels remain *in situ*.

The nest-holes

The whole interior is occupied by an irregular chequer pattern of nest-holes, except where they have been disturbed by rebuilding (figure 90); they continue into the north jamb of the original doorway. The entrances are 6 inches high by 7 inches wide, varying slightly, separated by hammer-dressed rectangular blocks of oolitic limestone. Inside the height is the same; in plan they open out to an asymmetrical bulb-shape, 11 - 12 inches wide and 20 inches from front to back.

Figure 91: Horsington: the north-west corner,
showing the original doorway (now blocked)
and an inserted doorway and window. There are
no nest-holes in the wall to the right, because it
has collapsed into the stream and been rebuilt.

Figure 90: Horsington: the south-east corner.
Note the blocked lower tiers of nest-holes.

All the nest-holes in one tier turn to the left, all those in the next tier turn to the right. 14 tiers are visible, from a few inches above the earth floor to the eaves; the two lowest tiers have been blocked with stone rubble. In the east and west gables they continue in diminishing tiers. 405 nest-holes are still open, in addition to a less easily determined number of blocked nest-holes. Allowing for these and the inserted apertures and substantial areas of rebuilt masonry there were probably about 600 nest-holes originally. There are no internal ledges.

The roof and former louver

The original roof structure is in two bays, with an in-pitch ridge and two butt-purlins in each pitch. Immediately west of the central truss a section of ridge-piece is omitted; a later timber has been inserted. This indicates the position of the former louver (figure 92). Its base was formed by two extra purlins and a collar which together enclose a rectangle 3 x 2 feet. Two posts are tenoned into the collar. The part above the roof has been cut away in order to lay tiles across the aperture. The present cladding is mainly of plain clay tiles, but five courses of stone tiles at the eaves indicate that originally the roof was clad with stone.

The nest-holes in the east elevation

In the east gable end of the eighteenth-century coach-house are two arched doorways of brick, a central first-floor window with a segmental brick arch and dropped keystone, and on each side of it a triangular pattern of nest-holes (figure 89). The southern group comprises four tiers of 1, 2, 3 and 4 nest-holes. The northern group comprises three tiers of 1, 3 and 3 nest-holes. They are formed in the thickness of the brickwork, and do not penetrate to the interior. Below each tier is an alighting ledge. Two large ammonites are set in the masonry.

Dating and use

Traditionally the rector of a parish had the valuable right to keep pigeons.[89] In some parishes pigeons were kept in part of the church;[70] the only example in Somerset which has survived is at Compton Martin, but there are others elsewhere. At Horsington a freestanding dovecote was built close to the stream, facing the house (as it was then) across a court. There is little evidence on which to date it, but the thickness of the walls and the shape of the nest-holes suggest that it is of the sixteenth century. A pigeon house was recorded in glebe terriers in 1613, and again in 1623.[90] There is no reason to doubt that these refer to the present building. The only way of establishing the origin more firmly would be by tree-ring dating of the timbers included (lintels and roof timbers).

In the eighteenth century the lower tiers of nest-holes were blocked for protection against brown rats (figure 90). Also in that century a stable and coach-house were added to the east, forming the present long range. The ammonites

Figure 92: Horsington: two extra short purlins in the roof indicate the position of the former louver.

built into the east elevation suggest that these alterations were by the Reverend John Wickham, who died in 1783; he is known to have been a keen naturalist.[91]

Then or in the early nineteenth century an access was made for horses through the east wall of the dovecote, and another in the west wall. For the latter dressed stones were re-used, possibly from the church.

The dovecote is still in use. At the time of inspection (October 2001) some 80 - 100 white fantails were in residence, which fly in and out through the west window.

The external nest-holes in the east elevation may have been occupied by pigeons occasionally, but they are mainly symbolic.

MANOR FARM, KELSTON (ST 698 670)

This is a rare example of a four-gabled dovecote of high quality which has never been adapted to later uses. Kelston is at the southern end of the Cotswolds on the north side of the Avon valley, three miles north-west of Bath. The dovecote stands 50 yards west-south-west of the parish church on land declining gently to the west. There are other redundant farm buildings immediately to the north, all much later in date. It is a rectangular building aligned east-west, 26½ feet long by 21 feet wide, 14½ feet high to the eaves (figures 93 and 94, between pp. 98 and 99). The doorway faces east, and there are windows in gables facing east and south. It is Listed Grade II*.

The fabric

It is built of blue and white lias coursed rubble with dressings of oolitic limestone, in lime mortar. A perching ledge all round at eaves level forms the bases of the gables, with a weathered upper surface and a concave soffit. The walls are 3 feet 2 inches thick. Open putlog holes are visible in the east gable.

The doorway

The jambs and lintel are formed of five massive blocks of freestone from different sources (figure 94). The doorway is 3 feet 5 inches high from the present concrete threshold, and 2 feet wide. Small doorways were normal at the period but this is so low as to be difficult to enter; as the earth floor is 8 inches below the threshold it is likely that originally the doorway was about 4 feet 1 inch high. Inside there are rebates 3 inches deep on the right, 2 inches deep elsewhere, for a door hinged on the right opening inwards; the hinges are missing. When Horne visited it in 1920 he reported that the original oak door with strap hinges was still present, with an inner door of elm planks. Both are missing now.

The windows

The windows are too high to be measured, but are estimated to be 2 feet high by one foot wide. Each jamb, lintel and sill is formed of one block of dressed limestone. The lintels are rebated on the outside and each has a single hole for a vertical bar to support a lattice (or possibly leaded glazing). The jambs of the east window are splayed internally; the south window, in a large dormer, is unsplayed (figures 95 and 97, opposite p.99).

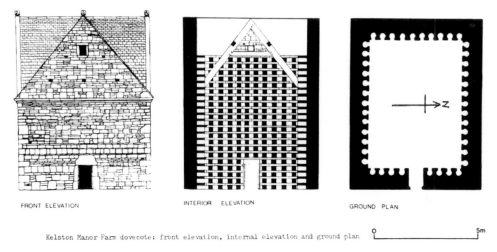

FRONT ELEVATION   INTERIOR ELEVATION   GROUND PLAN

Kelston Manor Farm dovecote: front elevation, internal elevation and ground plan

0   5m

Figure 95: Measured drawings of Kelston dovecote, from *Bristol Archaeology Research Group Review* no. 2, 1981. By courtesy of Robert Sutcliff.

The nest-holes and internal ledges

From the earth floor to half-way up each gable the walls are occupied by nest-holes in regular grid pattern, formed of dressed Bath stone (figures 93, 94 and 96). The entrances are 8 inches high by 7½ inches wide. Internally the same height is maintained; in plan they form exact circles 13 inches in diameter. There are 17 tiers to eaves level, with 46 nest-holes in each tier, a further 31 in each main gable and 30 in each dormer gable. Allowing for those omitted for the doorway this makes a total of 892. There are ledges all round to the sixth and tenth tiers (at heights 5 feet and 9½ feet); they are 3½ inches wide and 5 inches deep, with deeply chamfered soffits.

The roof and louver

Each gable has a plain coping with a cruciform finial. The roof is of butt-purlin construction in three bays with two purlins in each pitch, a ridge-piece, and straight collars between the principal rafters (figures 95 and 97). Some main timbers, the valley-boards and all the common rafters were renewed in 1982-3, and the roof was re-clad with stone tiles. The louver is a modern construction, but closely follows the decayed louver it replaced (figure 2). It is rectangular, with two inclined boards in each side, the lower part clad with weatherboards. It has a steep pyramidal roof clad with sheet metal. Horne's photograph taken in 1920 confirms that it has been restored accurately. He reported: 'Inside the building, beneath the exit hole, is a square board with a large circular hole in the centre. A trap-door, worked with a wire that hangs down on one of the side walls, enables the exit hole to be closed'. These internal features are missing. The skeleton of a pipe has been reconstructed without the boarding, which suggests that part of the original pipe survived until 1982.

Figure 96: Kelston: inside the west end. Note the ledges, and the regularity of the nest-holes.

Dating and use

This is a superb example of the four-gabled type of dovecote which was developed in the late sixteenth century, and became quite common in the seventeenth century. There are several in the Cotswolds and the West Midlands, and other examples in Hampshire, Oxfordshire, Leicestershire, Flintshire and elsewhere. Another one stood at Langford Manor, Fivehead, until the early twentieth century, since demolished (page 211). The particular merit of this type of roof is that it provided sloping surfaces facing in all directions on which the pigeons could perch and sun themselves at all times of day, and where they could obtain shelter from strong winds from any direction. The small doorway confirms that the dovecote has never been adapted for other uses.

The Listed Building entry associates it with Sir John Harington, 1561 - 1612, godson of Queen Elizabeth I and High Sheriff of Somerset (better known to posterity as the originator of the water closet). He completed a new manor house in Renaissance style in 1589, and evidently built this dovecote then or soon afterwards to supply the large number of squabs required when he entertained Queen Elizabeth and her court in 1592. (Like many of her hosts he ruined himself financially in preparing for her visit). His manor house stood immediately west of the church, between it and the dovecote. It was demolished in 1764 to build another in Palladian style, which has been demolished too.[92] The dovecote was restored in 1982-3. A dozen pigeons were in residence when examined.

Pevsner wrote that Kelston dovecote is 'said to have more nesting holes than any other in the county'.[93] It has substantially fewer than those at Fivehead, Long Sutton Court House and Shapwick House.

THE OLD RECTORY, WEST CAMEL (ST 578 245)

West Camel is on the River Cam, a tributary of the Yeo, six miles north of Yeovil. This handsome cylindrical dovecote is situated 40 yards south-west of The Old Rectory, a house of Regency appearance externally but of medieval origin, and the same distance south of a contemporary barn, on the boundary between the garden and a paddock. It is 22 feet in external diameter and 15 feet high to the eaves (figure 98, opposite p.112). The doorway faces north-west. There are no windows.

The fabric

It is built of blue lias rubble and lime mortar, with cement pointing. The wall is 3 feet 8 inches thick. It has a weathered plinth and four stepped buttresses 1½ feet wide, extending 1½ feet. Just below the eaves is a plain perching ledge 4 inches wide. Cement mortar has been laid on it to form an inclined upper surface.

The doorway

This is 4½ feet high by 2 feet 5 inches wide, with a wide segmental arch, and is rebated inside for a door opening inwards (figure 99). Two wrought iron pintle hinges remain in the right jamb. Four original oak lintels 8 inches deep remain *in situ*, the inner one shaped to the curvature of the wall. The ledged and boarded door is nineteenth-century. The

Figure 99: West Camel Old Rectory: the doorway.

threshold is of concrete. When examined a deposit of pigeon droppings nearly two feet deep was mounded on the floor.

The nest-holes

The interior from the earth floor to the roof is occupied by a chequer pattern of nest-holes (figure 100). The entrances are 6½ inches square; inside they are of symmetrical bulb-shape, 10 inches wide and 20 inches from front to back. There are 16 tiers, with 41 nest-holes in a complete tier. 15 nest-holes are omitted for the doorway, making a total of 641, all still in good order. There are no internal ledges.

The roof and louver

The roof structure is modern, clad with plain clay tiles. One course of stone tiles at the eaves survives from the earlier cladding. The modern wooden louver has eight arched flight holes, a conical roof clad with red clay tiles and a weather-vane.

Figure 100: West Camel Old Rectory: the north-western part, with a deep accumulation of pigeon droppings obstructing the doorway.

Figure 98: The dovecote of The Old Rectory, West Camel, from the south-west. The small aperture at the base was made for hens.

Figure 107: The dovecote of the Shapwick House Hotel, Shapwick, from the south-east.

Figure 101: Hinton Priory: the chapter house, with a fragment of the sacristy to the right. The lower pigeon-loft is above the three-light window. The upper pigeon-loft occupies the four-gabled roof, lit by the single-light window.

Dating and use

The Listed Building description states that this dovecote was probably built in the seventeenth century as part of the Grange estate attached to Muchelney Abbey, but it appears older. However, it was not included in a glebe terrier of 1606, which mentioned the dwelling house, barn, stable, garden and orchard.[93] The only way of obtaining a more definitive date of construction would be by tree-ring dating of the lintels built into the structure.

When Horne visited in 1922 it was in use as a chicken-house, with a small aperture low in the south side. The small doorway and the absence of windows show that this dovecote has never been adapted to any other secondary use. It is occupied by about thirty pigeons still.

THE CHAPTER HOUSE OF HINTON PRIORY, HINTON CHARTERHOUSE (ST 779 592)

Hinton Charterhouse is six miles south-east of Bath. The Carthusian Priory of Locus Dei was founded here in 1232 and dissolved in 1539. Most of it was demolished the same year, but two monastic buildings survive on the level site, the refectory, now standing isolated, and the chapter house, with a fragment of the sacristy which formerly linked it to the Priory church (figure 101). The site is Scheduled as an Ancient Monument and the remaining buildings are Listed as Grade I.

The chapter house is built of oolitic limestone rubble with dressed quoins in Early English style. Since the Dissolution two pigeon lofts have been made in the roofs, one at a higher level than the other. They are reached by a winding stone stair north of the former sacristy (figure 102).

The lower loft

This is over the eastern bay of the chapter house, above the triple lancet window in figure 101, some 21 feet above ground (figure 102). From the winding stair and a short passage one enters a well-lit chamber of two bays with quadripartite vaults which was built as the monks' library (figure 103). At the eastern end a tall doorway leads into what was the inner room of the library, but is now a pigeon-loft (figure 104). The doorway has been reduced in height to 7 feet 2 inches wide by timber lintels, and the upper part has been blocked with masonry. Internally this loft is 18 feet 4 inches by 9 feet 8 inches; the height to the ridge is 15 feet. There are no windows. At the doorway the wall thickness has been increased to 5 feet by the construction of a lining of Bath stone containing the nest-boxes, supported over the doorway by a stone lintel.

This inner lining continues all round the interior to meet the roof, with nest-boxes in regular chequer pattern. The entrances are 7½ inches high by 6½ inches wide. Inside they are of the same height, elliptical in plan, 11½ inches wide and 13½ inches from front to back, neatly lined with lime plaster. The shape is clearly revealed where some stones above have fallen away, and shows that they were formed with an elliptical template. The inner gable (with the doorway) has 16

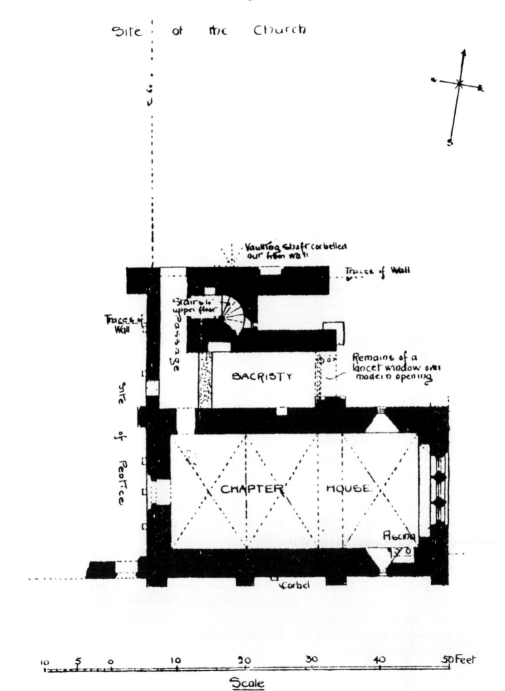

Figure 102: Plan of the chapter house and sacristy of Hinton Priory by R. W. Paul. From *Somerset Archaeology and Natural History* volume 41, 1895. By courtesy of the Society.

Figure 103: Hinton Priory: the former library, facing east. The doorway leads to the lower pigeon-loft.

Figure 104: Hinton Priory: the lower pigeon-loft, facing south.

diminishing tiers of nest-boxes, making 98. In the side walls the upper tiers have been damaged, but 13 nest-boxes remain of an estimated 32 originally. In the outer gable all the nest-boxes are in good order; there are 90. They enclose a collar of the roof, showing that the roof is of the same period as the nest-boxes. Above it they are made slightly differently; the floors are formed of one-inch hardwood boards. In this loft 211 nest-boxes remain of an original total of about 230.

There are no alighting ledges. A set-back in the east gable wall forms a horizontal surface 3½ feet above the floor.

The upper loft

is in the main four-gabled roof, some 30 feet above ground. A short passage from the head of the winding stair leads to a framed oak doorway 3 feet 9 inches high by 2 feet 4 inches wide, rebated for a door opening inwards, with two wrought iron hinges (figure 105). This loft is 21 feet long by 19 feet wide. In the east gable is a single lancet window 5 feet 8 inches high by 11 inches wide, shown in figure 101. The north, west and south gables are fully occupied by nest-boxes of Bath stone, made to the same size and pattern as those below. In this loft 246 nest-boxes remain of an original total of 250. There are no nest-boxes in the east gable (with the lancet window).

In the north and south gables there are ledges 2½ inches wide and 2½ inches thick with chamfered soffits, 9½ feet above the floor.

This makes a total for the whole building of 480 nest-boxes originally, of which 457 remain.

Figure 105: Hinton Priory: the upper pigeon-loft, facing north-west, with the original doorway.

The roofs

Both roofs are of butt-purlin construction, with straight collars between the principal rafters, evidently built in the seventeenth century. They were substantially repaired in 1950; some timbers were replaced, following the form of the existing structure. They are clad with stone tiles.

Dating and use

At the Dissolution the property was acquired by Walter, Lord Hungerford, of Farleigh Castle. Apart from a brief interval in the 1550s the property remained in the Hungerford family until 1674. It is not known which of them is responsible for this construction. A mansion called Hinton House (now Hinton Priory) was built nearby partly of re-used stone from the monastic buildings, and altered at several periods.[94]

An engraving published in 1813 shows the chapter house already in disrepair; the roofs were thatched, with a louver on the ridge of the lower pigeon-loft (figure 106). The upper pigeon-loft is depicted without a louver, but with triangular flight holes in each gable.[97]

Figure 106: Hinton Priory in 1813. The lower pigeon-loft is at left, with a louver. The upper pigeon-loft has triangular flight holes high in the gables. Both roofs are shown as thatched. From *The Gentleman's Magazine*, 15 December 1813 (supplement), in the Braikenridge Collection. By courtesy of the Somerset Archaeological and Natural History Society.

A hand-written recipe book compiled by Mrs. Mary Day, mistress of Hinton House from the 1820s to the 1840s, includes a recipe:

'Broil pigeons whole'

'Cut off the Wings and Neck close, leave the Skin at the Neck to be closed, then have some grated Bread, two Pigeons' Livers, one anchovy, a quarter of a pound of butter, half a nutmeg grated, a little Pepper and Salt, Thyme & sweet Marjoram, stand all together, put a piece as big as a Walnut into each Pigeon, [illegible word] up their rumps & necks, strew a little Pepper, Salt and Nutmeg on the outside, broil them on a very slow charcoal fire on the hearth, baste and and turn them very often, [illegible word] is Melted Butter or rich Gravy if you like it'.

At the end of the book other recipes have been added by Mrs. Newman Barwick, one of which is:

'Stew pigeons'

'Stuff the pigeons with the livers, some thyme, parsley, pepper, salt, cloves, a little mace, & a bit of butter.

Fry them just enough to brown them; then stew them softly over a slow fire for an hour in rich gravy, enough to cover them'.[98]

SHAPWICK HOUSE HOTEL, SHAPWICK (ST 417 387)

This is a rare example of an hexagonal dovecote, the only one in Somerset. It is situated on level ground 68 yards south-east of the Hotel, a manor house of seventeenth-century appearance but with a medieval core. To the south it is closely bordered by a haha, with parkland beyond. Each facet of the hexagon measures 17 feet; it is 20 feet high to the eaves, with a doorway to the west (figures 107, opposite p.112, 108 and 109). There are no windows.

Figure 108: The dovecote of Shapwick House Hotel, from the south-south-east.

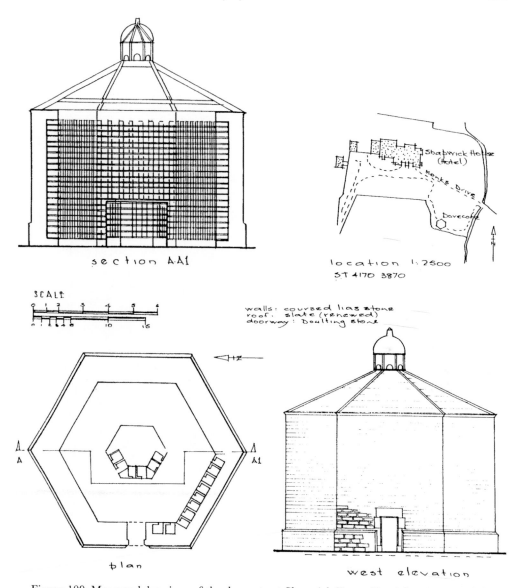

section A·A1

location 1:2500
ST 4170 3870

Shapwick House
(Hotel)

Monks Drive

Dovecote

SCALE

walls: coursed lias stone
roof: slate (renewed)
doorway: Doulting stone

plan

west elevation

Figure 109: Measured drawings of the dovecote at Shapwick House Hotel, by courtesy of the
Somerset Vernacular Building Research Group.

The fabric

It is built of even courses of blue lias, very neatly squared, with such precision
that after more than three centuries it still looks new. There is a weathered plinth
2½ feet high of blue lias rubble, and no other projections. The walls are 3 feet
thick.

The doorway

The square-headed doorway is 4½ feet high by 2 feet 2 inches wide, formed of large blocks of Doulting stone, chamfered all round. Inside there are three hardwood lintels of horizontal section, two 5 x 8 inches and one 5 x 10 inches.

The nest-holes

Tiers of nest-holes in regular grid pattern occupy the interior from 14 inches above the earth floor to the roof (figure 110). The sides and fronts are formed of sections of lias 2 inches thick. Each entrance is 7 inches high by 5½ inches wide. Inside is a rectangular space 11½ inches wide and 16 inches from front to back. The floors are formed of slabs of blue lias 1½ inches thick which project to form alighting ledges 1½ inches wide. There are 22 tiers, with 48 nest-holes in each complete tier. Allowing for those omitted for the door this makes 1,008 nest-holes in the walls. This regular pattern is not disturbed at the angles of the hexagon; the sides appear to butt together.

In addition there is an hexagonal column 6 feet high in the middle which provides six tiers of 12 nest-holes (figure 111). They are made in the same as those in the outer walls, except that at the angles the rear parts of the nest-holes are 'pinched'; the floors and alighting ledges are only 1 inch thick. This adds another 72 nest-holes, making a total of 1,080, nearly all of which are still in good order. It is possible that the central column was taller originally.

Figure 110: Inside the dovecote of Shapwick House Hotel.

Figure 111: Shapwick House: the central structure comprising 72 additional nest-holes.

The roof and cupola

The pyramidal roof is modern, clad with blue slate. The hexagonal cupola has a leaded dome. There is one arched flight hole in each side.

Dating and use

An English Heritage assessment of its significance describes it as: 'A rare example of an early hexagonal dovecote and the only early one surviving which is constructed of stone. It was built of the highest quality in 1630, of blue lias, for the Lord Chief Justice of the time, Sir Henry Rolle . . . and probably represents the use of dovecotes as status symbols in local rivalries'.[99]

The dovecote is shown on an estate map of *c*.1754.[100] The haha on the boundary of the park departs from a straight course to enclose it, indicating that it was formed when the dovecote was already present. At the time of the 1839 tithe survey this property was owned by George Warry and occupied by Sarah Taylor. The 13-acre plot was described as 'Mansion House, Offices, Gardens, Pleasure Ground, Cottage, Island and Orchard'.[101]

The small doorway and the central column show that it has never been adapted to a secondary use. Hope Grange reported in 1937 that the roof had been repaired by Colonel Barry about 1911; probably he was responsible for the present louver.[102] It may be compared with the earlier – but much repaired – round dovecote at Shapwick Manor School, only 300 yards away (page 84).

Our enquiries indicate that the dovecote at Shapwick House is unique in England. There are a few other hexagonal dovecotes, mostly of brick, but nothing comparable with this one.[103]

HALSWELL HOUSE, GOATHURST (ST 253 338)

This is 3 miles south-west of Bridgwater. Halswell House is a major country house which has been a subject of concern for many years to those who care about historic buildings. The cylindrical dovecote is 20 yards south of the house. Despite introductions from impeccable intermediaries the owners, an Arab property company, have flatly refused to allow us to visit. This is the only dovecote in Somerset where our interest has not been welcomed. Therefore we can only assemble information from other sources.

A photograph of the dovecote in *Country Life* in November 1908 shows it covered with ivy, having a bell-shaped roof without a louver. It was Listed Grade II in July 1950, and re-Listed in January 1987, described as seventeenth-century, of rubble with some roughcast, with an ogival slate roof, an open turret with an arcade of turned balusters, a zinc cupola, a small door opening to the east, and an interior completely lined with nest-holes. It is shown distantly in an engraving of Halswell Park published in 1791. C. J. Bond described it as **early** seventeenth-century, and wrote in 1998 that a section of **cob** walling had suffered a serious collapse. Three Crown Copyright photographs taken in August 1986 show it in a neglected garden (figure 112).

Figure 112: The dovecote of Halswell House, Goathurst, from the south-west. © English Heritage, NMR, by courtesy of the National Monuments Record, Swindon.

Halswell House was put up for sale – again – in 2002. The sale catalogue reproduced a photograph of the dovecote taken from the south-south-west. It shows it as cylindrical, the outside newly rendered, with a high window to the south-west. The bell-shaped roof is fitted with modern guttering, and has no louver; scaffolding is in place. As the open turret with an arcade of turned balusters and zinc cupola mentioned in the List description of 1987 were not present when it was photographed in 1908 they may have no historical basis. The house is described by Robert Dunning in *Some Somerset Country Houses*, but the dovecote is not mentioned.[104] If Bond is right that it is of cob, as he is likely to be, it is the only cob dovecote in Somerset which has survived. One at Durleigh collapsed in 1967 (page 214).

HILL FARM, KINGSTON ST. MARY (ST 219 298)

We often see flight holes high in a house, barn or stable, indicating that there has been a pigeon-loft there (figure 113), but usually there is nothing left to see inside. This is the only exception we have come across. Kingston St. Mary is 2½ miles north of Taunton. Hill Farm is a medieval house on the northern edge of the village,

Figure 116: The dovecote of The Court House, Long Sutton, from the north.

Figure 122: The dovecote of Godminster Manor from the south-west.

Figure 125: Godminster, from the south. The louver is four-gabled, but the roof has been rebuilt with plain inclines to the east and north. The nest-holes of inverted-U shape are copied from the photograph of *circa* 1890.

Figure 127: Manor Farm, Southstoke: The great barn from the south-south-east, with the combined pigeon-loft and stable set in its south-eastern angle.

Figure 113: The roof of the south wing of Hill Farm, Kingston St. Mary, showing the pigeon-loft at right.

with jointed crucks, internal walls of cob, and heavy smoke-blackening over the hall, datable to the fifteenth century. The original house is aligned east-west. From the western (high) end a seventeenth-century parlour wing extends to the south, with an external chimney stack at the south end. Beside the stack is an original stair-turret. The pigeon-loft is above it (figures 114 and 115). It came to light when the roofs were taken off for major repairs.

Figure 114: The pigeon-loft of Hill Farm, Kingston St. Mary, showing the access from the house at left.

Figure 115: The pigeon-loft of Hill Farm, Kingston St. Mary. The flight hole is at centre right.

The fabric and pigeon-loft

The south wing, stair-turret and pigeon-loft are fully integrated, built of uncoursed Devonian shale rubble in clay mortar, without quoins. The original walls are 16 inches thick. At a later date they have been raised. The later parts are 6 inches thinner than those below, and have quoins formed with bricks 9 x 4½ x 2¼ inches, also laid in clay mortar. The stair rises through a half-circle, re-entering at first-floor level. The upper doorway was only 5 feet high when built, although a late Georgian alteration has made more headroom. The pigeon-loft is above it in the small space below the roof, having a floor of thick elm boards. Internally it is 3 feet 9 inches from east to west and 2 feet 10 inches from north to south; it is only 4 feet 2 inches high at the high end.

The nest-holes

Nine nest-holes are arranged in four irregular tiers in the east wall of the loft, against the stack. There are two more low in the south wall, and two more in the west wall. They vary greatly in size and shape, formed by irregular slabs of rubble, but all are wider inside than at the entrance. From front to back most are 14 to 17 inches deep, although one low in the east side is 2 feet 2 inches deep! (Its remotest part is in the rubble between the flue and the inside of the house). Some of the roofs of the nest-holes are of slabs of shale; others are of sawn boards. One is formed from a re-used curved timber 10½ by 1½ inches, apparently part of the wind-brace of a medieval roof. Others are of boards ¾ or 1 inch thick. In addition to the nests *in situ*, originally there were two more in the west wall, above the two existing and immediately below the low part of roof. The wooden floor below them is still present, retaining ghost images of the former nest-holes.

The door

There is no aperture a human being could pass through. A re-set unglazed window forms the only access from the house, 14½ inches high by 10½ inches wide, level with the floor of the pigeon-loft (figure 114). It is chamfered all round towards the loft, with diagonal stops. A square-set central mullion has been sawn off against the frame. From inside the house this door is immediately over the upper entrance to the winding stair. It is closed with a roughly-shaped board hung on two nails.

The flight hole

This faces south, and is 4 feet 2 inches above the loft floor, 13 feet above ground (figure 115). Externally it is 6 inches high by 5 inches wide, without a perching ledge. On the inside it opens out to 12 inches wide but is only 4 inches high. The inside of the flight hole has been crudely plastered and lime-washed. There is no other source of light or ventilation.

The roof

The roof of the south wing is in three bays, with principal rafters tenoned and bridled at the apices, straight collars, a square-set ridge-piece, and two purlins in each pitch, which are scarfed with dovetail joints near the south end. It was thatched originally. Most of that structure is still present, but in the late Georgian period a higher roof was built, at a shallower pitch to accommodate double Roman tiles. The pigeon-loft has remained undisturbed (and inaccessible) since then, until the roof cladding was removed in 2002.

Dating and use

The pigeon-loft is of the same origin as the south wing, datable to the mid-seventeenth century by the roof structure. One might wonder how it was used, if no human being could enter it. The owner, Lloyd Dormer, suggests that the squabs were tempted to the small door with corn or other food as soon as they could leave the nest, and taken for slaughter there. The accumulated droppings could only be removed through the same aperture. Probably the two missing nest-holes were destroyed when the roof was raised.

We know of no evidence that Hill Farm was ever a manor. As any freeholder could keep pigeons after 1619, the owner of this property evidently decided to incorporate a small pigeon-loft when he extended the upper end of the house in the seventeenth century. The flight hole is quite inconspicuous when seen from ground level. There was no prestige involved, just the utilitarian purpose of keeping a small number of pigeons for household consumption.

THE COURT HOUSE, LONG SUTTON (ST 466 259)

The Court House is a fourteenth-century manor house situated on the south side of the main road from Langport to Podimore. The dovecote is 12 feet west of it, 28 yards south of the road, on ground declining to the south. It is a rectangular stone building 27 feet long by 23 feet wide aligned north-west to south-east, 16 feet high to the eaves (figure 116, opposite p.122). At the north-west end a pitched roof abuts to form a covered wagon-way to farmland at the rear, connecting the dovecote to a later barn range on the same alignment.

The fabric

The walls are built of coursed blocks of blue lias in clay mortar, varying in thickness from 2 feet 9 inches to 3 feet 3 inches. The outside has been pointed with lime mortar. Two spur walls abut at the south-east end, enclosing a small yard. A stone buttress has been added at the west corner, at the lowest point of the slope.

Figure 117: The original north doorway of the dovecote at The Court House, Long Sutton, from inside, blocked, and the stone platform built against it later.

The original doorway

The original door aperture is at the western end of the long north-east elevation (facing the road), 5 feet 5 inches high by 3 feet wide; the missing door-frame would have reduced this to about 4 feet 11 inches x 2½ feet. It is neatly blocked externally with coursed blue lias to form a flush surface, leaving a recess 11 inches deep inside (figure 117). Two original oak lintels 7 inches square are visible, one of which is still in excellent condition. Others may be present, concealed by the rubble infill.

The inserted doorways

Doorways have been inserted in both gable ends against the rear wall, one of which (at the north-west end) has been blocked later. Two other doorways have been inserted in the rear (south-west) wall. One is now fully blocked with stone, the other partly blocked and reduced to a window.

The window and pitching hole

The window is high in the front (north-east) wall, 4 feet square, with modern glazing, splayed asymmetrically to the inside. Its original size is unknown - if there was a window in that position. A pitching hole 5 feet high by 4 feet 3 inches wide has been made high in the south-east gable end, now closed with modern materials (figure 118).

The nest-holes and platform

Inside, a stone platform 12 - 14 inches high and 3 feet wide has been built round three walls since the dovecote passed out of use for its original purpose. At each end it terminates clear of the inserted doorways, showing that it was built after them (figure 118). What is probably the lowest tier of nest-holes is an inch or so above this platform. They are simple box-shaped recesses arranged in chequer pattern, averaging 6 inches high by 6½ inches wide, and 16 - 18 inches from front to back (figure 118 and 119). The tiers align at the corners, and extend into the original doorway in the north corner. In the south-east gable end there were originally 19 tiers of 13 nest-holes to eaves level, and a further 93 nest-holes in diminishing

Figure 118: The north corner of the dovecote of The Court House, Long Sutton. Note the low platform, built after it ceased to be a dovecote.

tiers in the gable, making 340. In the north-west gable end there was one tier less (because of the gradient), making 327 nest-holes. In the front (north-east) long wall there are 18 tiers, each complete tier comprising 18 nest-holes, but 35 were omitted for the original doorway, and 42 spaces are occupied by the present window. This makes a minimum of 247 nest-holes, but there would have been 260 or more before the window was enlarged (or inserted). The rear (south-west) long wall has two extra tiers of nest-holes because of the inclination of the ground, so originally there were 20 tiers of 18 nest-holes, uninterrupted by door or window apertures, making 360 nest-holes. Thus the dovecote originally had at least 1,287 nest-holes. This is large within the range of dovecotes

Figure 119: The south-east end of the dovecote of The Court House, Long Sutton.

nationally, most of which have between 300 and 1,000 nest-holes, and the second largest in Somerset. There are no internal ledges.

The roof

The gables have coped parapets on simple convex kneelers, with carved finials, typical of the eighteenth century. In the south-east gable inclined straight joints at a slightly steeper pitch show that the parapets were added after the initial construction. (At the north-west end the gable is concealed by the abutting roof). The upper courses of the long walls have been rebuilt in a better quality of masonry than the main fabric, also in the eighteenth century.

The roof has been rebuilt twice. The existing roof is in three bays with two purlins in each pitch, simply carpentered of local hardwood; the beams are waney at the arrises. In 1937 Horne wrote 'The roof was of stone slabs but these were removed by a local builder to use elsewhere, and tiles, helped out by corrugated iron, have taken their place'. Two courses of stone tiles at the eaves confirm that earlier it was clad throughout with stone tiles, but now above them are red clay pantiles. Further repairs and reinforcements were executed in 1998. The entrance for the pigeons would have been a louver – or because there were so many of them, probably two louvers – on the ridge of the roof, but no evidence remains.

The alterations

The first major alteration was the reconstruction of the roof in the eighteenth century. When this building ceased to be used as a dovecote it was converted into a dairy or cider-house with a loft above. The two doorways in the gable walls were inserted, the window in the front wall was enlarged, and the low platform was built round three sides. A floor was inserted at mid-height, and the pitching hole was inserted to give access to the loft from the covered wagon-way. The floor has been removed subsequently; as the joists were supported in the nest-holes it has left no trace, but it can be deduced from the high pitching hole. The asymmetrical splays of the north-east window suggest that it occupied only the north-western half of the building. Many of the former nest-holes have been eliminated by the numerous inserted apertures, filling of the masonry around them, and repairs to cracks in the structure. Of the original complement about two-thirds remain open.

Origin and use

This building has been much altered over the years, so its origin is difficult to determine. It is probably of the seventeenth century, and may have been built originally by Thomas Spigurnell, who greatly altered the fourteenth-century manor house and left an inscription on the porch with his name and the date 1658.[105] The integral lintels of the original doorway may be datable by dendrochronology.

In the eighteenth century the walls were raised with parapet gables, and a new roof was built at a slightly shallower pitch. Alterations continued to be made to adapt the building to the constantly changing economics of farming. None of the doorways is large enough to admit a wagon, so despite its barn-like appearance it has never been used as a corn barn. In the depression years of the early twentieth century it was neglected, and most of the stone tiles were stripped from the roof. The dovecote was carefully repaired and reinforced in 1998.

KENN COURT, KENN (ST 414 687)

Kenn is on the plain north of the Congresbury Yeo, two miles from the Bristol Channel. This fragment of a former dovecote is situated on level ground 50 yards south-west of Kenn Court, which is of sixteenth-century origin. It is 31 feet long by 18 feet wide, aligned north-east to south-west (figure 120). The present wide doorway to the north-west is inserted. The end walls, originally gabled, have been cut down to form a monopitch roof of corrugated asbestos, which was in disrepair when inspected. Another farm building abuts to the south-west. A dense growth of nettles limited examination of the outside, and an accumulation of junk obstructed the inside. It is not Listed.

Figure 120: The ruined dovecote at Kenn Court, Kenn, from the west-north-west.

The fabric

It is built of coursed Triassic red sandstone rubble with clay mortar, without quoins. Buttresses have been added at the north corner and in the middle of the north-western elevation. There is a deep vertical crack near the west corner.

The nest-holes

The nest-holes are in the north-east and south-west walls only. Six feet above the earth floor is a ledge 4 inches wide and 2½ inches thick; they are all above that (figure 121). The entrances are 6 inches square; inside they are of L-plan, 20 inches from front to back and of irregular widths. The lowest tier is mainly blocked, but five tiers (including that) are discernible, with 10 nest-holes in each. 45 remain in the north-east wall, and about the same number in the wall opposite. In the south-west wall a doorway has been inserted and later blocked.

When Horne visited this building in 1928 he counted 135 nest-holes in the north-east wall 'which runs right up to the point of the gable' and 84 in the south-west wall. He reported that 'the roof was thatched until a few years ago, when the walls were lowered by about four feet and a new roof was put on'. Apparently the walls have been lowered by more than 7 feet since 1928. Before that they were 18 feet high to the points of the gables, and perhaps 22 feet high earlier. It is not clear why nest-holes were not provided in the other walls, or in the lower six feet of the two walls which have some. The buttresses were added when the walls began to spread. The crack near the south-west corner was caused by the absence of a buttress there.

Dating and use

There is little evidence on which this building can be dated; probably it is seventeenth-century. An estate map of 1780 shows Kenn Court and a range of ancillary buildings to the south-west (which would include the dovecote) enclosed by three arms of a rectangular moat; but the range is simply represented as a continuous building.[106] The building is used now only for junk.

GODMINSTER MANOR

By request of the owner this dovecote is not identified further. It is situated on level ground 30 yards north-east of the manor house, which is of medieval origin, with a walled-in garden 5 yards to the east. It is 24 feet square and 19 feet high to the eaves (figure 122, opposite p.122). The doorway faces south-south-west. Horne reported in August 1921 that it was 'a complete ruin'; his photographs show that the walls then stood no more than 11 feet high (figure 123). By 1923 it had been rebuilt, perhaps due to his influence, taking the design from a photograph taken about 1890 (figure 124). It is Listed as Grade II*.

Figure 121: Kenn: inside the north-east end.

Figures 123: Godminster: Horne's photographs taken in August 1921 show that at that time it was a ruin, standing only about eleven feet high. By courtesy of Somerset Archaeological and Natural History Society.

The fabric

It is built of oolitic limestone rubble with ashlar dressings of Cary stone, with cement pointing overall. The walls are 3 feet 2 inches thick.

The doorway

At first glance the doorway appears to be original, 6 feet 10 inches high by 3 feet 4 inches wide, as it appears in the photograph of c.1890. However, it may have been enlarged earlier, for smaller doorways were common when this dovecote was built. Over it is a massive oak lintel of horizontal section, 24 x 5 inches, with a smaller modern one inside. The roll-moulded door-frame and ledged and braced oak door were made in 1922, and by now are sufficiently weathered to be mistaken for original work. The stone threshold is 2 inches above ground level, which is the same inside and outside. Above the door is a square recess containing a sundial, slightly angled to face due south. It was empty in Horne's photograph of 1921; earlier it may have contained an initialled datestone.

The roof and louver

The roof has large gables to south and west each containing a window, and plain inclines to north and east; it is clad with stone tiles (figure 125, opposite p.123). The four-gabled louver is also clad with stone tiles. Each of its gables is weather-boarded, with a triangular pattern of flight holes of inverted-U shape in four tiers of 2, 4, 6 and 8. Below each tier is a narrow wooden perching ledge on wooden brackets.

Figure 124: Godminster: the dovecote as it was in about 1890. By courtesy of Somerset Archaeological and Natural History Society.

The gable windows

The windows are of three lights, estimated to be 2½ feet by 10 inches, with ovolo-moulded mullions and jambs. Evidently in 1921 enough remaining freestone components were found to rebuild only two of the four original windows, with a small insert of new freestone in the head of the west window and a complete new head to the south window. The original windows had a vertical bar in the middle of each light. The holes where they were sunk are present in the original stone, absent in the stone cut in 1922. Both windows have original stone drip-moulds.

The interior and nest-holes

Solid masonry containing original nest-holes crosses the corners of the interior. From one foot above the earth floor to the roof the walls are occupied by nest-holes in chequer pattern; the sides are formed of hammer-dressed freestone, the floors of rubble slabs 3½ inches thick, with lime mortar (figure 126). The entrances are 6½ inches high by 6 - 7 inches wide. Inside they all turn to the left to form asymmetrical bulb-shapes, about 13 inches wide and 17 - 18 inches from front to back. There are 20 tiers, with 41 nest-holes in a complete tier. About 15 were omitted for the original doorway, so when first built there were about 805. They were lined from the outset with clay daub, applied from above as each tier was completed; in some the lining has survived intact; in others it has nearly all gone.

Above the door, and elsewhere above a height of about 11 feet the nest-holes were rebuilt in 1922, mostly re-using the original freestone blocks at the sides but with new stone to replace the old floor slabs. The re-built nest-holes are above the white pointer in figure 126.

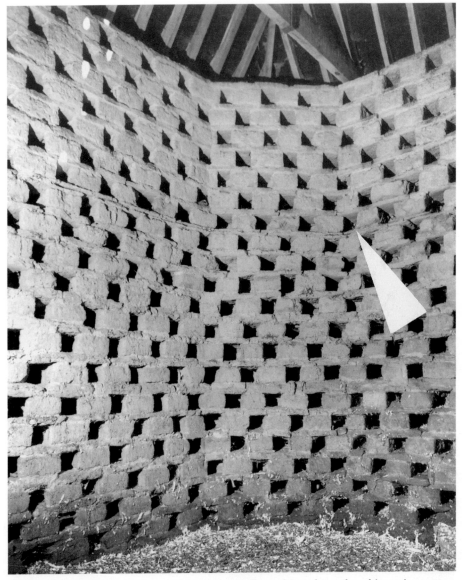

Figure 126: Godminster: the south-east corner. Everything above the white pointer was
rebuilt in 1922-3.

Dating and use

Four-gabled stone dovecotes are fairly common in the west Midland counties;
some bear seventeenth-century inscribed dates. This form of roof provides sloping
surfaces facing in all directions on which the pigeons could sun themselves, sheltered
from wind from all directions.

Figure 132: The dovecote of
Heale House, Curry Rivel,
from the south-east.

Figure 134: Curry Rivel: the interior,
facing west.

Figure 136: The dovecote of Abbey Farm, Montacute, from the south-south-west.

Figure 137: The original south-west
doorway.

The photograph of *c.* 1890 shows the building rendered overall, the recess over the door empty, and the roof in disrepair. There was a lean-to shed against the west elevation; fruit trees were trained against the south elevation. The dovecote has been rebuilt without external render, but owing to the cement pointing overall there is no visible indication from outside that the walls above 10 - 11 feet have been wholly rebuilt. Inside, the junction with the newer work is clearly visible.

Originally the four-gabled louver would have had open gables, as found elsewhere. It has been rebuilt with closed gables and multiple flight holes, copying the form it had reached by 1890, by which time it had already been adapted for keeping a small number of ornamental pigeons (figure 124). It is still in use, with some white fantails in residence.

It is remarkable that most observers have described this building as four-gabled; it is not. They include the writers of the Listed Building reports of 1961 and 1984, the authors Peter and Jean Hansell in two publications, and the *Victoria County History*.[107] It is most easily approached from the south-west, and that aspect has been much photographed, but Horne's photograph of 1923 shows that the roof was built then with only two gables, and plain inclines on the other two sides, as it remains to this day (figure 125). Only the modern louver is four-gabled.

MANOR FARM, SOUTHSTOKE (ST 747 612) ───

Southstoke is two miles south of central Bath, on the northern slope of the valley of the Cam Brook, a tributary of the Avon. This example is a pigeon-loft over a stable, a handsome construction originally designed for those purposes. A fifteenth-century barn of seven bays is aligned north-south with a porch to the east, on land declining to the south. South of the porch is a small lean-to. The stable/pigeon-loft is set in the south-east angle, between the lean-to and the south bays of the barn (figure 127, opposite p.123). Therefore the only elevations face south and east. Externally it is 20½ feet north to south by 15 feet 4 inches east to west, and 13½ feet high to the eaves. It is fitted against the barn built two centuries earlier so neatly as to mislead some writers into believing that they are both of the same construction.[109] It is Listed as Grade II*.

The fabric

It is built of coursed oolitic limestone rubble with quoins and other dressings of Bath stone, in lime mortar. The outer walls are two feet thick.

The doorway and windows

The stable doorway faces east and is 6 feet 8 inches high by 4 feet 3 inches wide. In the same elevation is a small window. In the south elevation is another small window and an ovolo-moulded two-light window with a moulded drip-ledge.

The external nest-holes

Above first-floor level the east (gable) elevation has eight tiers of nest-holes in chequer pattern facing outwards, with five perching ledges – one below and one above the assembly, and one to each second tier (figure 128). The entrances are 6

Figure 128: Manor Farm, Southstoke: the gable facing east. Originally the nest-holes and perching ledges continued across the gable uninterrupted. When it ceased to be used for pigeons a pitching hole was inserted, later converted to a window.

inches square; inside they are of the same height, but cut to a distinctive plan (figure 188), 13 inches wide and 15 inches from front to back. A loading hole 3 feet 8 inches high by 2 feet 5 inches wide has been inserted into the pattern, and later converted to a casement window, leaving 73 of an original set of 91 nest-holes in this elevation. The perching ledges are 3½ inches wide, with chamfered soffits; the lowest is 10 feet above ground.

In the south elevation are three tiers of similar nest-holes and three perching ledges – the upper one immediately below the eaves (figure 129). When photographed by Horne an inserted pitching door interrupted the tiers of nest-holes. It has been restored to almost its original form, a dormer window of two lights with ovolo-moulded jambs and mullion; but the lower part of the inserted aperture is blocked by a large blank stone. Parts of the window are original – particularly the jambs and the drip-ledge above. This alteration and minor repairs have left 18 of an original set of 28 nest-holes in this elevation.

Figure 129: Manor Farm, Southstoke. The south elevation.

Figure 130: Southstoke: nest-holes in the internal gable wall, against the barn.

The internal nest-holes

The first floor is reached by a wooden stair immediately inside the entrance. The gable wall and the wall opposite (against the main barn) are occupied by sets of similar nest-holes in chequer pattern, but without ledges (figure 130). The east gable wall has 32 nest-holes, and the west wall 40. Adding the external and internal nest-holes together, this makes a total of 191 originally, of which 163 remain in good order.

The flight holes

In the east gable, above the tiers of nest-holes, is a rectangular flight hole 2 feet high by 11 inches wide, splayed to the inside, with original timber lintels. In the south elevation, above the window, is an arched flight-hole 1 foot 8 inches high by 11 inches wide (figure 131). Both are now glazed.

The roof

This is aligned east-west. The east gable and south dormer have plain copings and cruciform finials. The timber structure is original, with two purlins in each pitch, secured by forelocks, and a ridge-piece. Like the barn it is clad with stone tiles.

Figure 131: Southstoke: the flight hole and restored south window.

Dating and use

This is a highly accomplished building which expresses a period of prosperity, and confidence in the owner's manorial status. It is datable by the window details to the seventeenth century. However, the economics of farming are constantly changing. The insertion of pitching doors in the pigeon-loft, and conspicuous ritual marks on the inside wall, indicate that what was built for pigeons has been used to store farm produce, probably cheeses, later in the seventeenth or eighteenth century.[108] In the east elevation the insertion of a low aperture, blocked later, indicates that at another period the ground floor has been used as a pig-sty. It has survived these changes with minimal alterations, and remains easily recognizable as a stable with pigeon-loft above, as it was built. The Listed Building report states that it was restored in the 'mid-late 1940s'.

THE DOVECOTE OF HEALE HOUSE AT HEALE WOLD, CURRY RIVEL (ST 382 256)

Curry Rivel is on the ridge between the River Isle and West Sedge Moor, two miles south-west of Langport. The dovecote is 260 yards west-south-west of Heale House. It was part of the home farm, but is now absorbed into Burton Pyenent Dairy Farm, in an abandoned farmyard 30 yards south-east of the nearest contemporary building, Heale Barn, a barn converted into a dwelling. It is 20½ feet long by 20 feet wide, and 14 feet high to the eaves; a door and a window face south-south-east (figure 132, opposite p. 134). A dense growth of elder and brambles obstructs the west end. There are tall trees in an overgrown hedgerow to the west and north.

The fabric

It is built of alternate thick and thin courses of blue lias in lime mortar. The thin courses are of softer stone and have weathered back to produce a ribbed appearance. Stone of the same quality is used for the nest-holes, where it exhibits fine cuboidal fractures, like dry rot in wood.[110] The walls are 2 feet 4 inches thick. There is a short buttress at the south-east corner, and two tie-bars have been fitted to prevent the eastern end from spreading. High on the south-east corner the masonry has been substantially repaired on the outside only.

The doorway and original door

The doorway is 4 feet 2 inches high by 2 feet wide, with a chevron head. It is formed of massive blocks of Hamstone, splayed to the inside, and rebated for a door opening inwards (figure 133). Both original pintle hinges remain *in situ* in the right jamb, with a wrought iron staple opposite to receive the tongue of the lock. Inside the arched head are two oak lintels 5 inches deep by 8½ inches wide. The original

Figure 133: Curry Rivel: the original door, now much decayed.

chevron-headed door is still present, severely decayed at the bottom, hanging from one hinge. It consists of two layers of oak boards, laid vertically outside, horizontally inside, secured by numerous square-headed nails clenched inside. It retains one strap hinge and a stock-lock.

The window

The window above the door is 2½ feet square, the sill 11½ feet above ground, with a decayed frame.

The nest-holes

From 2½ feet above the floor to the roof the walls are occupied by a grid pattern of box-shaped nest-holes, 8½ inches square and 14 inches from front to back (figure 134, opposite p.134). They were made with the entrances 5 inches wide, but in many one piece of stone has been removed (or has fallen out), widening it to 8½ inches (figure 135). There is one plain ledge 2 feet 3 inches above the floor, 2½ inches wide and 3 inches thick.

In the front and rear walls there are 12 tiers of nest-holes, with 13 in a complete tier. In each gable wall there are 12 in each tier, and diminishing tiers up to the apex, making an additional 140. Allowing for those omitted for the door and window this makes a total of 740 nest-holes, all still open.

Figure 135: Curry Rivel: detail of the nest-holes. In some a piece of stone which formerly reduced the width of the entrance has been removed.

The floor has been paved with stone flags, but it has been so comprehensively undermined by brown rats that it now appears to be of a random mixture of earth and stone.

The roof and former louver

The gable parapets have stepped plain copings. The much-repaired roof structure is in three bays, with a ridge-piece and two joggled and tusk-tenoned butt-purlins in each pitch. The original wall-plates are present, chamfered below, with some minor repairs. Some of the purlins are of ash retaining bark. One principal rafter is made from a re-used cruck blade with the curvature reversed. The common rafters in the two outer bays are of hardwood of square section; those in the middle bay have been replaced with modern softwood. In the middle bay there is no ridge-piece, and the upper purlins exhibit water staining and some decay where the louver was formerly mounted. The cladding is of red clay plain tiles. Horne's photograph of 1939 shows a simple louver with a pyramidal roof, but he commented: 'The exit on the roof may follow in design the one that was there before, but there is no opening beneath it, into the building'.

Dating and use

This is a seventeenth-century building, designed to make a bold impression when it stood isolated; but the growth of trees and the remote position have left it quite obscure now. The small doorway shows that it has never been adapted for secondary use. Hope Grange reported in 1937 that it had no windows, and that the interior was very dark, from which we can deduce that the only window aperture had been blocked; it is open now.[111] The roof has been repaired at various dates; originally it was clad with stone slates.

A lease of 1795 between Samuel Alford of Heale House and Thomas Lockyer and William Stuckley, yeomen, refers to Pigeon House Plott but excepts it from the land leased. That is, Alford reserved the dovecote for his own use although he was content to let others farm the adjacent land.[112] Large-scale pigeon-keeping ceased soon afterwards, as reported in Chapter 4.

Evidently the louver photographed by Horne was purely ornamental. In the first few years of the twentieth century Mildred Berkeley campaigned by lectures and magazine articles to persuade the owners of dovecotes to restore them to good order.[4] The effect was mostly to regard them as ornamental garden buildings, and to restore them as such. The louver may have been one result of her influence.

ABBEY FARM, MONTACUTE (ST 497 169)

The dovecote is isolated in a paddock declining gently to the east, 30 yards south of the parish church, and 90 yards east-south-east of Abbey Farmhouse, formerly the gatehouse of the Cluniac priory. The site is enclosed by the wooded conical hill which gives Montacute its name 500 yards to the north-west, and a long ridge to the south and south-west. There is a pond 60 yards to the south-west. The dovecote is 17 feet 8 inches square and 13 feet high to the eaves, with an original doorway in the south-west side and an inserted doorway opposite (figure 136, opposite p.135). It is Listed Grade II and is included in the Scheduled site of the priory.

The fabric

This is of uncoursed Hamstone rubble with quoins of re-used ashlar (probably from the demolished priory) in lime mortar. It has been re-pointed locally with cement mortar. There are no windows, perching ledges or cornices. The walls are 1 foot 8 inches thick.

The doorways

The original doorway is 4 feet 2 inches high by 2 feet wide with a shallow chevron arch formed from a single block of ashlar 3 feet wide by 2 feet 2 inches high (figure 137, opposite p.135). It is chamfered all round, and rebated on the inside for a door opening inwards. The inserted doorway facing north-east is 4 feet 10 inches high by 3 feet 7 inches wide, with lintels formed from re-used timbers, and a concrete threshold. Both have modern doors.

Figure 138: Montacute: The interior and roof, facing south-west.

The interior and nest-holes

The whole interior has been rebuilt in response to the hazard of brown rats in the eighteenth century. The lowest tier of nest-holes is 5 feet 2 inches above the stone floor, with plain rubble below. Immediately below it is a ledge projecting 5 - 6 inches composed of the old stone tiles of which the floors of the nest-holes are formed. The tiers are arranged in three bands of three separated by bands of plain rubble 13 inches high (figure 138). Most of the nest-hole entrances are in grid pattern, but over the inserted doorway they form a chequer pattern. The sides and fronts are formed of bricks 9 x 4¼ x 2½ inches; they are of a plan which has not been observed elsewhere (figure 188, page 202). Stretchers at the front form a tunnel behind, having two entrances each 6½ inches high by 6 - 8 inches wide. The whole is 2 feet 1 inch wide by 13 inches from front to back. The height is 6½ inches throughout. There are 40 nest-hole entrances in each tier.

The roof and former louver

The roof forms a truncated pyramid, composed partly of machine-sawn timber, partly of original components. Hip rafters and principal rafters in the middle of each side support a square frame at the apex, with an aperture 2 feet square through which the pigeons flew in and out. Joggled purlins at mid-height support the common rafters (figure 138). At the eaves it is clad with three courses of stone tiles, indicating the original cladding. Above them are red clay tiles; most are hand-made, with some local repairs in machine-made tiles. There are blue clay ridge tiles on the hips. The square aperture at the apex was covered by clear plastic sheeting when seen in July 1999.

A louver was still in place when Horne visited in 1937, and is shown in his photograph (figure 139). It consisted of four posts and a pyramidal roof, open on all sides, with a shallow segmental arch over each. He wrote: 'The exit is now permanently closed down'. Local informants report that the louver was present until 1958-9.

Dating and use

This dovecote was built in the seventeenth century and altered in the later eighteenth century by various members of the Phelips family.[113] The original nest-holes would have been formed in the rubble fabric from a little above floor level.

Figure 139: Montacute: Horne's photograph taken in 1937, showing the louver still in place.
By courtesy of the Somerset Archaeological and Natural History Society.

When brown rats presented a new hazard in the eighteenth century the inner layer of rubble was stripped out and replaced by the present lining containing brick nest-holes. As they are over 5 feet above the floor, additionally protected by a stone ledge below, this was probably done when brown rats first arrived in the area, for later it was realised that a sheer wall 3 feet high provided sufficient protection.

The double nest-holes are ingenious. The breeding cycle of pigeons is so short that young breeding pairs may be still feeding one pair of squabs while incubating the next clutch of eggs. By the early nineteenth century J. C. Loudon was advocating that all nests should be arranged in pairs.[114] The arrangement here is more flexible, allowing each nest-hole to be used either as one or two.

The wide doorway inserted in the north-east elevation is as high as it can be without interrupting the tiers of nest-holes above, but it is too low for practical secondary uses. Part-floors have been improvised against the walls which do not have doors. The building is used only for miscellaneous storage.

MANOR BARN, QUEEN SQUARE, SALTFORD (ST 685 675)

Saltford is between Bristol and Bath. The ancillary building illustrated in figure 140 is associated with Saltford Manor. In August 2003 an enquiry arranged by *Country Life* found that this house is twelfth century, the oldest **continuously inhabited** house in Britain; the building shown is a later addition. It is situated on level ground 50 yards west of the parish church and 4 yards north of Manor Barn. It is aligned approximately east-west, 18 feet 4 inches by 13 feet, and 12 feet high to the eaves. The doorway is in the east gable end, and there are other apertures to east, south and west. When examined in June 2001 a heavy growth of ivy covered both gables and the roof. The building is disused and difficult to approach; a raised flower-bed has been built against the entrance to a depth of three feet. The west and north elevations are obstructed by dense growths of nettles, elder and ivy.

The fabric

The walls are of local oolitic limestone rubble with ashlar quoins of Bath stone. They are 1 foot 10 inches thick.

The apertures

The size of the doorway indicates that its last use was as a stable. In the same gable end there is a first-floor aperture 3 feet 4 inches high by 1 foot 10 inches wide, without a frame. In the south elevation is an unglazed window 2 feet 2 inches high by 2 feet wide, 4½ feet above ground level, with a jointed and pegged oak frame with one mullion, and three horizontal straps of wrought iron secured by hand-made nails. There is a small unglazed window low in the west elevation.

The floor and roof

An original floor in ruinous condition consists of one transverse beam with scroll stops and hand-sawn joists of 4 x 3-inch vertical section. The roof structure is of butt-purlin construction in two bays, with a ridge-piece; it is clad with red clay pantiles. There is no evidence of a former louver.

Figure 140: The combined stable and pigeon-loft at Manor Barn, Saltford, from the east-south-east.

Dating and use

In 1951 this building was Listed as a dovecote, 'possibly seventeenth-century', mentioning 'upper openings in gables with perches'. Owing to the enveloping ivy these features were not visible when examined in June 2001. The scroll stops confirm the period. The walls do not contain nest-holes, but wooden nest-boxes could have been provided, leaving no evidence when they were removed. The first-floor doorway is of a size likely in a pigeon-loft over a stable, and is too narrow to be used easily as the pitching hole to a hay-loft.

THE DOVECOTE, CLAVERTON, NEAR BATH (ST 788 643)

Claverton is on the west bank of the Avon valley, two miles east of central Bath. This is now a private house, converted in 1986 from a farm building (figure 141). In 1928 Horne wrote: 'The dovecote is situated in the farm yard [of Claverton Manor Farm] and has very little left to show that it was once a columbarium. It is much changed inside in order to convert it to a barn for farm use, a floor having been made through the middle of the building, and windows have been placed in the walls. The place is about 24 feet square inside and although most of the nest holes have now been filled, they must originally have numbered about 300 . . . The roof is new'.

Figure 141: The former dovecote at Claverton, now converted to a dwelling, from the north-west.

The fabric

It is built of oolitic limestone rubble with ashlar quoins in lime mortar.

The conversion

Horne's photograph shows the building just outside a high garden wall, the roof clad with double Roman tiles (as it is now), with a door and two windows in the west elevation. The door has been converted to a window, and another ground-floor window and two half-dormers have been inserted on this side. His photograph shows a ledge on brackets high on the north gable, evidently for the pigeons to perch on; it has been removed. A small lean-to extension has been built at this end, and twin lancet windows have been inserted above it. It was in use as a garage when re-Listed in the late 1980s. Most of the nest-holes were plastered over when it was converted to a dwelling. So much has changed that it is impossible now to deduce much about it when it was a dovecote.

The nest-holes

The only indication that it was one is a chequer pattern of six nest-holes exposed in a first-floor bedroom. The entrances are 7 inches square, 10 inches apart in the same tier, and 3½ inches above the tier below. They are L-shaped in plan, 11 inches wide and 11 inches from front to back, and were lined with lime plaster from the outset.

KING'S LOOD, KINGSTON ST. MARY (ST 220 299)

This is three miles north of Taunton. In 1939 Horne described this building as a stable with dovecote above. Since then it has been converted to a dwelling, and some of the original features are now missing or concealed by modern plaster. However, enough remains to be worth illustrating (figure 142). It is situated some

Figure 142: King's Lood, Kingston St. Mary, from the east-north-east.

20 yards south-west of the Manor House with which it was formerly associated, on land declining gently to the south-west. It is 34 feet long by 20 feet wide, and 16 feet high to the eaves. The door and the coach-house doors were in the long elevation facing east-north-east; the latter is now converted to a window. High in each of the two long elevations are two original oval flight holes, and in the south gable end two more, one above the other. On the outside at first-floor level there are two tiers of nest-holes, visible on the east and south elevations, concealed by a modern lean-to on the west elevation.

The fabric

It is built of uncoursed rough red sandstone rubble from the Quantocks, with clay mortar. Above first-floor level it incorporates some brick.

The external nest-holes

There are two tiers of nest-holes, the lower 9½ feet above ground. Each entrance is 7 inches high by 4¾ inches wide. Inside they are of the same height, L-shaped in plan, 16 inches wide and 15 inches from front to back. Below each tier is a perching ledge of slate, 4½ inches wide and 1½ inches thick. At the south gable end the lower tier is interrupted by the concrete lintel of a modern window (already present in 1939), and in the east elevation some nest-holes have been lost above the door and coach-house doors. In Horne's photograph the vertical surface between the ledges was rendered with lime plaster, forming a conspicuous white band; that plaster is now fragmentary. The nest-holes in the rear elevation are accessible in the roof space of the lean-to extension.

Figure 143: King's Lood, Kingston St. Mary: nest-holes in the south gable.

The internal nest-holes

Most are now concealed by modern materials, but some are exposed in the south gable, within what is now an attic (figure 143). Nine diminishing tiers of nest-holes are arranged in chequer pattern up to the apex, formed with bricks and lime mortar in the same way as those outside, with an alighting ledge of slate to each tier. The ledges project 2½ inches. The entrances are the same size as those outside. The nest-holes which could be examined are 12 inches wide and 13 - 14 inches front to back, but in the gable they are necessarily irregular. Immediately inside the entrances they are whitened with lime mortar. Although the gable was partly obscured by stacked lumber when inspected a calculation suggests that 45 nest-holes are present there, from the modern attic floor up to the apex. Horne reported that there were no nest-holes below first floor level, so we may assume a further four tiers of nest-holes below those which are visible, down to the level where the walls are occupied by external nest-holes. Horne counted 266. The north gable is obscured inside by an inserted chimney, but it seems reasonable to believe that nest-holes were present in this wall originally, already obscured by 1939. Therefore there may have been 350 - 380 nest-holes inside, and about 104 outside.

The flight holes

Each flight hole is formed of a solid plate of Hamstone 1 foot 8 inches square, with an oval aperture 15 x 13 inches. They are now glazed.

The roof

The building retains its original roof structure, of butt-purlin construction in five bays, with two purlins in each pitch. The principal rafters are notched and pegged at the apex. Straight collars are pegged and spiked to them. The principals bear assembly marks in Roman numerals, cut with a chisel, numbering from south to north. There is no ridge-piece. All the common rafters are original, of 4 x 4-inch section. It is clad with double Roman clay tiles.

There is no gap in the roof structure where a louver could have been, so as Horne deduced, the pigeons flew in and out of the oval apertures in the walls.

Dating and use

The Manor House was built *circa* 1560, with alterations dated 1702 by inscription. The combined stable, coach-house and dovecote was built of similar Quantocks stone. The roof structure and the bricks indicate that it is of late seventeenth-century origin. An internal chimney was inserted at the north end some time before 1939. Human access to the loft was by an internal ladder, still present when Horne was there. It has been used as a dwelling since 1944, and has been more comprehensively converted in recent years. Now it has modern windows and doorways outlined in brick.

CHARLTON HOUSE, CHARLTON MACKRELL (ST 529 291)

Charlton Mackrell is two miles east of Somerton. Charlton House is an early Georgian mansion facing west-south-west. Its dovecote is 6 yards north-east of the house (figure 144, opposite p.152). The ridge of the roof is aligned parallel with the house although it is 22 feet across the gable ends, 20 feet 9 inches in the other dimension; it is 17½ feet high to the eaves. The pigeon-loft is on the first floor. The first-floor doorway faces east-north-east, away from the house. There are no windows in the pigeon-loft.

Figure 145: Charlton Mackrell: a perching ledge on the west elevation.

The fabric

The walls are of coursed blue lias, neatly hammer-dressed and squared, in lime mortar. Above a weathered plinth the wall is 2 feet 10 inches thick. There are two perching ledges 3 inches wide on the west elevation only; one is 6½ feet high, the other 16 feet high, just below the eaves (figure 145). The upper ledge extends round the returns. At the same level a horizontal slab projects from the north-east corner (figure 3, p.29). The broken stub of a similar slab projects at the south-east corner.

The doorway

The doorway is 5 feet 10 inches high by 3 feet 4 inches wide. Because the ground level rises to the east it is reached by a flight of only ten stone steps, with a wrought iron hand-rail. The nineteenth-century door is hung on pintle hinges in the right jamb to open inwards. It is ledged and boarded, with fine roll-mouldings throughout, and is fitted with a stock-lock.

The inserted window

In the south wall beside the door is an inserted window 3 feet 2 inches high by 2 feet 4 inches wide, later blocked with masonry and rendered.

The roof

The coped gables have cruciform finials. The original roof structure has two pairs of principal rafters each with two collars lap-dovetailed and pegged, and two purlins in each pitch. Between the principals is a space 5½ feet by 2 feet in which the louver was formerly mounted. Some of the common rafters are original. The present cladding is of Welsh slate.

The nest-holes

The walls are occupied from floor to roof by a regular chequer pattern of nest-holes, extending up the gables (figure 146). The entrances are 7½ inches high by 8 inches wide. Inside they are of the same height; in plan they form oblique parallelograms 8 inches wide by 19 inches from front to back, very neatly executed (figure 188). The lower parts of the walls are obscured by grain bins and apple racks, so not all the nest-holes can be seen, but a calculation indicates that originally there were at least 516 – or a few more if the doorway has been enlarged. Only 43 can be seen to be blocked, mostly in the east wall. There are no internal ledges.

Dating and use

The house was built by Thomas Lyte in 1726. Originally the road from Kingweston to Ilchester passed close to the front elevation, but between 1800 and 1806 the owner, John Jerritt, was authorised to divert the public road to form a

Figure 146: Charlton Mackrell: nest-holes in the south gable wall, with apple racks below.

wide loop to the south-west. He enclosed that part and retained the old road as a carriage entrance.[115] Whereas the house was evidently designed by an architect, the dovecote is more traditional in design and construction, and could be older. External features which suggest an earlier origin are the cruciform ornaments crowning the gables, the high perching ledge extending round the corners, and the projecting stone slabs high on the north-east and south-east corners. Similar corner ledges have been observed on a sixteenth-century stone dovecote at Newton-in-the-Willows, Northamptonshire, and on seventeenth-century stone dovecotes at Westington and Broad Campden, Gloucestershire.[116] Their function was to prevent polecats and martens from climbing the corners of the building to gain access to the interior. Similar protective features are fairly common in France, where the stone marten, a related species, is (or has been) common.

The parallelogram plan of the nest-holes is unique in Somerset, and is rare elsewhere. Nest-boxes of similar shape but constructed in wood are present in a Worcestershire dovecote.[117]

This building has been used as a granary, and still has incomplete grain bins against the north wall. Those against the south wall have been replaced by apple storage racks. The present doorway and the flight of stone steps date only from the early nineteenth-century granary phase. The doorway was probably smaller originally, accessed by a removable ladder. The ground floor is devoted to ancillary uses associated with the house.

MANOR FARM, CHURCH PATH, WEST CAMEL (ST 579 246)

West Camel is on the River Cam, a tributary of the Yeo, half a mile south of the road A.303 and 5 miles north of Yeovil. The house is mainly eighteenth-century, retaining some fifteenth-century features. It is 25 yards west of the parish church, orientated east-west. Over a large bread oven outside the west gable a pigeon-tower has been built (figure 147, opposite). The entrance to it is at first-floor level, originally accessible by external ladder, now enclosed by a modern extension. There is one window in the west wall, and a set of flight holes in the gable.

The fabric

It is built of coursed blue lias rubble with clay mortar. The doorway is of normal human size, now modernized. Inside, the pigeon-tower is 9 feet 8 inches by 6 feet 4 inches, and 15 feet 8 inches high from the first floor to the eaves. The floor has been concreted.

The flight holes and window

In the west gable is a triangular pattern of ten flight holes in four tiers, with a perching ledge below each tier (figure 148). Externally the flight holes are of an elegant two-centred shape, cut in freestone. On the inside each forms a square aperture in the rubble fabric, with a thin wooden board between tiers. Below them is a window 8 feet 4 inches above the internal floor, 2 feet 3 inches square with a modern frame, splayed to the inside, with two oak lintels 4 inches deep. The inner lintel is 14 inches wide.

Figure 144: The dovecote of Charlton House, Charlton Mackrell, from the east.

Figure 147: Manor Farm, West Camel, from the south-west. The pigeon-tower is at left, now enclosed by a modern extension. The parish church is at right.

Figure 150: The pigeon-tower of Widcombe House, Bath, from the east-south-east.

Figure 148: Manor Farm, West Camel: the flight holes and perching ledges.

The roof

The west gable has a plain coping with a cruciform apex and ball finial (figure 148). The roof is modern, clad with red clay plain tiles.

The nest-holes

The north, west and south walls are occupied from 1½ feet above the floor to the roof by a regular grid pattern of nest-holes (figure 149). The entrances are 6 inches square. Inside they are of the same height, forming reversed wedges in

Figure 149: Manor Farm, West Camel: nest-holes in the south and west walls, and an original window.

plan, 9½ inches wide and 16 inches from front to back. In the north and south walls there are 17 tiers of nest-holes, and 19 in the west (gable) wall, with 21 nest-holes in a complete tier. There are an additional 72 nest-holes in the east wall (against the house), arranged less regularly; part of it is occupied by a flue. Allowing for those omitted for the door and window this makes a total of 417. All are open and in good order. Traces of whitewash remain outside the nest-holes.

Dating and use

The tithe map of 1839 shows that Manor Farm formerly stood just to the rear, 12 yards north-west of the church; it has been demolished. The present house has acquired the name. The pigeon-tower was built over an existing bread oven. It is difficult to date, but is believed to be of the early eighteenth century. It has never been adapted to any other use, and remains in perfect condition today. It is within 150 yards of the dovecote at The Old Rectory (page 109).

WIDCOMBE HOUSE, WIDCOMBE, BATH (ST 761 638)

This unusual pigeon-tower is of distinguished architectural design, handsomely executed in golden Bath stone. It is octagonal, of three storeys with a cupola (figure

150, opposite p.153), situated 10 yards south-west of Widcombe House (formerly the coach-house and stable range of Widcombe Manor), in a garden declining steeply to the south-west. Each side of the octagon is 5 feet 10 inches; it is 25 feet high to the eaves. It is exceptional in having external nest-holes in addition to those within the pigeon-loft. The arched doorway and a smaller door to the pigeon-loft face north-east; on the first floor there are windows to west and south-west. A chimney in the thickness of the south-east wall serves fireplaces on the ground and first floors.

The external features

At first-floor level the elevations facing north, north-east and east (towards Widcombe House) incorporate a regular grid pattern of nest-holes facing outwards. The entrances are of inverted-U shape 7 inches high by 5 inches wide. The nest-holes are L-shaped in plan, 11 inches wide, 14 inches from front to back. Each wall has eleven tiers of four nest-holes, 132 in all. Below the lowest tier is a moulded perching ledge all round the building, 3½ inches wide, 5½ inches deep. At 16 and 24 feet above ground are two wider moulded perching ledges, the upper one just below the eaves. Each facet of the octagon displays a blank medallion below the upper ledge.

The lower storeys

The ground and first-floor rooms are designed for human use, connected by a winding stair. Each has a coal-burning hearth. On the ground floor there is a blocked window facing south-west. The upper room has two sash windows of 9 + 9 lights, and a fixed wooden bunk. There is now a trap-door to the pigeon-loft above but this is not original; formerly the only access to the pigeon-loft was by ladder.

The roof and cupola

The roof is clad with stone tiles. The pigeons entered by an octagonal stone cupola (figure 151, opposite p.160). In the early twentieth century a surveyor found that it was inadequately supported on two crossed tie-beams, and was subsiding. The ceiling of the pigeon-loft was replaced by a solid concrete floor which now supports the cupola, with a trap 2 feet square through it. The arched apertures of the cupola are 2 feet 3 inches high by 1 foot 2 inches wide; four of them have been blocked. It is finished with a ball finial and weather-cock.

The pigeon-loft and internal nest-holes

The pigeon-loft was entered by an arched doorway 4 feet high by 2 feet 3 inches wide from a removable external ladder; it retains the original ledged and boarded door (figure 152). At that point the wall is 1 foot 8 inches thick. Six sides of the interior are occupied from floor to ceiling by a regular grid pattern of nest-holes in eight tiers; there are three tiers above the doorway. The south-east wall (containing the flue) is blank. All have rectangular entrances 8½ inches high by 6 inches wide. The nest-holes are of the same height, L-shaped in plan, 13 inches wide by 13 inches from front to back. There are 18 nest-holes in a complete tier, making 153 in all. There is a plain ledge at mid-height 3 inches wide by 4 inches deep. The whole is finely executed in Bath stone. There is no trace of whitewash.

Figure 152: Widcombe House: in the pigeon-loft, with the original door.

Dating and use

The best evidence of date is a landscape sketch of Bath by Thomas Robbins which clearly shows Widcombe pigeon-tower; it is dated 1748. The building was probably fairly new at the time, as this property was not developed until 1728.[118] The first-floor room was evidently designed as a garden pavilion providing long views to south and west. The ground-floor room was mainly for servicing it. It is now used for storage.

The nest-holes inside and outside the building total 285. Whether the external nest-holes facing the cold north-to-east quadrant were as attractive to pigeons as the more commodious ones inside the dark loft seems very doubtful. They may never have been occupied, except perhaps in summer.

Horne quoted a passage from Jane Austen's *Sense and Sensibility*, ostensibly describing the fictional 'Delaford' where she stayed, but which seems to describe Widcombe Manor: 'Then there is the **dovecote** and delightful stewponds, and a pretty canal . . . and moreover it is close to the church and only a mile from the turnpike road'.[119]

WHITESTAUNTON MANOR, WHITESTAUNTON (ST 280 104)

Whitestaunton is 1¼ miles east of the River Yarty, ½ mile north of the road A.30 and three miles west of Chard. Whitestaunton Manor is a major house of mid-fifteenth-century origin standing south-west of the parish church. The dovecote is one of a range of outbuildings bordering a court between them, 15 yards from the house. The ground level is several feet below the churchyard. It is 29 feet long by 24 feet wide, and is 21 feet high to the eaves (figure 153). The doorway and two high windows face west. It has been comprehensively converted to a granary, and remains in that form today.

Figure 153: The dovecote of Whitestaunton Manor, Whitestaunton, converted to a granary, from the west-north-west.

The fabric

Outside it is built of coursed rectangular blocks of local greensand and chert. Inside it is the same up to the nest-holes; they are made of limestone blocks with Hamstone dressings. The walls are 2 feet 11 inches thick.

The doorway

This is 5 feet above the level of the yard, now approached by a modern terrace, but formerly high enough for sacks of corn to be loaded to and from a cart. The aperture is 6 feet 8 inches high by 4 feet 7 inches wide, with a shallow segmental arch over, slightly splayed to the inside. It retains a jointed and pegged door-frame and double doors.

The windows

Immediately below the eaves are two window apertures 3 feet 2 inches high by 3 feet 9 inches wide, deeply splayed to the inside, fitted with modern casements.

The nest-holes

The nest-holes (which are all blocked) are arranged in regular grid pattern, the lowest 4 feet 9 inches above the modern concrete floor (figures 154, 155 and 156). Each is a simple box-shaped recess 7½ inches square and 16 inches from front to back. There are 13 tiers, with 62 nest-holes in a complete tier. Therefore originally there were at least 806 nest-holes; and as the original roof was probably gabled with nest-holes extending up each gable, likely to be nearer 900.

Below most of the tiers of nest-holes is a ledge of Hamstone, projecting 1½ inches, 1½ inches thick, and chamfered above and below. Evidently these are alighting ledges, intended for the pigeons to perch and parade on; they are deliberately made too narrow for birds of prey, and have part of that surface set at an angle. Below the lowest tier is a ledge which projects 3½ inches, is 2½ inches thick, and is unchamfered. Above the sixth tier, at a height of 9 feet 9 inches, the wall thickness is reduced to 2 feet 7 inches, and there is a ledge 4 inches wide, 2½ inches thick, also unchamfered. The purpose of these ledges is less clear, but they may have been provided for the pigeon-keeper to climb on while collecting the squabs.

Figure 154: Whitestaunton: above the inserted floor, showing the north and east walls, and the stair trap at bottom left.

Figure 155: Whitestaunton: the alighting ledges have been cut back at intervals, and the nest-holes have been blocked with limestone, for use as a granary.

As a dovecote

It was built after the introduction of brown rats, and was designed from the outset to be elaborately rat-proof. The floor and entrance were raised 5 feet above the yard, and the nest-holes were raised almost 5 feet above that, additionally protected by a ledge below them. This is well above the height to which brown rats can jump or climb, but evidently it was designed at a time when the owner was unsure how much height was necessary for protection.

The insertion of a large granary door has destroyed all evidence of the original doorway; it would have been in the same position as the present one, but much smaller. If it were less than 5 feet high, as in many other dovecotes, it would not have interrupted the lowest tiers of nest-holes. The entrance for the pigeons would have been a louver on the ridge.

As a granary

When this building passed out of use as a dovecote it was converted to a granary. The doorway was enlarged, and windows and a floor were inserted. To support the floor, intended to be heavily loaded with corn, a longitudinal wall of stone rubble was built just forward of centre, leaving a gap 4 feet wide in the middle for access.

Figure 156: Whitestaunton: the trap in the north-east corner. The lowest tier of nest-holes is set five feet above the floor for protection from brown rats. When it was converted to a granary the joists of the inserted floor were lodged in the fifth tier of nest-holes. The others were neatly blocked with limestone.

The joists were inserted into the fifth tier of nest-holes in the long walls, and the remainder of each nest-hole was filled (figure 156). A trap was formed in the rear right corner; a ladder leads up to it. At the front the original wall is still almost complete to full height (apart from the insertion of windows), but elsewhere some upper tiers of nest-holes were taken down, and the wall was repaired with solid rubble above the remaining nest-holes (figure 154). The gables were taken down, and a hipped roof was built.

Subsequent developments can be deduced from curious slots in the ledges. When corn bins were built the nest-holes were blocked at first with vertical boards. Sections of the alighting ledges were cut away to allow them to lie flat against the wall, and the exposed surfaces were lime-washed. Evidently this was found to be unsatisfactory; grains fell into the nest-holes, became mouldy and contaminated the stored crop. Later the boards were removed, and each hole was neatly filled with a block of limestone cut to size, and all gaps were sealed with lime mortar (figure 155). Where it is possible to measure the depth, the limestone blocks are 5 inches thick.

Figure 151: Widcombe House: the cupola and chimney, from the east-south-east.

Figure 157: Sutton Hosey Manor house and dovecote from the south.

Figure 160: Sutton Hosey; regular eighteenth-century nest-holes and the window of the western cell.

Figure 161: Sutton Hosey: the east end, showing the large east window of the chapel, blocked and almost filled with eighteenth-century nest-holes. Irregular nest-holes were cut in the east wall. The regular nest-holes in the south wall were built in the eighteenth century. Part of the broken cross-wall is visible at the bottom.

The roof

The present roof dates only from the building's use as a granary. It is hipped, constructed of hand-sawn local hardwood with some exposed bark. Principal rafters rise from the corners and the walls, and support purlins at mid-height, which support the common rafters. It is clad with blue slates. On the front wall an incomplete wall-plate from the original roof remains *in situ*.

Dating and use

Sir Abraham Elton of Bristol bought the manor from the Brett family in 1718, and it remained in the family until 1920.[120] Probably this dovecote replaced another elsewhere on the manor which had been made useless by rat infestation.

It was converted to a granary after 1793, when the economics of farming were totally changed by the French Revolutionary Wars. As pigeon-keeping declined the price of corn boomed, so it became desirable to provide an efficient granary. It may be possible to check this by dendrochronology, for the surviving wall-plate may date the original building, and the timbers of the inserted floor and the present roof may date the conversion to a granary.

In 1947 the lower storey was fitted out as a generator house for the village. This required no substantial alterations, other than a vent for exhaust gases. Much of that equipment is still present. It passed out of use in 1953 when mains electricity became available. The building is now used only for minor storage.

SUTTON HOSEY MANOR, LONG SUTTON (ST 469 260)

(Formerly known as Manor House Farm and Chard's Farm). Externally the manor house is of eighteenth-century appearance, but it is of medieval origin. The dovecote was formed in the late eighteenth century from the remains of a medieval chapel. It is described at this point in the chronological series because in its present form it is essentially an eighteenth-century dovecote. It is 47 yards south of the house on land declining gently to the south. It is orientated WNW – ESE, and is 25 feet long by 17½ feet wide, and 18 feet high to the eaves (figure 157, opposite p.159). It has been converted into a double garage, obtaining the required length for vehicles by a short lean-to extension to the north. There is one high window to the south.

The fabric

The walls are of coursed blue lias rubble with lime mortar, 2½ feet thick, pointed outside with modern mortar. At the east end it is medieval – the east gable wall, a small part of the north wall, and a larger part of the south wall (figure 158). The remainder is of eighteenth-century construction. A transverse wall divides the oblong plan into two equal cells, which in the lower storey have become two garages.

The eighteenth-century nest-holes

This is the easier part to describe. Tiers of nest-holes in regular grid pattern occupy most of the interior – to be precise, the whole west wall, the western end and upper part of the south wall, the north wall above the vehicle entrances, and both sides of the partition wall (figures 159 and 160, opposite). They are of simple

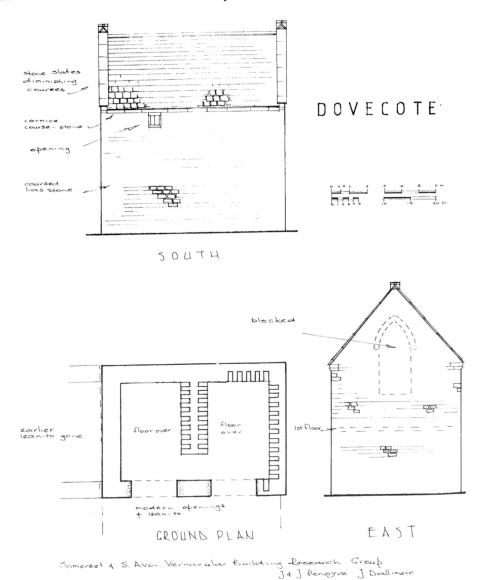

Figure 158: Measured drawings of the dovecote at Sutton Hosey Manor, Long Sutton (formerly called Manor House Farm), by courtesy of the Somerset Vernacular Building Research Group.

box shape, 6 - 7 inches high, 5½ - 6½ inches wide, and 16 - 18 inches from front to back. The lowest tier is 2½ feet above the concrete floor. The number of tiers varies from wall to wall. In the west wall the nest-boxes continue almost to the apex of the roof. In the partition wall some are omitted for a connecting doorway; the top of the wall is broken away. In the south wall they were built up to within 9

Figure 159: Sutton Hosey: in the eastern of the two garages, showing regular nest-holes in the eighteenth-century cross-wall at right, original solid rubble at left and rear, in which some nest-holes have been cut and later blocked.

inches of the wall-head, but the lower east triangle of it was of a much earlier build, and is completely different. The lower part of the north wall has been perforated for the garage entrances, but above that level the tiers of nest-holes continue to the roof.

The medieval part

The east wall and the remaining part of the old south wall are quite different. They were built as solid walls for the medieval chapel, but a number of irregular nest-holes have been made in them later where the rubble construction permitted. The large east window aperture has a two-centred arch, and is splayed to the inside. It has been blocked on the outside with rubble so that its original outline is barely perceptible, but on the inside it is clear. It has been built up to within two feet of the top with regular tiers of the same eighteenth-century nest-holes provided elsewhere (figure 161, opposite p.161).

Formerly there were at least 500 of the regular nest-holes constructed in the eighteenth century. A much smaller number of the irregular nest-holes cut into the older fabric remain, but many have been blocked by modern repairs. In the second half of the eighteenth century there were 600 - 700 nest-holes in all.

The windows

Each cell had a small window. The east window of the medieval chapel has been described already. When the eighteenth-century nest-holes were built a small aperture was left within the two-centred arch; it has been filled with plain rubble more recently. The western cell has a window aperture 1 foot 3 inches square at the head of the south wall, slightly splayed to the inside (figure 160).

The roof

There are parapets on both gables, with cruciform finials. The remainder is of modern construction, dating only from 1936. It has been partly clad with diminishing courses of old stone tiles. They cover the south pitch (facing the approach), and the lower half of the north pitch. The remainder is clad with modern regular stone tiles.

Dating and development

Horne first visited the building in 1920; the north wall was then complete. He reported that the building was in poor condition, and was 'being destroyed by ivy on its walls, and it has not many years of life unless something is done to save it'. In the roof were two 'exit holes' for the pigeons, one over each cell. His photograph shows that these were in the form of small dormers high in the south pitch of the roof. Both the windows described above were still open. Later he reported: 'In the summer of 1937 the place had been thoroughly repaired, changed inside, and made into a car house'.

This building originated as a medieval chapel. The *Victoria County History* reports that in Long Sutton there were two chapels whose sites have not been identified. They survived the Dissolution and were still in use in 1563; they were leased for secular purposes in 1572.[121] They were medieval buildings, and would not have been properly maintained since the 1530s, so may have been in a poor state of repair even then. Evidently this is one of them. Initially it was adapted as a dovecote by blocking most of the windows and cutting nest-holes in the solid fabric. By the late eighteenth century some of the older masonry was in poor condition (or had already collapsed), so the western end was rebuilt from the firmer masonry near the base. By that time the hazard of brown rats was well understood, and it was known that to set the lowest nest-holes three feet above the floor gave sufficient protection. The opportunity was taken to build a cross-wall, both to stabilise the building and to increase the number of nest-holes. With accommodation for a much larger number of birds two louvers were provided, one above each cell.

Hope Grange reported in 1937: 'the roof of this cote had become so unsafe that only about twelve months ago it had to be renewed, and while the old roof was off an east window was found which had been filled with pigeon nest-holes'.[122]

This is not the only dovecote which has been formed from a medieval church or chapel. Two are reported in *The Dovecotes of Suffolk*, one still extant, the other long gone. Another is known at Empingham in Rutland.[123] There must have been others, for numerous religious buildings were released into secular hands by the Dissolution, and one possible use for them was as dovecotes.

In recent years a modern floor has been inserted 8 feet above ground, the ground floor has been built up with concrete, and the remaining part of the east window has been blocked. The part above the floor continued to be occupied by feral pigeons, which have left a deep accumulation of droppings on the inserted floor. They entered and left by the window in the south wall until the growth of wisteria eventually obstructed it.

THE TOWER AT BRUTON (ST 684 344)

In a commanding position on the summit of a hill 350 yards south of Bruton parish church is a roofless tower (figure 162). It is of three storeys, 20½ feet square, with a door facing north-east and windows on all sides at each floor. C. R. B. Barrett expressed the view of an earlier generation of historical writers when he wrote in 1894: 'It is the remains of the columbarium of the abbey, peculiar from the fact that the lower part thereof had evidently been intended for the habitation of the keeper'.[124] All architectural details are of high quality, evidently intended for fashionable human use; but the tower was not built until many years after Bruton Abbey was dissolved. The Berkeleys acquired the lands of Bruton Abbey at the Dissolution, and established a deer park of 60 acres. They built this as a prospect tower commanding views over the park. It was converted into a dovecote only after the surrounding land was disparked in the late eighteenth century.[125] It is Listed II*, belongs to the National Trust, and is always accessible.

Figure 162: The tower at Bruton, from the east-north-east.

The fabric

It is built of coursed oolitic limestone rubble with quoins and dressings of Doulting stone in lime mortar, 2 feet 8 inches thick at the base. It has been patched with modern freestone and re-pointed with modern mortar. Three of the gables have plain copings of modern freestone with cruciform finials, the other has collapsed. The floors are missing.

The doorway

This has an ovolo-moulded arch and jambs, and a stone threshold. It is 5 feet 9 inches high by 2 feet 8 inches wide, and is rebated for a door opening inwards; it retains evidence of a hinge on the left and a lock on the right.

The windows

The windows on the first floor, and at the third floor front, are of two lights; the others are of one light. All are square-headed and have sunk chamfers, and diamond-shaped holes above and below for stanchions which formerly supported panels of leaded glazing. In addition the north-west and south-west windows on the ground floor have small holes inside the jambs where secondary grills have been fitted. Most of the windows were blocked with stone when the tower was converted into a dovecote, and some are still blocked.

The nest-boxes

From first-floor level nest-boxes were built across the corners and along the sides to form octagonal tiers. Only six tiers of nest-boxes remain *in situ* but there were many more earlier. Their sides are formed of rectangular blocks of tufa and their floors are of thin stone tiles (figure 163). Tufa is a lightweight material, ideal for this use because when first built the nest-boxes were supported on the first floor. Some nest-boxes have been reconstructed in modern freestone. They are too inaccessible to examine, but they appear to be simple rectangular recesses 8 inches square and 16 inches from the front to the structural wall at the back. Originally the nest-boxes extended much higher, probably up to the roof. When the floor timbers deteriorated triangular piers of rubble were built up from the ground to support the nest-boxes.

There are 40 nest-boxes in a complete tier, and there is sufficient height for about 22 tiers. A few were omitted for the one window which was left open. Therefore there were at least 850 nest-boxes, perhaps more if they extended up the gables. The octagonal arrangement of nest-boxes suggests that a revolving ladder could have been provided, but if so no evidence of it survives.

Dating and development

Ovolo mouldings were not used in England (other than in royal works) before the 1570s; they became common in the seventeenth century. The shape of the doorhead suggests the early-mid seventeenth century. Some original lintels remain *in situ*, from which the prospect tower could perhaps be tree-ring dated.

By 1773 the direct line of the Berkeleys had died out; the manor was sold to the Hoare family. The mansion house was pulled down, and the park became

Figure 163: Bruton: the nest-boxes, originally built on a wooden floor, are now supported on piers of rubble.

redundant.[126] The tower was converted to more mundane uses. An entrance for cattle was made in the south-east wall (which has been blocked since) and the part above the first floor was adapted for keeping pigeons. As pigeon-keeping was in decline from 1794 it cannot have been used for long in this way.

When examined in 1913 there were still remains of plaster on the inside, and a wooden window-seat survived on the ground floor.[127] Horne's photograph of 1938 shows scaffolding on the south-east elevation.

CLAVERHAM COTTAGE, STREAMCROSS, LOWER CLAVERHAM, YATTON (ST 443 662)

Claverham is four miles from the Bristol Channel, on the flat land immediately north of the range of wooded hills which terminates at Congresbury. The small pigeon-tower stands some 50 yards west of Claverham House, with which it was formerly associated. The property has been divided by stone walls; most of the building is now in the small garden of another house formed from part of the servants' quarters. It is a two-storey building of Triassic sandstone rubble in lime mortar, 10½ feet by 6½ feet, and 13 feet high to the eaves, with doorways at two levels facing north-east (figure 164, opposite p.170).

The lower storey

This has a door of normal size and two oval windows (or *oculi*) cut in stone plates, facing south-east and north-west; the former is 13 x 11 inches, the latter 9 x 8 inches (now blocked). The interior is lime-plastered.

Only the loft was intended for pigeons. The floor is mainly modern, but retains two wide joists of re-used timber from a much earlier building.

The doorway

The original access was by a first-floor door 4 feet 1 inch high by 2 feet wide, accessible by removable ladder (now enclosed in the adjacent property). The original ledged and boarded door remains *in situ*, hinged on the right to open inwards.

The nest-holes

They are built into the fabric of the upper storey, arranged in chequer pattern in five tiers. The entrances are 6 inches high by 5 inches wide. Inside they are box-shaped, 11 inches wide and 15 inches from front to back. There are 15 in the front wall, 15 and 18 in the two side walls, and 27 in the the rear wall, making a total of 75, all still in good order. The interior was formerly lime-plastered. There are no windows in the pigeon-loft.

The roof and louver

The rebuilt pyramidal roof is clad with red clay pantiles, with a weather-vane. The louver has been rebuilt in the original form. Inside it is 2 feet square and some 3 feet high, with a pyramidal roof clad with slate. There is one rectangular flight hole facing south-east.

Dating and use

This type of small dovecote became quite common in the eighteenth century, to provide modest gentry households with a supply of squabs for domestic use. The lower room is under 9 feet by 5 feet, so could not have had many practical uses, but the elegant oculi indicate that this building was designed to be an ornament to the garden. It would have passed out of use for pigeons between 1800 and 1850. It is reported to have been used as a boiler house to heat the nearby greenhouses, but it could not have been used in that way while it still housed pigeons. The building was sensitively restored in 2001.

FAIRFIELD, STOGURSEY (ST 187 431)

Fairfield is one of the major houses of the county, situated on the plain 2 miles east of the Quantocks, within 1½ miles of the Bristol Channel. It has the general appearance of an Elizabethan E-plan house, although it contains a medieval core, and exhibits alterations of all periods.[128] It faces south-east across a park. At the rear, 18 yards from the house and parallel with it is a stable-block 31 yards long which, together with the north wing and a link wall, enclose a rectangular court. The dovecote is built over an archway 6 feet wide through this stable-block (figure 165, opposite p.171). Externally it is 26 feet long by 10½ feet wide. The floor is 10 feet above ground; the eaves are 12½ feet above that.

The fabric

The stable range is of grey Triassic rubble. The way through it is covered by semi-elliptical arches of red brick. The dovecote is built of finely-made bricks 9 x 4½ x 2¾ inches with lime mortar in irregular Flemish bond. Four courses rise 11¾ inches. The brickwork was rendered externally from the outset, leaving some architectural details exposed. Some of the render has fallen away or has been removed; in the north-west elevation the brickwork is wholly exposed. The gable walls are 1 foot 6½ inches thick.

The access

The doorway faces south-east into the courtyard. It is reached by a flight of ten cast iron rungs projecting 14 inches from the wall of the stable block, with a wrought iron hand-rail (figure 166, opposite p.186). At the head is a concrete platform (replacing an original stone platform) on stone brackets, and another short hand-rail. The doorway is 4 feet 10 inches high by 2 feet 10 inches wide, with an arched head of 'Tudor' curvature framed by a single course of headers, left unrendered. The hardwood door-frame is rebated inside for a four-panelled door hinged on the left. Inside, the floor is of clay tiles.

The windows and blind recesses

In the elevation facing the house are three windows. Above the door is a pair of arched lights set in a brick surround shaped to form a 'Tudor' arch; the frame of headers is left unrendered. Inside there is a top-hung shutter. Above it in the gable is a glazed oculus 1½ feet in diameter, also framed by exposed headers.

In the north-west elevation blind recesses of the same shape and size as the arched window and oculus are formed in the brickwork (figure 167). In small gables to north-east and south-west are similar blind oculi, also surrounded by exposed headers.

Figure 167: Fairfield, Stogursey. The stable range and dovecote from the north.

The nest-holes

The interior is occupied from floor to ceiling by nest-holes in regular chequer pattern (figure 168). The entrances are 5¾ inches high by 5 inches wide. Inside they are L-shaped in plan, 7 inches high, 9½ inches wide, and 14 inches from front to back. The backs of the nest-holes are formed by bricks laid on edge. (This can be seen from outside in the blind apertures. The pattern of nest-holes continues regularly across them, showing that they were never intended to be open). Below each nest-hole is an alighting step of slate 6 inches wide which projects 1½ inches. Some are broken; they have been replaced by iron plates of the same size. There are 12 tiers of nest-holes, making a total of 654.

Above the highest tier of nest-holes are wooden shelves 6 inches wide, extending 4½ feet from the gables. Their purpose is unknown. All surfaces are painted with early white paint, including the insides of the nest-holes.

The revolving ladders

There are two revolving ladders, both complete and in working order – rare survivals. They are finely made, with tapering arms, and all arrises chamfered. Each incorporates three feeding platforms, diminishing in diameter from the base (figure 168). The contemporary ladders are secured to blocks on the arms by hand-made hooked bolts. The whole structures are finished with early white paint.

The roof, louver and pipe

The stable range and dovecote are clad with double Roman clay tiles. The roof of the dovecote is gabled at each end; smaller gables to each side form a symmetrical cruciform plan. Over the centre is a wooden louver formed by four posts with 'Tudor' arches between them; and on that is a pyramidal roof clad with slate, with a weather-vane (figure 169, opposite p.186). Inside the dovecote the soffit is lathed and plastered to form intersecting barrel vaults. From this a conical funnel or pipe of sheet copper 2½ feet deep leads up to the louver (figure 170). At the base the diameter is 3½ feet, tapering to 2 feet 4 inches at the top.

Figure 170: Fairfield, Stogursey. Looking up at the pipe and louver. Part of one blind oculus is shown at the bottom.

Figure 164: The pigeon-tower at Claverham Cottage, Yatton. The door to the pigeon-loft is on the other side of the high party wall at right. Photograph by courtesy of Pat Kington.

Figure 165: The dovecote at Fairfield, Stogursey, from the south.

Figure 168: Fairfield, Stogursey: the interior, facing south-east. The revolving ladders with original feeding platforms are complete and in good order.

This is the only authentic pipe which has been found in Somerset. Several pipes have survived in Suffolk dovecotes, although these are rectangular, made of wood. The pipe was an ingenious protective device against sparrowhawks, which could sometimes penetrate the louver and descend into the interior of the dovecote. Unlike pigeons they cannot fly up vertically. The pipe was always made with a smooth inner surface, which ensured that a sparrowhawk could not get out again. Unable to perch anywhere it would fall to the floor, where it would be despatched by the pigeon-keeper. The round apertures in conical stone roofs at Selworthy and Henstridge functioned similarly.

Dating and use

There was a dovecote at Stogursey manor by the late thirteenth century, for it is recorded that at that period sales of cheese, fish, **pigeons,** fleeces, livestock and pasture accounted for more than rents. In 1297 the dovecote was let to farm.[129]

The stone stable range with a way through was already present when the dovecote was added.[130] Several indications suggest that the dovecote was built in the early nineteenth century:

(1) From 1800 there was a strong incentive to build dovecotes in enclosed yards or over ancillary buildings close to the house, to prevent wholesale thefts to supply the new pigeon shooting clubs (see page 28). Probably a free-standing dovecote elsewhere in the park was demolished when it became too vulnerable to theft.

(2) The semi-elliptical archways and 'Tudor' detail of the windows were favoured architectural devices of the period.

(3) Although cast iron was available in the final decades of the eighteenth century it came into common use only in the early nineteenth century.

(4) Elsewhere, in the early nineteenth century feeding platforms were nailed to existing revolving ladders as a response to the changing economics of pigeon farming (see page 15). Here the feeding platforms are designed integrally with the revolving ladders, attached to the axes by hand-made woodscrews.

From 1815 Sir John Acland created the park and carried out major alterations to the house.[131] The dovecote was probably his work too.

This dovecote has never been altered or adapted to a secondary use. It has been well maintained, and apart from some broken plaster it survives complete, a near-perfect example of its period. At present it is Listed as Grade II, but it amply qualifies for being up-graded to Grade II*.

CHELVEY COURT FARM, BROCKLEY (ST 466 684)

This is on the River Kenn, 1½ miles south of Nailsea. The fifteenth-century great barn of Chelvey Court Farm is situated 40 yards south of the parish church on land declining gently to the south. The original barn is of seven bays, aligned east-west, with a central wagon-porch to the north. At the eastern end the long walls have been extended by 14 feet to meet an early nineteenth-century building (figure 171). Against the original east end wall of the barn an extra cross-wall has been

Figure 171: The great barn of Chelvey Court Farm, Brockley, from the north-east. The pigeon-loft is at left.

built containing nest-holes above 8½ feet. The pigeon-loft thus formed is 12 x 21½ feet internally. The original access was by external ladder. The floor has been rebuilt, with a modern stair.

The fabric

This is of coursed rubble with freestone dressings. There is no perceptible difference between the rubble of the barn and its eastward extension, except that the diagonal buttresses at the north-eastern and south-eastern corners have been rebuilt at right-angles to the long walls. The wall containing the nest-holes has straight joints at each end where it meets the long walls; it has no other function than to provide nest-holes. A connecting doorway has been formed at ground-floor level against the north wall, allowing access from the barn to this extension.

The first-floor doorway

The entrance to the pigeon-loft is in the north elevation, 9 feet above ground, finely formed in freestone (figure 172). It is 4 feet high by 3 feet wide, with an arch of 'Tudor' shape (see Glossary), deeply chamfered outside, and rebated 2½ inches deep for a door opening inwards. Inside the arch are two hardwood lintels approximately 6 inches square. The door is mounted on original pintle hinges in the left jamb.

Figure 172: Chelvey: the doorway, with an arch
of 'Tudor' shape.

Figure 173: Nest-holes at Chelvey.

The nest-holes

The nest-holes are arranged in chequer pattern, without alighting ledges (figure 173). The entrances are 6 inches high by 5½ inches wide. Inside they are of the same height, of asymmetrical bulb-shape in plan, 11 - 13 inches wide, 16 inches from front to back. All the nest-holes in one tier turn to the left, all those in the next tier turn to the right. There are 9 complete tiers of 11 nest-holes to eaves level, and 11 diminishing tiers up to the apex, making 154 nest-holes in all. Nearly all are open and in good order. There are no nest-holes in the other three walls of the loft. The wall has been white-washed.

The roof

This is modern, clad with double Roman clay tiles.

Dating and use

This building has no datable features except the high entrance of 'Tudor' shape, but in its present form it is essentially an early nineteenth-century pigeon-loft. The freestones of the entrance may have been re-set, or may have been made in conscious imitation of the earlier style. Lintels over the internal connecting doorway and over the first-floor entrance may be datable by dendrochronology. The pigeons would have entered by a louver on the roof, of which no evidence remains. Nest-holes of asymmetrical bulb plan are normally associated with the medieval period. Is the wall containing the nest-holes a fragment of a much earlier dovecote, incorporated in the later building? Or were the nest-holes formed in the early nineteenth century to reproduce those of an earlier dovecote which had given good service elsewhere on the manor? This was a period when outlying dovecotes were being demolished, and when pigeon flocks were being reduced to the small number of birds which could be fed in the farmyard.

We are grateful to John Thorp of Keystone Historic Building Consultants for informing us of this building.

HOLBROOK HOUSE HOTEL, BRATTON SEYMOUR (ST 690 285)

This is 1½ miles west of Wincanton. The cylindrical dovecote is situated on the crest of a low hill 70 yards north-west of the eighteenth-century manor house, and 5 yards west of its coach-house. It is 17 feet in external diameter, and 13 feet high to the eaves (figure 174). The door and a window above face south-south-east, and there is a matching window opposite. A group of tall conifers stands to the west.

The fabric

The main fabric is of coursed rubble with lime mortar, rendered with lime plaster, over which is modern roughcast. Inside it is built of the same rubble to a

Figure 174: The dovecote at Holbrook House Hotel, Bratton Seymour, from the south-south-west.

height of 3½ feet, above which nest-holes are formed of finely-made bricks 9 x 4¼ x 2⅜ inches laid in lime mortar. The wall is 2½ feet thick.

The doorway

This is 4 feet 8 inches high by 2 feet 4 inches wide, with a segmental arch and a stone threshold. The pegged and jointed door-frame has decayed, leaving only the left jamb and lintel *in situ*. They are rebated for a door hinged on the left opening inwards, retaining one pintle hinge. Over it are three oak lintels 5 inches deep, the inner one shaped to the curvature of the building.

The windows

These are 2½ feet square, the sills 9 feet above ground, with three plain mullions. The jambs are rebated inside for grills or lattices.

The nest-holes

Above the stone base there is a regular grid pattern of brick nest-holes (figure 175). The entrances are 5½ inches high by 6½ inches wide. Inside they are of the same height, L-shaped in plan, 13½ inches wide and 15 inches from front to back. There are 14 tiers with 30 nest-holes in a complete tier; one tier continues above the windows. Allowing for those omitted for the door and two windows this makes

Figure 175: Bratton Seymour: the interior, with the original north window.

a total of 375 nest-holes, all still in good order. At the backs lime plaster is visible; that is, the wall of stone rubble was plastered before the brick nest-holes were built against it. The whole interior has been been treated with whitewash, extending into the entrances of the nest-holes. There are no internal ledges.

Evidence of a former revolving ladder

Above the brick nest-holes are two shallow courses of stone rubble, into which are let long timber pads to west and east, shaped to the curvature of the wall. On these are mounted an original beam to support the upper bearing of a revolving ladder. In 1921 Horne noted that the iron plate in which the upper pivot revolved was still present; now only the nail-holes remain. He could not search for a lower bearing 'as the place was full of wood'. The floor has been concreted recently.

The roof and louver

The roof structure is original. It consists of eight principal rafters, with four parallel common rafters in each sector, side-nailed to the principals. At the apex they meet a ring of solid timber with a hole 2 feet in diameter through which the pigeons entered. The cladding is of red clay plain tiles, with a single course of stone tiles at the eaves. The louver consists of a freestone cap with a ball finial supported on bricks on end, mounted on a slate platform (figure 176, opposite p.187). It is netted to keep out birds.

Dating and use

This dovecote was built in the early nineteenth century. By that time brown rats had become a familiar hazard, so the lowest nest-holes were set 3½ feet above the floor, a height that had been found by experience to provide adequate protection. The single course of stone tiles indicates that originally the whole roof was clad with stone tiles. The stone louver and finial are original.

Before boundary changes in 1886 this was in a detached part of Charlton Musgrove parish. Holbrook was a manor; the house dates from the second quarter of the eighteenth century. In 1786 the owner, Samuel Farewell, left to live in Wincanton, and the mansion house was leased. In 1823 it was bought by Robert Page, together with some land; he remained in possession until 1848.[132] This is the period when the dovecote is most likely to have been built. Originally it stood isolated on a low hill 70 yards from the nearest building. The stable block which now reaches to within 5 yards was built in 1848-9 by the next owner, and the tall conifers to the west had not been planted.

The round plan, the use of stone rubble, stone tiles, and the low doorway suggest that its external appearance was intended to resemble more ancient dovecotes – perhaps to suggest that the manor was of greater antiquity than the eighteenth-century house indicated. The interior was up-to-date in design and construction. It mainly follows the recommendations of the anonymous writer of 1740 who expressed his ideas about pigeon-keeping in rhymed couplets.[133] Passages will be quoted in Chapter 7, but in brief he advised that a new dovecote should be sited on the highest eminence, that it should be whitened to attract pigeons, and that the nest-holes should be of brick.

This dovecote would have passed out of economic use at the same period as others in Somerset, but the low doorway shows that it has never been adapted to a secondary use. It has remained in good condition. When Horne visited it in 1921 the exterior was covered by ivy, and it was in use as a wood-shed. In 1937 Hope Grange reported that it had been repaired recently. Evidently the roughcast render was new then, for he thought the fabric was of brick.[134] It is used now only for storage.

HOME FARM, WEST QUANTOXHEAD (ST 105 430)

West Quantoxhead is between the northern end of the Quantocks and the Bristol Channel. The pigeon-tower is situated 36 yards north-west of Home Farm on land declining to the north, within a few hundred yards of St. Audries Bay. It comprises a base 13½ feet square (called the Harness Room) with an octagonal pigeon-loft above (figure 177). The tower is 20 feet high to the eaves. Originally it stood isolated, but it now forms the entrance to a modern bar to the west. The doorway faces south. There are tall trees immediately to the north.

Figure 177: The harness room and pigeon-loft at Home Farm, West Quantoxhead, from the south-east.

The exterior

It is built of uncoursed red sandstone rubble, with quoins and dressings of freestone; the walls are 1½ feet thick. From a square base it reduces with broached corners to an octagonal tower. In the lower stage there are two slit windows 3 feet high by 5 inches wide facing south. In the upper stage there are similar blind recesses facing south, west, north and east.

The interior and nest-holes

An internal stair of nine concrete treads with a door at the bottom leads up to the pigeon-loft, which now has a floor of concrete. The walls are wholly occupied by a regular grid pattern of nest-holes formed in brick (figure 178). The entrances are 6 inches high by 4½ inches wide. Inside they are of the same height, L-shaped in plan, 10½ inches wide by 11½ inches from front to back. There are 14 tiers of nest-holes from 14 inches above the floor to the roof, with 24 to a tier, making a total of 336; all are still in good order. Below each entrance a slate alighting step 5½ inches wide formerly projected 4 inches, although many of these are broken.

The whole interior has been treated with whitewash, including the insides of the nest-holes. Above the highest nest-holes is a ledge 6 inches

Figure 178: West Quantoxhead. The nest-holes and iron revolving ladder.

wide of slate, all round. The only source of daylight is the louver above.

The revolving ladder

This is of unique design, made entirely of iron (figure 178). From a central shaft a wrought iron arm with two long brackets supports the base of a cast iron ladder inclined at a convenient angle. The upper part has been damaged, but evidently another arm formerly extended from the upper part of the axis to support the top of the ladder. This illustrates the Victorians' enthusiasm for iron; numerous artefacts which earlier had been made of wood were made of iron in that period.

The roof and louver

The pyramidal roof is clad with fish-scale clay tiles. The wooden louver consists of eight posts with arched openings between, and a tented pyramidal lead roof on which is mounted a weathervane dated 1855. The pigeons alight on an octagonal ledge, pass through the arched openings and down through a round hole about 1½ feet in diameter to the interior (figure 179, opposite p.187).

Dating and use

In 1836 Sir Peregrine Acland bought the manor of West Quantoxhead for his daughter Isabel, who married Sir Alexander Acland-Hood. They lived there after their marriage in 1849. The manor house was much altered, and a new farmstead was established at its present site in 1855. The architect of Home Farm and the dovecote was John Norton of London.[135]

The combined harness room and pigeon-loft was built in 1855 as a functional building designed to be an architectural ornament to the estate. In the Second World War the roof and interior were damaged by an unexploded bomb; they have been carefully repaired. The present holiday centre which encompasses it came in the 1970s.

About 30 white fantail doves were in residence when examined. The entrances to the nest-holes are smaller than is desirable, evidently determined more by the size of bricks used than by the requirements of the doves. Some were nesting on the floor.

THE MULBERRY COMPANY (DESIGN) LTD., SHEPTON MALLET
(ST 627 435)

In the capacious landscaped grounds of this manufacturing firm is a building known as the Round House. It is situated on level ground beside a lake, 4 yards east of a gateway into Kidd's Lane, and 150 yards south-east of the nearest contemporary building, a former cotton mill. It is 18 feet in external diameter, and 10½ feet high to the eaves (figure 180). It has been incorporated into the boundary wall to the south. There is a doorway to west-north-west, and two windows to north-north-east, one above the other.

The fabric

It is built of coursed Mendips stone rubble pointed with cement mortar, and plastered internally. The wall is 2 feet thick.

The doorway

This is 6 feet 4 inches high by 3 feet 2 inches wide, with a segmental arch. It has a jointed and pegged door-frame and a ledged and braced door with a wrought iron bolt and staple.

The windows

Each window is 3 feet square, splayed to the inside, fitted with a modern double casement. The upper aperture is original. The lower one has been inserted later to match it in size and design.

Figure 180: The Round House at Shepton Mallet, from the west-north-west. The stone cap of the louver has been dropped to close it.

The interior

Against the south wall is a blocked coal-burning fireplace, the flue of which has been truncated at eaves level. The Listed Building description reported in 1984 'Interior contains nesting boxes for doves', but there were none when examined in December 1999. A rail at half-height against the south-east wall perhaps indicates that they were formerly fitted above that level.

The roof and former louver

The conical roof is clad with machine-made red clay tiles, and is plastered to the soffit. At the apex is a round hole about 2 feet in diameter, sealed against leakage. Above it is a stone cap, now set firmly down against the hole; but when the louver was in use it would have been raised about six inches above it.

Origin and use

This is a nineteenth-century dovecote which was never intended to provide large numbers of squabs. Later it was converted to a garden pavilion by installing a fireplace and making a window at low level to provide a view over the lake. It is now used as a boat house. The only feature which indicates its original use is the round aperture in the apex of the roof, where the pigeons entered.

There has been a water-powered fulling mill here at least from the sixteenth century. In the nineteenth century silk was produced, and later crepe. The ornamental lake was made from an existing mill-pond early in the twentieth century by Ernest Jardine, a lace manufacturer from Nottingham. He formed the ornamental garden, which was re-designed in the early 1960s by Francis Showering, the originator of Babycham perry. We believe the dovecote/pavilion was built by Ernest Jardine. For this background we are grateful to Fred Davis.

BANWELL

Innkeepers and farmers continued to keep pigeons for meat well into the nineteenth century, long after the practice had ceased to be associated with high social status. To an innkeeper pigeons were 'a ready viand for the sudden traveller', as Ferguson observed.[55] To a farmer they were an extra cash crop. A rare picture by John Buckler (figure 181) illustrates this form of pigeon-keeping, which has left no surviving examples in the county. The device illustrated, known to contemporaries as a standard box (i.e. a box on a standard), is based on a redundant cartwheel, and was erected in a farmyard near Banwell, three miles east of Weston-super-Mare. It was built within the vernacular tradition, entirely different from the architecturally designed dovecotes introduced by Lutyens, Gimson and other designers early in the twentieth century. At the time a thatched roof was the cheapest form of roofing. The detailing of the post displays good craftsmanship. The projections on each side of the base were to protect

Figure 181: A standard box in a farmyard near Banwell. From a drawing of 1812 by John Buckler in the Piggott Collection. By courtesy of the Somerset Archaeological and Natural History Society.

it from passing carts. (The tradition of standard boxes has remained alive in Germany and Austria, where one may still see these structures in farmyards).

RUISHTON COURT NURSING HOME, RUISHTON, NEAR TAUNTON
(ST 261 245)

This small pigeon-loft brings the present chronological series to an end. It is mounted above a former stable block 25 yards north of Ruishton Court, formerly a nineteenth-century country house called Ruishton House. It is now surrounded by tall trees.

The stable block is aligned approximately east-west. The dovecote is mounted on the west gable end of the roof, 16 feet above ground, and is made of wood throughout (figure 182). It is 5 feet square and 5 feet high to the eaves, with a pyramidal roof surmounted by a weather-vane. In each side there are seven flight-holes of inverted-U shape arranged in two tiers, with a perching ledge below each tier. On the west side, facing the entrance drive, is a decorative plaster panel bearing the letters RMS and the date 1899. There is no access to the interior now.

This dovecote was made for ornamental pigeons rather than to produce meat. The keeping of pigeons purely for ornament was fashionable in Queen

Figure 182: The pigeon-loft at Ruishton Court, Ruishton.

Victoria's reign, and was promoted by her example at Windsor.[136] In 1870 *Cassell's Household Guide* wrote of pigeons: 'Their variety and beauty of plumage, the tenderness of their voices, their absurd antics and small vanities, their struttings and love-makings, all combine to render them an endless source of amusement and pleasure to every properly organised mind. No country house, or, indeed, any house where pigeons can be kept is, in our opinion, complete without them'. This pigeon-loft is an example of the fashion. It could not have operated successfully if the surrounding trees had been present when it was in use, as they would have masked the approach of sparrowhawks.

The Somerville family for whom this house was built owned the paperworks at Creech St. Michael. There is a memorial to them in the parish church.

Chapter 6
Some Oddities

LYTES CARY, CHARLTON MACKRELL (ST 534 266)

A building 120 yards north-east of the National Trust house Lytes Cary is Listed
Grade II as a dovecote, 'possibly eighteenth century' (figure 183). The description
includes the qualification 'Interior not seen'. If the Listing officer had been able to
see the interior he would have known that is not a dovecote. It was built in the early
twentieth century as a pump house, but because it is prominently situated on the
axis of the garden it was disguised as a traditional dovecote. The house underwent
a major renovation in 1907 for Sir Walter Jenner; the architect was O. E. Ponting.
Probably he designed the imitation dovecote too.

Figure 183: The imitation dovecote at Lytes Cary, Charlton Mackrell, with the house beyond.

PRIORY FARM, STOGURSEY (ST 204 428)

A round building 20 yards north-west of Priory Farmhouse appears from the outside
to be a medieval dovecote, and is Listed Grade II as of historical interest (figure

Figure 184: The building at Priory Farm, Stogursey, which has replaced the former dovecote. The stone steps are the oldest part, dating back to the conversion into a cool store, as at Wellow.

184). It is 21 feet in diameter, 18 feet high to the eaves, with a doorway and a window at ground and upper floor level, and a thatched conical roof. Apart from the stone steps to the upper floor it was wholly rebuilt in 1925. There was a dovecote here earlier, the only remnant of the Benedictine Priory which formerly adjoined St. Andrew's Church, but by the twentieth century it had long ceased to be used as such, and had been converted to a game larder or cool store, as at Wellow. It was still in that form when Arthur O. Cooke wrote about it in 1920. He said the nest-holes were 6 - 7 inches square, 'enlarged inwards', and that many had been blocked; the wall was about three feet thick.[137] Horne visited it in 1936; he reported that the owner had decided it was unsafe, and had rebuilt it in its game larder form on the same foundations, without nest-holes.

At the time of the tithe commutation of 1839 this farm was the property of the Merchant Adventurers of the City of Bristol, and was let to James Rich.[138]

LITTLEFIELDS FARM, SHEPTON BEAUCHAMP (ST 414 167)

An isolated building 40 yards south of Littlefields Farm is Listed Grade II as a 'former granary or dovecote', and is known to the owners as 'the old dovecote'. It is of two storeys, with a high timber floor dating from the seventeenth or eighteenth century. It could not be properly examined, for the floor was said to be unsafe, and the loft door could not be opened more than a few inches. There are no nest-holes sunk in the fabric, but it is possible that it was provided with wooden nest-boxes earlier. It appears to have been built as a stable with loft above, as it remains today.

THE GRANGE, WOOLAVINGTON (ST 346 416)

In 1983 E. H. D. Williams of the Somerset Vernacular Building Research Group examined a round stone building at The Grange, and identified it as a seventeenth-century cockpit. It is 20 feet in external diameter, 14 feet high to the eaves, with a thatched conical roof. There is a considerable amount of supporting evidence for that interpretation; but three factors suggest that it may have been a dovecote earlier – the thickness of the wall, 3 feet 2 inches, the four symmetrical stepped buttresses and the proximity to a house of early origin. It is possible that careful archaeological examination would reveal blocked nest-holes within the fabric.

THE DOVECOTE, QUANTOCK LODGE, OVER STOWEY (ST 186 377)

Quantock Lodge is a mansion built in 1857 for Henry Labouchere, who became a Minister in Lord Melbourne's government of 1839-41, and the first (and only) Lord Taunton. The architect was Henry Clutton. At that time it was the centre of an estate of 10,000 acres. A long coach-house range has at its northern end a coachman's cottage, to a design copied from an elaborate French dovecote (figure 185), which is called 'The Dovecote'. It has a four-gabled roof and a conical tower crowned by a large conical louver. Sixty triangular apertures in the tower imitate flight holes for pigeons, but

Figure 185: 'The Dovecote', Quantock Lodge, Over Stowey.

Figure 166: Fairfield, Stogursey. The cast iron steps, wrought iron handrail, and entrance.

Figure 169: Fairfield, Stogursey. The louver and one blind oculus.

Figure 176: Bratton Seymour, the original louver.

Figure 179: West Quantoxhead. Pigeons alight on the octagonal platform below the louver.

there is no evidence inside that there were ever any nest-boxes. It is an elaborate folly. It is set among tall trees on the lower edge of Great Wood, ancient woodland which extends up the Quantock Hills, a most unlikely site for a working dovecote. The upper part subsided owing to decay of the timbers, and has been carefully restored by the present occupiers.

Since Quantock Lodge ceased to be a private house it has been a sanatorium and a co-educational boarding school; it is now a sports and conference centre.

THE COUNTY PRIMARY SCHOOL, KEINTON MANDEVILLE (ST 549 306)

A building in the south-east corner of the grounds of this modern school is Listed Grade II as a dovecote, and is known to the school as 'the old dovecote' (figure 186). On examination it proves to be a winter bee-house – a building primarily intended to accommodate bee skeps; in one wall there are nest-holes for a small number of pigeons. It is a lean-to structure aligned east-west, built against a high stone wall to the south which evidently extended further originally. It is 23½ feet long by 12½ feet wide, and is 6 feet 3 inches high to the eaves (on the low side). The fabric is of blue lias rubble with some freestone in clay mortar; the wall is 1 foot 10 inches thick. There are wide door apertures to east, north and west, only the last having a door-frame. The roof is modern, clad with red clay pantiles.

Figures 186: The winter bee-house at Keinton Mandeville County Primary School, with nest-holes for pigeons.

Figure 187: Keinton Mandeville; the nest-holes and perching ledges.

The nest-holes

In the outside of the west wall, above the doorway, are 12 nest-holes in diminishing tiers of 6, 4 and 2 (figure 187). Each entrance is of inverted-U shape, 4½ inches high by 3 inches wide, cut in vertical slabs of local lias. Inside, the nest-holes are 10 inches high and oblong in plan, 11 inches wide and 16 inches from front to back, with the entrance in the middle of the front (short) side. A perching ledge below each tier projects 5½ inches and is 2½ inches thick, with a similar ledge above the highest tier. The lowest ledge is 7½ feet above ground.

The bee boles

Inside the building are recesses called bee boles made for bee skeps (the conical hives wound from straw rope, which were used before the modern beehive was introduced). In the low north wall are 3 tiers of 7 bee boles; each is 1 foot high by 1 foot 5 inches wide, and 1 foot from front to back. Below each tier is a stone ledge 5 inches wide. One similar recess is built into the east wall. The wide doorways on three sides, all over 3 feet wide, are to facilitate the movement of bees.

Dating and use

The International Bee Research Association states that this is a winter bee-house, and that there is only one other in Somerset.[139] It is the only example known in Britain of a bee-house combined with accommodation for pigeons. Several are known in France. It was built (probably in the eighteenth century) against an existing high wall of similar stone. The nest-holes in the west wall are of ample size inside, but have remarkably small entrances, the smallest found in the county. Probably the intention was to make them so small that no bird of prey would attempt to harass the pigeons inside, for there was no other protection. No evidence has been found of the house or estate with which it was associated.

BRYMPTON HOUSE, BRYMPTON D'EVERCY (ST 521 154)
A few yards south of the house is a structure intended to house ornamental doves, consisting of a short Doric column on a chamfered square block on three circular stone steps, with a wooden nest-box above. This pedestal was built early in the twentieth century from re-used components from the old Town Hall of Yeovil, destroyed by fire. Other components were used to build a classical temple at the same house.[140]

Chapter 7
Comparisons and conclusions

Forty-nine dovecotes and pigeon-lofts have been described, together with some dubious or misleading buildings. We can now draw some conclusions from the survey. Somerset was chosen for this study because it is so different from Suffolk, of which a similar study was published in 1998.[141] The differences of building materials and climate suggest numerous comparisons. This chapter has been arranged under the same subject headings as the Suffolk study, as far as the subject matter permits.

STATUS

Sixteen of these dovecotes are medieval or sub-medieval. All those built before the seventeenth century were for lords of manors, whether personal or corporate. Of the pre-Dissolution dovecotes two were at Carthusian granges (Witham and Norton St. Philip), two were for the Benedictine Abbey of Glastonbury (Pilton and West Bradley), and one was for a Priory of the Benedictine Abbey of Bath (Dunster). The other medieval dovecotes were built for secular lords – Wellow, Stoke-sub-Hamdon, West Coker, Norton-sub-Hamdon, Somerton, Selworthy, Kingweston, Shapwick Manor, Henstridge and Ham Farm, Yatton. Not all of these manors were large or important, but a minor manor had the same privileges in common law as a major one.

Of the dovecotes which were built after the Dissolution four were established on sites which earlier had belonged to religious houses – Monkton Combe, Hinton Charterhouse, Montacute and Bruton; and the dovecote at Sutton Hosey Manor was formed from a medieval chapel. Two were built for prominent lawyers – at Shapwick House for Sir Henry Rolle, Lord Chief Justice, and at Cathanger Manor, Fivehead, for John Walsh, then a Serjeant-at-Law, who later became Chief Justice of the Common Pleas. Kelston was built for an aspiring courtier who became High Sheriff of Somerset. The others were built for secular lords whose status we cannot determine now.

Four were built for rectories – Stanton Drew, Horsington, West Camel Old Rectory, and the 'pigeon house over the chauncell' of Compton Martin church.

Although after 1619 it was legally possible for a freeholder who was not lord of a manor to build and stock a dovecote, we have found only one in Somerset which comes into this category, at Claverham Cottage, Yatton. There must have been others in Somerset, for they are known elsewhere.[142] As small buildings they were perhaps less easily converted to secondary uses, or they have not survived in sufficiently unaltered form to be identifiable today.

THE SITES

In 1740 an anonymous writer described the ideal site for a dovecote:

That situation will your doves delight,
Where the Air's pure, and nothing stops the sight.
Then place your Cote, where from the rising Ground
The Fields in Prospect lye around.[143]

Because pigeons are instinctively attracted to high places it was desirable to set the dovecote on the highest part of the site, but in practice it was not often achieved. In this series Norton St. Philip and Bratton Seymour are the only dovecotes sited on eminences (and Bruton tower, which was not built originally as a dovecote). In some cases existing buildings already occupied the ideal site. As reported in Chapter 1, when a new dovecote replaced an older one the old dovecote could not be demolished until the pigeons had moved into the new building. If the earlier dovecote was ideally sited on the summit of a hill, the newer one had to be built elsewhere.

The same writer advised that the dovecote should be situated well away from woodland:

For oft the Grove's deceitful shade
The Hawk his Prey is ready to invade.

In 1698 Roger North expressed similar advice, already quoted (page 28). None of the dovecotes described here is near ancient woodland. Where now there are tall trees nearby it can be shown by measuring the girth that they have grown since the dovecote passed out of use in the nineteenth century.[145]

North wrote of pigeons: 'If they are among too much buissness and noise, they will be frighted. If retired, the hauks will be too saucy; the passing of men too and fro frights them'.[146] In this survey the distance from the nearest contemporary building has been stated (disregarding most later buildings). With a few exceptions (Manor Farm, West Camel, West Coker Manor, Southstoke, Hill Farm, Kingston St. Mary and Fairfield, Stogursey) they were formed as free-standing buildings – although the distance from contemporary buildings varies widely, from 4 yards at Somerton to over 50 yards at Shapwick House, Wellow, Montacute, Henstridge and Bratton Seymour.

PLAN FORMS

Of the freestanding dovecotes which survive in Somerset, 13 are round, 23 are rectangular, two are octagonal and one is hexagonal. There have been claims that the plan forms of dovecotes developed in an identifiable typological sequence, from round to rectangular to polygonal, but this survey finds no correlation between the plan shapes and the ages of the buildings. Some of the earliest medieval dovecotes are round, some are rectangular. It is impossible to show that the round ones are earlier than the rectangular ones. The only hexagonal dovecote (at Shapwick House) is of the early seventeenth century, and the two octagonal ones (at Widcombe House and West Quantoxhead) are respectively of the mid-eighteenth and mid-nineteenth century.

The advantages claimed for a round dovecote were that it did not require freestone for quoins, and it avoided the possibility of four-legged predators climbing the corners. (Its suitability for use with a revolving ladder was not relevant before the eighteenth century, as there is no evidence that they were used in Britain before 1698).[146] The disadvantage was that the roof structure of a round building was complicated to build, and could force the head of the wall outwards. This inherent weakness derived from the desire to eliminate tie-beams, because a bird of prey which penetrated to the interior could settle there, out of reach of the pigeon-keeper. (North wrote 'the thrust would drive out the walls . . . and that winged vermin might have no means to fly out, if once ventured in, wee could not have any cross-girders').[147] The main advantage of a rectangular dovecote was that the weight of the roof was carried by purlins mounted on the gable walls; it did not place an expanding strain on the long walls.

BUILDING MATERIALS

Building stone is available in most parts of Somerset, but much of it is of poor quality – adequate for use as rubble, but incapable of being finely cut for quoins, doorways, windows and other dressings. The few freestones of good quality in the county are identified by the quarries or districts they came from – Doulting, Cary, Dundry, Bath, and Hamstone. These freestones have been mentioned often in the text; their characteristics are summarized in the Glossary. The only dovecotes composed wholly of this superior stone are those at Kelston, Monkton Combe, Montacute, Norton-sub-Hamdon, Southstoke, West Coker, Stoke-sub-Hamdon and Widcombe House; and six of them are mainly built of rubble. Only in the last two is it used dressed throughout (figures 20 and 150).

In an intermediate category are blue and white lias. These sedimentary rocks were laid down in the Jurassic era in beds of even thickness. When quarried they break easily into rectangular blocks, and can be laid to produce remarkably regular courses. In the best work, walls built of blue and white lias appear as smooth and regular as good brickwork – as in the medieval rectangular dovecote at Crane Farm, Somerton, or the seventeenth-century hexagonal dovecote at Shapwick House Hotel (figures 46 and 107). Blue lias contains a variable proportion of clay, which can greatly reduce its weathering properties. At Curry Rivel courses of soft blue lias have weathered so badly as to recede from the face of the building (figure 132). Even inside, protected from the weather, blue lias of this poor quality exhibits numerous fine cracks (figure 135).

White lias is displayed at its best in the interior of Fivehead (figure 75); although where it is exposed to driving rain it has been seriously eroded – after more than four centuries (figure 73).

In practice the quality of stone available locally seems to have made little difference to the design of dovecotes. In every case the rubble which made up the greater part of the building was extracted near the site. If freestone was required for dressings quite small amounts were transported from the nearest convenient source. One round dovecote (Stoke-sub-Hamdon) is within 200 yards of Ham Hill, where there was an abundance of good freeestone, and another is only a mile away (Norton-sub-Hamdon). There are rectangular dovecotes where the freestone had to be brought from a distance (as at Pilton and West Bradley), and others in which no freestone was used (as at Somerton and Kenn). Evidently it was the client who determined the general design. The master mason carried out his requirements, obtaining whatever stone was necessary.

THE MORTAR

Dovecotes of the highest quality, for the wealthiest clients, were built with lime mortar. This includes some of the earliest examples, at Witham, Stoke-sub-Hamdon and Pilton. The burning of lime, its transport to the site, and further preparation there added greatly to the cost of building. Others were built with clay mortar dug locally, involving minimal cost.

To what extent the use of lime mortar has extended the life of these buildings is difficult to assess. Historic buildings do not fall into disrepair simply by the passage of time, but because they are neglected or abused – for instance, by the insertion or enlargement of apertures. The removal of six buttresses out of eight at Pilton was done for no practical reason, only to make what became a nineteenth-century stable appear more in accordance with the architectural preference of the time. Inserted apertures reduce the stability of walls. The round dovecote at Stoke-sub-Hamdon, built with dressed freestone in lime mortar, has been roofless since the late nineteenth century. The one at Kingweston was built of blue lias rubble with lime mortar, has two or three inserted apertures, and has been standing roofless for at least 82 years, perhaps substantially longer. Some dovecotes built with clay mortar appear to have lasted almost as well as those built with lime mortar, unless there are other structural problems, such as an unstable site.

Lime mortar became generally available in Somerset in the eighteenth century as bricks came into fashionable use, but clay mortar continued to be used for lesser buildings of stone well into the nineteenth century. This survey suggests that the use of lime or clay mortar is a better indicator of the original status of the building than of its age.

It is interesting to note the use of clay mortar with brick quoins at Hill Farm, Kingston St. Mary, in a late Georgian alteration. This is the only instance known.

THE USE OF BRICK

Most of the dovecotes of Somerset are built of stone throughout, but there are a few exceptions:

(1) At King's Lood, Kingston St. Mary, external and internal nest-holes were formed of bricks, in a late seventeenth-century building which otherwise is built of Quantocks rubble (figure 142).

(2) and (3) At the nineteenth-century dovecotes at Bratton Seymour and West Quantoxhead the nest-holes were built originally of brick, where the main structure is of local rubble (figures 175 and 178).

(4) At Montacute nest-holes formed of bricks and old stone tiles have been inserted in an earlier dovecote built of rubble and re-used freestone (figure 138).

(5) At Henstridge an early eighteenth-century brick lining containing nest-holes has been inserted in an older dovecote of local rubble (figure 81, opposite p.85).

(6) The only dovecote built wholly of brick is the early nineteenth- century one at Fairfield, Stogursey (figure 165, opposite p.171). Brick was late in being adopted in Somerset, compared with some eastern counties where stone was not available.[148]

COB

is hardly represented in this series, the only exception being the much-repaired dovecote at Halswell House, Goathurst, which we have not been permitted to examine (page 121 and figure 112). A seventeenth-century cob dovecote at Durleigh was demolished in 1967 (figures 193 and 194, p.215). It was fully recorded by R. F. Taylor, whose description is summarized in Chapter 8.[149] In 1726 the Reverend John Laurence described how he made a dovecote of cob in Northamptonshire:

'The cheapest Way possible for building a Dove-House, is to make the Walls with Earth or Clay mixt with Straw, in the same way they make their Mound-Walls in Northampton and Leicestershire; which are not only durable and cheap, but singularly warm. I made a Dove-House myself in this manner; which answered my Expectations well, and cost me I think about Five Pounds; being (if I remember) about Four Yards square in the clear within-side. I made the Walls Four Foot thick and Twelve Foot high; and before I set on the Roof, and whilst the Walls were a little greenish, with a coarse Chisel I ordered a proper Number of Holes to be cut out square; which was done with a greal deal of Ease, the Walls being, as I said, not quite dry. The Holes were made (as they should be) a little dipping backward, and about Fourteen inches deep: So that when the walls were covered with a Roof and become perfectly dry, they made a warmer Habitation for the Pidgeons than any other sort of Building made with Brick and Stone, tho' framed with Wood: And accordingly the Pidgeons prosper'd to a Wonder whilst I was in Northampton-shire'.[150]

Cob is particularly vulnerable to neglect, and to thoughtless repairs with inappropriate modern materials.[151] As it was widely used for houses and ancillary buildings in Somerset it is reasonable to believe that many other dovecotes were built of cob, but they have not survived.

DOORWAYS AND DOORS

At many dovecotes the doorway has been enlarged for a secondary use, but twenty examples retain their original doorways unaltered. They are less than 5 feet high; four of them are less than 4 feet high. Because of changing ground levels we cannot always be sure of the original height, but this finding matches county surveys in Suffolk and East Lothian which indicate that low doorways were general in dovecotes built before the eighteenth century.[152] Two reasons have been advanced for the small size:

(1) the pigeon-keeper could block the aperture with his stooping body as he entered to prevent birds escaping

(2) doorways occupied wall space which might have been better devoted to nest-holes. In 1698 North wrote 'I set in the door, 4½ foot high (enough for entrance, and more had robbed the walls of holes'.[153]

The widths vary more, from 1 foot 8 inches at Dunster to 3 feet at Chelvey. From the eighteenth century considerations of visual proportion tended to determine the size of the doorway, but low doorways at first-floor level occur at Widcombe House, Claverham Cottage, Yatton, and Fairfield, Stogursey.

In 1735 the anonymous author of *The Sportsman's Diary* wrote that the door of a dovecote should be visible from the house 'because the master of the family may keep in awe those that go in and out'.[154] In some cases the contemporary house has not survived, but where the evidence is clear, 22 of the doorways were visible from the house, five were not.

Contemporary writers expressed dogmatic opinions about which way the doors and windows of a dovecote should face. For instance, in 1785 Daniel Girton wrote: 'It should also be a standing rule, that there be no door, or other aperture towards the east; these should always face the south, pigeons being very fond of the sun, especially in the winter'.[155] However, their recommendations did not agree with each other. In practice, doors and windows have been found facing in every direction.

A few original doors survive. At Curry Rivel much of the seventeenth-century door is still present, although severely decayed at the bottom (figure 133); it is not beyond skilled repair. Original doors in good condition survive *in situ* at:

1. the seventeenth-century upper pigeon-loft at Hinton Priory,
2. the early eighteenth-century pigeon-loft at Widcombe House, Bath,
3. the late eighteenth-century pigeon-loft at Claverham Cottage, Yatton
4. the early nineteenth-century dovecote at Fairfield, Stogursey,
5. possibly the early nineteenth-century pigeon-loft at Chelvey,
6. and if it can be called a door, the tiny entrance to the pigeon-loft at Hill Farm, Kingston St. Mary.

At Dunster the present door is not original but it is certainly old, possibly dating from the eighteenth-century alterations.

WINDOWS

At least 15 of these dovecotes had no windows originally; for light and air they relied on what came through the pigeon entrance. There may have been more. Where the existing window shows evidence of alteration (e.g. by revealing incomplete nest-holes), one cannot always know whether it has been enlarged from a smaller aperture or punched through a previously unbroken wall. Although the absence of windows is often considered a characteristic of early dovecotes, this study has found examples in the seventeenth, eighteenth and nineteenth centuries.

In almost all cases the windows were unglazed, protected against winged predators by a wooden lattice or wire grill. (A wooden lattice survived at Kelston to appear in Horne's photograph of 1920, although it has gone since). The only possible exceptions are at Monkton Combe, Kelston and Godminster – and even there it is far from certain that they were glazed. Sixteenth and seventeenth-century window glass was fragile and impermanent; contemporary household accounts record frequent visits by the glazier to replace broken panes. Therefore dovecote windows would have had to be protected with a lattice or grill even if they were glazed. The anonymous author of 1740 offered advice about 'windows' in dovecotes, by which he evidently meant unglazed apertures:

> *Two windows will let in sufficient Day,*
> *One to receive in Winter the warm Ray,*
> *Full-south: Another in the Dome above,*
> *For Light, and easy Passage for the Dove.*

There was a gradual change of practice in the seventeenth and eighteenth centuries. More and larger windows were provided, and dormers became more common (although in Somerset dormer windows are present only at Norton-sub-Hamdon). The merit of a dormer window was that it provided light without occupying wall space which otherwise could be devoted to nest-holes. Windows continued to be undesirable in the smallest dovecotes, like that at Claverham Cottage, Yatton.[156] As late as 1855 the dovecote at West Quantoxhead was built without windows.

EXTERNAL LEDGES

Pigeons like to perch and warm themselves in the sun, but they try to find shelter from strong winds. Some dovecotes have external ledges on which the pigeons could perch in windy conditions. They are most common at exposed sites near the coast; they are provided on almost all dovecotes in Scotland, where strong winds from all directions are common. At inland sites in England they are found much less often, but a few have been recorded in Somerset:

(1) At the four-gabled dovecote at Kelston there is a ledge all round the building at eaves level, with an inclined upper surface (figure 93, between pp. 98 and 99). Pigeons, being a rock-nesting species, have no difficulty in perching on an inclined stone surface, but tree-nesting birds of prey cannot.

(2) At the almost square dovecote at Charlton Mackrell there are two plain perching ledges 3 inches wide on one elevation only, facing west towards the house. One is 6½ feet high, the other is 16 feet high, just below the eaves (figure 146).

(3) At the round dovecote at West Camel Old Rectory there is a plain ledge 4 inches wide all round, just below the eaves (figure 98, opposite p.112). Elsewhere, external ledges occur only with flight holes and external nest-holes. At Manor Farm, West Camel, there is a ledge below each tier of flight holes (figure 148). When Horne photographed the much-altered dovecote at Claverton in 1920 it had a plain stone ledge on brackets on the front gable, about 12 feet above ground; it has gone since. At the dovecotes at Kingston St. Mary, Southstoke, Horsington and Widcombe House, and at the bee-house at Keinton Mandeville, there are ledges below the nest-holes (figures 142, 128, 89, 150 and 186). The architect who designed the dovecote at Widcombe House provided perching ledges 3½ inches wide below the external nest-holes, and wider ledges at 16 feet and 24 feet above ground (figure 150). Whether he thought Bath was a particularly windy place, or

whether he was more familiar with dovecotes in a windier part of Britain must remain a matter of speculation.

Ledges occur also outside the flight holes of small pigeon-lofts in other buildings. At Stanton Prior there is a triangular pattern of flight holes with ledges below each tier in the gable of an eighteenth-century barn, leading to a former pigeon-loft inside (figure 195/1). A similar assembly occurs in a gable of Rowley Grange, Farleigh Hungerford, in the gable of a former coach-house in the main street of Wellow, and on a cartshed/granary at Dillington House, Ilminster. No. 6, Cheap Street, Frome, has flight holes in the rear gable with irregularly disposed stone ledges (figure 195/4). Carey's Mill Cottage, Martock, has a round flight hole with a stone ledge below (figure 195/3). A barn at Church Farm, Sutton Montis, has a triangular pattern of ten flight holes in the gable, with a wooden ledge below each tier (figure 195/2). This study has not attempted to find all the evidence of minor pigeon-lofts in other types of buildings; mostly nothing survives inside the building.

The curious belief that external ledges high on a dovecote were intended for protection from rats occurs only in twentieth-century writings; it has been examined at length in an earlier publication.[157] There is no need to reconsider it here, except to say that it is a modern myth. The word 'rat-ledge' did not exist before the twentieth century.

ROOFS

All the round dovecotes which have roofs at all have conical roofs except Goathurst, where it is bell-shaped (figure 112). At Selworthy and Henstridge the stone roofs are self-supporting without timber. They appear to be similar but are constructed on different principles. Selworthy functions as a dome, while Henstridge has a corbelled vault (figures 52 and 82). Most of the conical timber roofs have been rebuilt at various times, but Wellow retains most of its medieval roof structure (figure 19).

Ten rectangular dovecotes still have their original timber roof structures, or substantial parts of them. Most had gabled roofs. At Montacute the eighteenth-century roof is hipped.

At Hinton Priory, Kelston, Fairfield (Stogursey) and Godminster the roofs were four-gabled originally; the first three survive almost as built (figures 101, 93 and 169). This is an interesting design which became quite common in the seventeenth century. Its great merit is that it provided inclined surfaces facing in all directions on which the pigeons could sun themselves at all times of day, and on which they could find shelter from winds from all directions. We should remember that the pigeons could perch and find shelter also on other roofs of the domestic complex, some of which may have gone now.

LOUVERS, CUPOLAS AND FLIGHT HOLES

It need not surprise us that few original louvers have survived; Somerset retains more evidence of louvers than many counties. All dovecotes passed out of economic use 150 years ago or earlier. The louver was the part most exposed to extreme weather and most difficult to reach for maintenance, so when the dovecote was no longer used as such the louver ceased to be maintained, and eventually decayed. A later owner would have the roof lathed and tiled continuously over the space where it had been. In 23 of these dovecotes there is no trace of the original louver – where the roof has been rebuilt, or where there is no roof at all. Six dovecotes have, or have had, modern louvers or cupolas built by twentieth-century owners or architects – at Dunster, Shapwick Manor, Shapwick House, Goathurst and West Camel Old Rectory (figures 11, 85, 108, 112 and 98). At Curry Rivel Horne noted that there was an ornamental louver without even an access for the pigeons, and at Dunster he wrote that the louver 'looks like the old one but the present arrangement of timber in the roof, at the apex, would prevent its being used'. These twentieth-century louvers cannot be regarded as historically authentic; they may or may not be reasonable copies of the louvers which were there earlier. At Halswell House, Goathurst, the arcaded louver which now crowns the bell-shaped roof was not in place when the building was photographed in 1908. Was it there in dismantled form?

Therefore the few original louvers which survive, or which retain any part of the original structure, are particularly valuable as evidence of what the louvers of working dovecotes were like. At Henstridge, Bratton Seymour, Shepton Mallet, Norton-sub-Hamdon and Selworthy the pigeon entrance originally took the form of a round hole at the apex of the roof with a stone cap over it. In two of these it survives, though now blocked (figures 80, 176, 180). At Norton-sub-Hamdon the turned stone cap and ball finial supported by baluster-shaped stone legs represent an alteration of the eighteenth century, but the dovecote was still in use then (figure 45, opposite p.67). At the National Trust dovecote at Selworthy there is only a round hole, now glazed to keep out feral pigeons and to protect the interior from rain.

The four-gabled dovecote at Kelston has a rebuilt louver which closely follows the louver photographed by Horne in 1920 (figure 2). The four-gabled louver at Godminster was rebuilt from a photograph taken about 1890 (figure 124). Evidently it had already been adapted to the keeping of a small number of ornamental doves, so it tells us little about the louver of a fully functioning dovecote. At Widcombe House the original stone cupola survives complete; it has been rebuilt to correct a structural failure (figure 151). At West Quantoxhead the cupola of the mid-nineteenth century dovecote was carefully rebuilt after war damage (figure 179). The early nineteenth-century dovecote at Fairfield, Stogursey, alone among the series, retains its original louver undisturbed (figure 169, opposite p.186).

In six timber roofs there is evidence of the base of the original louver, though all the upper parts have gone – at Charlton Mackrell, Curry Rivel, Horsington (figure 92), Norton St. Philip (figure 61), Montacute and Wellow (figure 19, opposite p.43). The first five evidently had a wooden turret comparable with that at Kelston. Wellow is an important survival. It retains the wooden frame on which the louver formerly stood, but at present this is almost inaccessible. Perhaps one day the roof will need to be re-thatched. We would welcome the opportunity to re-examine it then.

At King's Lood, Kingston St. Mary, Southstoke and Manor Farm, West Camel, there never were louvers. Instead, flight holes were provided high in the walls (figures 142, 34, 131 and 148). The first of these is unique, with its six oval flight holes at two levels.

THE FLIGHT HOLES OF MINOR PIGEON-LOFTS

The flight holes of minor pigeon-lofts in houses, barns and other ancillary buildings have been mentioned already (page 197 and figure 195); in most cases nothing survives inside the building. Other examples have been observed at Chitcombe Farm in Huish Champflower, East Hall Farm in Compton Pauncefoot, Lodge Farm in Norton St. Philip, The Greenway in Dulverton, Cottles in Publow, Pensford, and at Bob's Cottage and The Old Ship in Porlock Weir.[158] No doubt there are many others, but the only small pigeon-loft we have seen which retains its internal features is at Hill Farm, Kingston St. Mary (page 122).

THE PROVISION OF NESTING PLACES

(a) Materials

In most Somerset dovecotes the nesting places were built of stone and were incorporated in the solid walls. The only exceptions are:

    (1) at King's Lood, Kingston St. Mary (figure 143);

    (2) at West Quantoxhead (figure 178);

    (3) at Fairfield, Stogursey, built wholly of brick (figures 168);

    (4) the demolished cob dovecote at Durleigh (figures 193 and 194);

    (5) at Saltford (figure 140), where there is no evidence of nest-holes in a stone building which in other respects appears to have been built as a stable with a pigeon-loft above. Nest-boxes of wood may have been provided, later stripped out and burned;

    (6) at Littlefields Farm, Shepton Beauchamp, a building Listed as a dovecote, and known to the owners as such, was also built as a stable with a loft above. Here too there may have been nest-boxes of wood, but if so they have not survived.

(b) Size of nest-holes – stone

In rubble construction the nest-holes inevitably varied one from another, both in size and shape. The entrances were more critical. They had to be large enough for the pigeons to pass through readily, but sufficiently restricted to give them a sense of security. The commonest building stone in Somerset is blue lias, which is easily hammer-dressed to exact shapes. In other areas dressed freestone was used to form the sides of the nest-holes, the rear parts being formed of rubble. One might expect that in all dovecotes the entrance holes would aspire to the same, ideal size. On the contrary, it is clear that there was no consensus among pigeon-keepers or builders as to what the ideal size was. Although many stone dovecotes have nest-hole entrances 6 to 6½ inches square, the heights vary from 5½ inches at Wellow to 8½ inches at West Coker Manor and Curry Rivel, and the widths vary as much. The smallest entrances of all are those at Keinton Mandeville (figure 187).

Figure 195: Flight holes and perching ledges of former pigeon-lofts:
(1) at a late eighteenth-century barn at Priory Farm, Stanton Prior
(2) at a barn at Church Farm, Sutton Montis, now enclosed by a covered way betweeen buildings
(3) at the eighteenth-century Carey's Mill Cottage, Martock
(4) in the seventeenth-century rear wing of no. 6, Cheap Street, Frome.

(b) Size of nest-holes – brick

Unlike stone bricks come in standard sizes. It is clear that builders allowed the bricks used to determine the size of the nest-holes. At Fairfield, Stogursey, the entrances are 5¾ inches high (representing two courses of bricks) by 5 inches wide. At West Quantoxhead they are 6 inches high by 4½ inches wide (two courses of bricks on edge). At Henstridge the entrances are 5½ x 5 inches, and at Bratton Seymour they are 5½ x 6½ inches (both of two courses). At King's Lood, Kingston St. Mary, an early instance of the use of brick, the entrances of the external nest-holes are 7 x 4¾ inches.

(c) Plan shapes of nest-holes

The various plan shapes are illustrated in figure 188. The commonest type, found in twelve dovecotes, is the asymmetrical bulb-shape, built in rubble with the entrances in chequer pattern. In one tier the nest-holes all turn to the left inside, in the next tier they all turn to the right. This form of construction provides maximum solidity in a rubble wall. At Dunster they are similar, but turning to the left in all tiers.

Nest-holes of symmetrical bulb-shape are found at eight dovecotes. At Hinton Charterhouse they are accurately formed to an oval plan, and are lined with lime plaster. Apparently a template was used to form them.

Three dovecotes have nest-holes of 'reversed wedge' plan. Two of them are medieval or sub-medieval (Somerton and Kingweston). The third is at Manor Farm, West Camel, much later in date.

Ten dovecotes have rectangular nest-holes. In most cases they are completely open at the front, but at Curry Rivel, Claverham Cottage, Yatton, Fairfield, Stogursey and Keinton Mandeville (the bee-house) the front was partly blocked by another slab or brick to form a smaller entrance.

Nest-holes of L-shape in plan, which are common in brick-building regions, are found here at four of the five dovecotes where the nest-holes are formed of bricks. In addition there are three examples formed in stone: at Widcombe and Claverton, where they were accurately constructed in dressed Bath stone, and at Kenn, where they were more roughly formed in blue lias rubble.

Kelston, a dovecote of the highest quality, has nest-holes of perfect circular shape 13 inches in diameter, formed with dressed freestone, with entrances 8 inches high by 7½ inches wide. As it is clear that no expense was spared, the owner evidently believed that that shape and size were ideal. An unusual plan shape occurs at Charlton Mackrell, where the nest-holes form oblique parallelograms in plan, made of blue lias. Nest-boxes of similar shape, but made of wood, may be seen in Worcestershire.[159] An ingenious design occurs at Montacute, where double nest-holes for flexible use are formed by providing each with two entrances. No exact equivalent is known anywhere.

As to the pattern formed by the entrances of the nest-holes, those in chequer pattern outnumber those in grid pattern in a proportion of three to two.

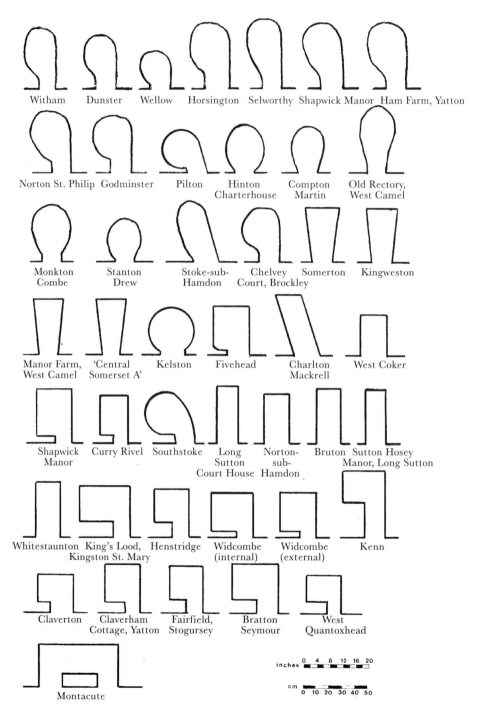

Witham　　Dunster　　Wellow　　Horsington　　Selworthy　　Shapwick Manor　Ham Farm, Yatton

Norton St. Philip　Godminster　　Pilton　　Hinton
Charterhouse　　Compton
Martin　　Old Rectory,
West Camel

Monkton
Combe　　Stanton
Drew　　Stoke-sub-
Hamdon　　Chelvey
Court, Brockley　　Somerton　　Kingweston

Manor Farm,
West Camel　　'Central
Somerset A'　　Kelston　　Fivehead　　Charlton
Mackrell　　West Coker

Shapwick
Manor　　Curry Rivel　　Southstoke　　Long
Sutton
Court House　　Norton-
sub-
Hamdon　　Bruton　　Sutton Hosey
Manor, Long Sutton

Whitestaunton　King's Lood,
Kingston St. Mary　　Henstridge　　Widcombe
(internal)　　Widcombe
(external)　　Kenn

Claverton　　Claverham
Cottage, Yatton　　Fairfield,
Stogursey　　Bratton
Seymour　　West
Quantoxhead

Montacute

inches 0　4　8　12　16　20

cm 0　10　20　30　40　50

Figure 188: Plans of typical nest-holes.

(d) Numbers of nest-holes

All the free-standing medieval dovecotes had between 300 and 1,000 nest-holes, the smallest being Selworthy with 320, the largest being Witham and Somerton, estimated to have had almost 1,000 nest-holes when built.

After the Dissolution there was more variation; a few dovecotes were built with more nest-holes – 1,470 to 1,845 (or perhaps more) at Cathanger Manor, Fivehead, 1,287 at Long Sutton Court House, and 1,080 at Shapwick House. Some had fewer – Chelvey (with 154), Southstoke (with 191), Widcombe (with 285) and Claverham Cottage, Yatton (with 79); they were pigeon-lofts in buildings partly devoted to other purposes.

Of the four dovecotes which served rectories Horsington originally had about 600 nest-holes, West Camel Old Rectory had 641, Stanton Drew had 470, and the fifteenth-century pigeon-loft in Compton Martin church had between 80 and 140 nest-holes.

One cannot calculate the number of adult pigeons in a flock simply by counting the nest-holes and multiplying by two. The breeding cycle of young adult pigeons is so short that two clutches may be in the dovecote simultaneously. As one writer said in 1735, 'each pair must be sure to have two nests, for before one pair can go out of the nest, or feed themselves, the old ones will lay and be sitting'.[160] The number of males did not always match the number of females, although pigeon-keepers tried to achieve that by culling. The higher nest-holes were more attractive to pigeons than the lower ones. Probably some of the lower nest-holes were often left vacant.

In 1611 Arthur Standish, arguing that pigeon-keeping was uneconomic, wrote: 'First, all men of experience know, that an ordinary Pigeon house of five yardes and a halfe square, and four yardes high to the evesings; in which house there may be contained twelve score paire of Pigeons'.[161] Taking these as internal dimensions, this is about the same size as the existing dovecote at Horsington, recorded at about the same time, which had some 600 nest-holes when built. Standish's figure implies that a substantial degree of under-occupancy was regarded as normal. It may be that the maximum number of pigeons which would willingly occupy a dovecote was determined more by its size than by the number of nest-holes provided. When there were many dovecotes about, it was always possible for pigeons which found the conditions too crowded to go elsewhere.

Few generalizations can be derived from this series of dovecotes, and they are not applicable in all cases:

1. Nest-holes of bulb-shape, whether symmetrical or asymmetrical, were common in the medieval period, uncommon later.

2. Nest-holes of rectangular shape were common in the eighteenth century.

3. Where the dovecote was built of stone rubble the nest-holes were more likely to be arranged in chequer pattern than where it was made of freestone, in which a grid pattern was more readily accomplished.

To every generalization there are exceptions. We have to conclude that at all periods, and particularly in the post-medieval period, the ideal form of nest-hole was very much a matter of opinion. This was confirmed by the anonymous versifier of 1740:

> *What various Forms Invention has display'd*
> *Of Nests in diff'rent Kind and Order made!*
> *I've known some Houses hung with Baskets round;*
> *In others, Boxes made of Wood are found;*
> *Some leave more wisely, as they think, a Place*
> *Betwixt the solid Stones of ample Space:*

LININGS IN NEST-HOLES

The writer continued:

> *The chilling stones will cold Distempers breed,*
> *And Wood will harbour Worms and Insect-feed.*
> *Of well-bak'd Brick be your Partitions made,*
> *Or else, with Mortar well-prepar'd inlaid;*
> *For thus no Vermin will their Holes infest,*
> *Or Winter rot the Eggs, and starve the Nest.*[133]

In seven of these dovecotes the walls of the nest-holes were lined from the outset with lime plaster (Witham, Wellow, Stoke-sub-Hamdon, Norton St. Philip, Stanton Drew, Hinton Charterhouse and Claverton). At Godminster they were lined with clay daub. The lining was applied from above as the mason completed each tier of nest-holes. (If it were attempted later, plaster or daub would be found on the roofs of the nest-holes; it is not).

Before this study of Somerset dovecotes was undertaken the earliest dovecote found in England having nest-holes lined with lime plaster was a small brick turret on the roof of a gatehouse tower at Hadleigh, Suffolk, built in 1495.[162] The Somerset examples cannot be dated so precisely, but it is likely that three or four of them were built earlier.

INTERNAL LEDGES

25 of these dovecotes do not have internal ledges of any kind. Four of them have an alighting ledge to each tier of nest-holes on which the pigeons could perch and parade, varying in width from 1½ inches at Whitestaunton and Shapwick House to 2½ inches at King's Lood, Kingston St. Mary. Of the four Wellow is the only medieval example; Whitestaunton is late eighteenth-century. The ledges were designed to be wide enough for pigeons to perch on, being a rock-nesting species, but too narrow for any tree-nesting bird of prey which managed to penetrate to the interior of the dovecote. Evidently they were not really necessary. (The earliest firmly dated dovecote in England, at Garway, Herefordshire, has an alighting ledge to every second tier of nest-holes).

At the nineteenth-century dovecotes at Fairfield, Stogursey, and West Quantoxhead there was originally an alighting step of slate to each nest-hole, projecting 1½ inches at the former, 5½ inches at the latter.

Ten of these dovecotes have a single ledge all round the interior, two of them have two ledges, and Fivehead has three. They vary considerably in height and width, as described in the text, but none exceed 4 inches wide; some are plain, some are chamfered above or below. These ledges had a different function. In 1887 Ferguson wrote: 'the attendant gets at the nests by climbing along the ledges in front of them, and holding on with his hands'.[163] Was this speculation, or was it prompted by a distant memory? The ledges may have been used to support staging while the dovecote was under construction, and later for occasional maintenance, or to support planks from which the pigeon-keeper could search the nests. We cannot know for certain, as no contemporary description has survived which would clarify their purpose.

The most intriguing internal ledges are those at Pilton (figures 28 and 29). The sloping wooden ledges on the gable walls could not have been used for staging, so they must have been for pigeons to settle on at first when they flew in through the louver. The equivalent ledges on the long walls do not have an inclined upper surface; white lias is difficult to cut at an angle. Perhaps an inclined upper surface was formed by the 'beam-filling' of clay daub, but has been removed since. Providing these ledges would accommodate pigeons' natural behaviour in the wild. Observation shows that when they arrive near the nesting site they perch for a few minutes nearby, checking for danger, and often perch again nearer to it before flying to the nest.[164]

REVOLVING LADDERS ('*POTENCES*')

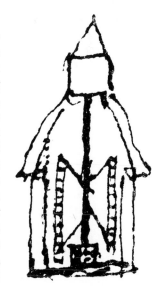

The best examples in Somerset are the early nineteenth-century specimens at Fairfield, Stogursey, each with three original feeding platforms, still in perfect order. At Dunster there is a (restored) eighteenth-century revolving ladder with two feeding platforms attached at a later date, in a dovecote built centuries earlier. New bearings have been fitted since 1936 – despite a local leaflet which asserted that they are medieval![61] At West Quantoxhead there is a unique example made wholly of iron. At Henstridge and Bratton Seymour revolving ladders have been used, for in each case evidence survives of the beam which supported the upper bearing. At present our earliest firm evidence of revolving ladders in England is from 1698, when Roger North described a device he proposed to instal in an octagonal dovecote at Rougham, Norfolk: 'On the inside it is intended (for it is not done)

Figure 189: A marginal sketch of a revolving ladder designed by Roger North for his dovecote at Rougham, Norfolk, drawn in 1698. From Howard Colvin and John Newman, editors, *Of Building: Roger North's Writings on Architecture*, Oxford, 1981. By courtesy of Oxford University Press and the authors.

to make an altar of holes round, and upon the center pitch an axis, which shall turne upon that and the midle cross peices of the lover. This axis is to carry 2 ladders, within 8 inches of the walls, and to be opposite each other, so as 2 persons may search the house at once, with the same movements'. He provided a rough sketch in the margin (figure 189). Note that his design does not provide a horizontal surface on which winged predators could perch – unlike later examples.[165] Balanced pairs of revolving ladders have been reported in East Lothian.[166] Where revolving ladders are found in much earlier dovecotes it is always apparent that the beam supporting the upper bearing has been inserted in existing nest-holes, or otherwise fitted after the main construction.

PROTECTION FROM BROWN RATS

It is not known when brown rats, *Rattus norvegicus*, reached Somerset. The first members of the species were established in London by 1730. By 1750 they had spread up the Thames river system to its remotest streams. As natural swimmers and riverbank feeders they spread most readily along watercourses and ditches, less easily across watersheds. They were reported in one of the Scilly Isles by 1755 and in Anglesey by 1762, so evidently they were carried from place to place by coastal shipping.[167] They would have reached Somerset ports by the same means, and from there spread up the rivers and numerous drainage channels. The naturalist Gilbert White reported that a remote farmstead on the chalk downlands of Hampshire, far from any streams or drainage channels, was infested with brown rats by 1787.[168] The evidence from Norton-sub-Hamdon and Horsington suggests that they became a hazard to pigeon-keepers in Somerset long before that, probably in the 1760s.

In five of the older dovecotes the lower tiers of nest-holes have been blocked with stone to a height of 4 - 5 feet (Somerton, Pilton, Kingweston, Shapwick Manor and Ham Farm, Yatton), to protect the stock from brown rats; and to lesser heights at Horsington, and perhaps at Dunster too. Later pigeon-keepers became better-informed about the behaviour of brown rats, and found that the stock was adequately protected if the lowest tier of nest-holes was 3 - 4 feet above the floor, particularly if the wall below was plastered to form a smooth surface. Twentieth-century research for the Ministry of Agriculture has shown that rats cannot climb or jump a smooth surface three feet high (provided that it is kept clear of clutter); and that buildings are sufficiently protected against undermining if they have foundations more than 1½ feet deep. Doors can be adequately protected by a metal plate one foot high.[169]

The dovecote which is most elaborately protected against brown rats is at Whitestaunton, which was new at the time. The doorway is five feet above the yard (then accessed by a removable ladder), and the nest-holes are nearly five feet above that. The medieval dovecote at Norton-sub-Hamdon was elaborately altered in 1785 to provide similar protection, having a sheer wall of ashlar more than 5 feet high below the lowest nest-holes. Nearby at Montacute a cheaper alteration was accomplished with stone rubble and bricks, the ledge below the nest-holes being formed of re-used stone tiles. At the later structures of Sutton Hosey Manor and Bratton Seymour the nest-holes were built well above ground, with a sheer wall below which in earlier dovecotes would have been occupied almost to the floor with nest-holes.

Fifteen of the dovecotes described here were built originally at first-floor height or above (Compton Martin, Hinton Charterhouse, Chelvey, Kenn, Kingston St. Mary (both), Southstoke, West Camel Manor Farm, Bruton, Charlton Mackrell, Widcombe, Claverham Cottage, Yatton, West Quantoxhead, Stogursey and Ruishton Court). They were approached by a ladder which was removed when not in use, or at Fairfield, Stogursey, by a flight of cast iron rungs.

That leaves a number of dovecotes where nest-holes were provided at or near floor level before the eighteenth century, and where there is no evidence that they have been altered later. If a stone dovecote was built well enough, with deep foundations and tight joints, it was inherently proof against penetration by brown rats – except via the door. One way of protecting it from gnawing was to fit an iron plate at the bottom. Another was to kennel a dog within reach. Where there is no evidence that anything was done to protect a pre-eighteenth-century dovecote from brown rats we must assume that one or other of these precautions was adopted, or that it passed out of use in the eighteenth century. This last may be what happened at Wellow. In the eighteenth century a floor was inserted at mid-height, and the space above was elaborately converted into a cold store. The lower part was not used again.

At Dunster the medieval door-frame is set high in the building, now reached by a short flight of steps. It appears to have been re-set at this height, and may have been at ground level originally. (Jenefer Chesher has pointed out that wooden door-frames often survive in this district, or are re-used, because the local stone does not lend itself to forming dressings).[170]

CONVERSION TO SECONDARY USES

When the medieval dovecote at Somerton ceased to be used as such it was comprehensively converted to a cider-house; the cider press is still present. Henstridge too was a cider house within living memory. Pilton, Horsington, Stanton Drew, Selworthy and Monkton Combe became stables, and the last has been used since to house cattle and pigs. What was left at West Bradley when it fell down eventually became a cow-shed. Norton St. Philip and Southstoke have also housed pigs at various times. The dovecote at West Camel Old Rectory was in use as a hen-house when Horne visited it. Charlton Mackrell became a granary, and later an apple store. Central Somerset A was converted into a coach-house, and Sutton Hosey became a double garage. Elsewhere the evidence of secondary uses is less clear, but general farm use can be deduced at many. The largest dovecote in Somerset, at Cathanger Manor, Fivehead, was converted into a corn barn, and was used as such almost to our own day; now it is used to store apples.

The dovecote at Whitestaunton was elaborately converted into a granary; since then it has been used as a generator house. The most complicated story of later uses is at the Carthusian dovecote at Witham, which may have passed out of use for its original purpose soon after the monastery was dissolved. Evidently it was well built, for it has passed through numerous phases of alteration. In 1747 it was described as a stable or stall; by 1812 it was a silk manufactory; by 1846 it was a pair of cottages. There is some possibility that it has been used also as a granary. In 1901 it was comprehensively converted into a village hall. More recently it has been a photographer's studio, and at the time of writing another use is proposed.

We should be grateful that thirteen of these dovecotes show no signs of having been converted to any secondary use. Fifteen dovecotes stand empty today, and their owners take a pride in them. Best of all, five dovecotes in Somerset are open to the public (Bruton, Dunster, Selworthy, Stoke-sub-Hamdon, and West Bradley). The owner of the dovecote at Norton St. Philip is usually willing to take interested visitors into his dovecote, and the key to the dovecote in Norton-sub-Hamdon churchyard is usually obtainable. Few if any other counties can match this degree of access.

Only three of these have been converted for residential use – West Coker, King's Lood and Claverton. The first two were already converted by 1940; at the latter, from Horne's description, there was not a lot to lose by the time it was converted. Five dovecotes are still used by pigeons – although not for producing squabs for eating, as they were intended.

Today many dovecotes are used for general storage. This use does no harm to the buildings, but sometimes makes difficulties for the photographer trying to photograph the interiors. Readers who wonder why the lower part of a particular interior is excluded from the photograph may safely assume that it was occupied by private possessions which are irrelevant to this study. The interiors which are empty or nearly empty have been illustrated in full.

DISTRIBUTION

The locations of surviving dovecotes are shown in figure 7. As they represent only a small proportion of those which were present earlier it would be unsafe to draw any conclusions about the original distribution. There may have been more losses in the cob-building areas than where building stone was readily obtainable.

THE DATING OF SOMERSET DOVECOTES

Only one of these dovecotes has been tree-ring dated, Pilton.[66] Only one dovecote displays inscribed dates, Norton-sub-Hamdon, and these refer to major alterations rather than the original construction. The ages of others are estimated from their physical characteristics, or are taken from reputable sources (which are all identified in the Notes). In a few cases one may reasonably associate a dovecote with a particularly prominent or wealthy owner of the manor, such as Sir Thomas Hungerford at Wellow, John Walsh at Cathanger Manor, Fivehead, John Harington at Kelston, and Sir Henry Rolle at Shapwick House. The only reliable way of dating them is by dendrochronology, where sufficient original oak timbers survive and prove to be datable. Regrettably, only six of them retain original timber roofs. Some retain lintels incorporated in the masonry. At present dendrochronologists cannot obtain dates from only one or two samples, or from timbers with less than fifty growth rings, as the science depends on statistical comparison. Elm, which is common in Somerset buildings, is not datable.[172]

Somerset dovecotes cover the range from the fourteenth century almost to the end of the nineteenth century. The latest example at Ruishton may have been used only for ornamental doves, but dovecotes were built to produce squabs for the kitchen on a major scale as late as the early nineteenth century at Fairfield, Stogursey, and on a lesser scale at West Quantoxhead in 1855.

Chapter 8
The dovecotes which have gone

From the thirteenth century every manor was entitled to have a dovecote; by the seventeenth century most manors had one. In 1611 Arthur Standish estimated that there were not less than 40,000 dovecotes in England.[173] Another observer asserted in 1655 that there were three in each parish 'taking one with another'.[39] With 363 parishes in Somerset this suggests that there were more than a thousand dovecotes at that time. Whatever the merits of these estimates, it is clear that the dovecotes which survive to our day represent only a tiny proportion of those which have existed.

From 1619 every freeholder became entitled to own a dovecote.[37] Only some freeholders chose to exercise the legal right, but evidently it led to the building of some modest non-manorial dovecotes, as at Claverham Cottage, Yatton. Comparable small dovecotes survive in Suffolk.[142]

Our information about the dovecotes which have gone depends mainly on chance. The sites of some are identified by field names. The name Culverhey meant a small enclosure in which a dovecote was situated, often of about one acre. Early seventeenth-century glebe terriers record *culverheys* at Bathealton, Blagdon, Doulting and Hardington Mandeville. Culver Hill in Wookey and Culver Street in Stogursey suggest other dovecotes.

A small triangular plot in Langport Westover (at ST 410 266) was described as Pigeon House Orchard in an estate map of 1777. The large field opposite was named Pigeon House Fardel, and was mentioned in a document of 1668.[174] (The site is now absorbed into Langport town). A map of Bristol and its environs published in 1769 has an enlarged inset of the neolithic stone circle at Stanton Drew. The site was described as 'Pidgeon House Close'.[175] A trawl through all the early estate maps of Somerset could perhaps identify other sites of former dovecotes, but it is too massive a task to contemplate.

However, field names are less informative than one might suppose. The largest source of old field names is the comprehensive large-scale survey conducted to administer the 1836 Tithe Commutation Act. Where a dovecote was close to the house or farm buildings the plot is usually identified in the tithe apportionment only as 'Farm House, Bartons, Gardens, etc.' or some similar phrase. Isolated round dovecotes at Selworthy, Henstridge, Norton-sub-Hamdon, West Camel Old Rectory and Bratton Seymour are not even shown on the tithe maps – perhaps because by then they had already fallen out of economic use. An isolated round building at Priory Farm, Stogursey, is shown; although as has been reported, it is not a dovecote now. The isolated square dovecote at Montacute is shown on the tithe map. Neither of these has conferred a name on the plot. The only surviving dovecotes which have given names to their plots are those at Selworthy and West Camel Old Rectory – the former as Dove Cote Orchard, the latter as Pigeons Close.

An engraving published in 1720 by Johannes Kip and Leonard Knyff showed the major mansion of Orchard Portman with its ancillary buildings, gardens and park in detailed perspective. A small cylindrical building on the boundary between an orchard and a paddock was probably a dovecote.[176] Since then the site has been cleared.

According to the guidebook of Somerset Rural Life Museum at Glastonbury, in 1517 the Abbey barn 'still stood in its farmyard by the Abbey precinct, surrounded by a pigsty, a dovecote, a slaughterhouse and 2½ acres of land'.

Horne and others collected some information on dovecotes which were derelict in the 1920s and 1930s, or which had been demolished in recent years:

(1) Langford Manor in the parish of Fivehead, one mile east of Cathanger Manor. A description and two photographs survive, showing it as a roofless ruin. It was rectangular with four gables, 20 x 14½ feet internally; it had about 1,000 nest-holes arranged in regular grid pattern, right up the gables. That is, it was similar in type to the surviving dovecote at Kelston, but rather larger. It was situated at the back of the manor house 'in a line with several out-buildings, stables, etc.' The range is identifiable on the tithe map of 1839, 12 yards east of the manor house, but the dovecote is not separately identified.[177]

(2) Manor Farm, Martock. In 1927 Horne described it as 'built into the later farm buildings . . . the divisions are very solid work of Ham Hill stone. The building is square'. It was demolished in 1931-2 to build a glove factory.

(3) The Manor House (Mallet Court), Curry Mallet. Horne described it as 'an oblong building divided down the centre lengthways, with nest holes in one half only, and in the gable of the House to which it joined … entirely destroyed a few years later, when the owner wished to build kitchens and other offices on the site'.

(4) In 1923 Horne mentioned that there was a dovecote at Chipley Park, Nynehead. Nothing else is known about it.

(5) In 1903 W. H. P. Greswell mentioned 'the remains of an old Columbarium' at East Melcombe in North Petherton.[178] In 1940 Horne searched for the remains, without success.

(6) Horne illustrated an excavated medieval dovecote at Butleigh (figure 190). He wrote that the internal diameter was 15 feet 3 inches, the wall was 3 feet thick, and stood nearly 4 feet high at the highest. The nest-holes were about 7 inches square and 1½ feet deep. Perhaps the most remarkable feature he found was a circular depression in the paved floor, 7 feet 2 inches in diameter and 2 inches deep, drained by a channel through the wall.[179] This resembles the unique dovecote at Garway, Herefordshire, built in 1326 by the Knights Hospitaller. The design seems to have been copied from a dovecote in the Mediterranean region, for the roof is dished to collect rainwater which drained into a central reservoir. This was necessary in the dry summers of that region, but not in Herefordshire.[180]

Figure 190: Horne's photograph of a medieval dovecote at Butleigh, excavated in 1923. By courtesy of the Somerset Archaeological and Natural History Society.

(7) A fragment remains of a late eighteenth-century dovecote at Spargrove Manor, two miles north-north-west of Bruton (ST 672 380). It was 17 feet square, built mainly of stone rubble; only one original wall survives (figure 192). There are 20 nest-holes in two tiers, formed of bricks 9¼ x 4¼ x 2½ inches laid in lime mortar. The lower tier is 5 feet above ground level. The entrances are 5½ inches high by 5 - 6 inches wide. Inside, each nest-hole is box-shaped, 8½ inches high by 10 inches wide, and 13 inches from front to back. They are built into the north wall, 2 feet 2 inches thick. It is 17 yards north-west of the manor house, in a yard with other ancillary buildings.

ARCHAEOLOGICAL EVIDENCE
A medieval dovecote has been excavated at Englishcombe (ST 729 620). It was of Bath stone, had nest-holes 6 - 7 inches square and 1½ feet deep (figure 191). A platform of lias projected one foot from the base of the wall, level with the base of the lowest tier of nest-holes, and a paved floor of lias extended into the porch. It had been roofed with pennant tiles. Probably it was associated with the deserted

Figure 192: The remaining fragment of a dovecote at Spargrove Manor.

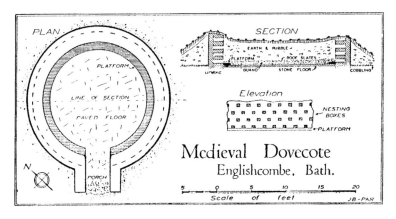

PLAN AND SECTION OF DOVECOTE AT ENGLISHCOMBE
Drawn by P. A. Rahtz from measurements by J. Bolwell

Figure 191: A medieval dovecote at Englishcombe, excavated by Philip Rahtz and J. Bolwell.
From *Medieval Archaeology*, volume 1, 1957, by courtesy of the Society for Medieval Archaeology and
Philip Rahtz.

medieval village of Barewe, which passed to the Crown in 1333. All the pottery sherds found in the immediate vicinity were of twelfth to fourteenth century date.[181]

Another has been excavated by local schoolchildren at Abbey Farm, Montacute (ST 497 168). No record of the excavated evidence has been traced. The site is Scheduled as an Ancient Monument.

At Low Ham in High Ham parish (ST 431 286) the site of a post-medieval dovecote described in 1779 as 'in decay' is marked by a large earthwork mound with a trench round, 32 feet in diameter. A five-acre field named 'Pigeon House' at the same site was recorded in a map of 1823.[182]

At Court Farm, Wookey, the Scheduled site of a medieval palace of the Bishop of Bath and Wells (ST 518 456) includes the remains of a medieval dovecote.

At Barlynch Farm, Dulverton (SS 929 290) there are remains of a medieval dovecote associated with Barlynch Priory.[183]

At West Bower Farm, Durleigh (ST 265 363), R. F. Taylor recorded a seventeenth-century cob dovecote which collapsed in 1967 (figures 193 and 194). His description is summarized below:

It was 28 feet in diameter, and stood 13½ feet high, with a doorway to north-west and a window to south-east. The conical roof was thatched, with a louver and weather-vane.

A plinth of sandstone rubble stood 3 feet high. The cob was made from red clay (not including stones) and chopped straw, built in rises of 1½ to 2½ feet, each allowed to solidify before the next was added. The nest-holes were arranged in grid pattern, and were of reversed-wedge plan, 6 inches square at the entrance, widening out to 10 or 11 inches at the back; from front to back they varied from 15 to 18 inches. Toolmarks showed that they had been cut with a paring-iron 5 inches wide before the cob was fully dry. Originally there were 13 tiers, with 60 in a complete tier, making about 730 originally, of which a few were lost in enlarging the doorway. Each nest-hole had a floor and alighting step of slate, projecting one inch. The whole interior was lime-plastered, the plaster extending 3 inches into the nest-holes.

The unglazed window at the head of the wall was 2½ feet square, with splayed jambs and a steeply sloping sill.

The roof had eight principal rafters, each resting on a wall-plate, with a curved bracket transmitting the thrust to an inner wall-plate and the inner face of the cob. There were two sets of curved purlins canted to the pitch of the roof, mortised into the principals. Four collars linked the principals above the upper purlins.

The louver rested on a circular ring-beam mounted on the principals, and consisted of six uprights supporting a conical thatched roof.[184]

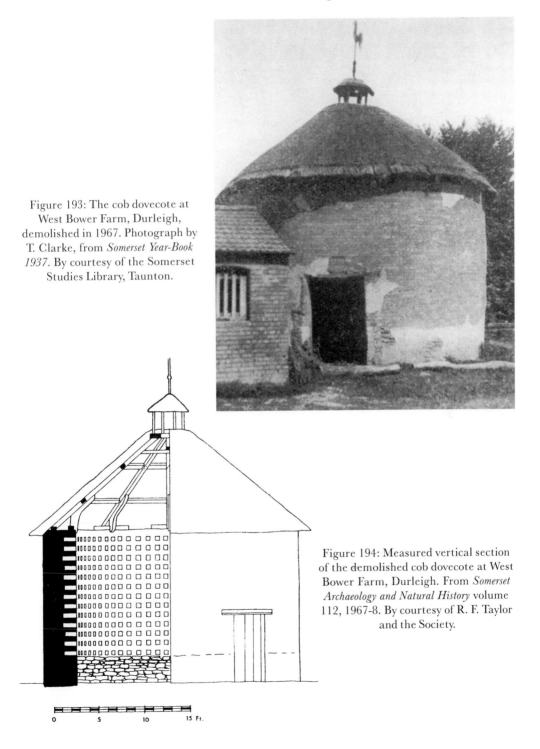

Figure 193: The cob dovecote at West Bower Farm, Durleigh, demolished in 1967. Photograph by T. Clarke, from *Somerset Year-Book 1937*. By courtesy of the Somerset Studies Library, Taunton.

Figure 194: Measured vertical section of the demolished cob dovecote at West Bower Farm, Durleigh. From *Somerset Archaeology and Natural History* volume 112, 1967-8. By courtesy of R. F. Taylor and the Society.

Chapter 9
Documentary Evidence

Where anything relevant to a standing building has been found it has been mentioned in the main text. More often documentary evidence is found of other dovecotes of which nothing else is known. Most early records are concerned only with property and revenue, so they may list a dovecote among other assets, but hardly ever its location. Sometimes they record the rent received, but nothing else about it. The earliest record found of a dovecote in Somerset is a brief mention in the customs of Meare in 1235; and at Newton Plecy a house called Newton Court was recorded in 1274 as having a dovecote and gardens.[185] Even these early records do not show that there were no dovecotes in Somerset earlier.

Medieval stewards' accounts survive only in exceptional circumstances. Sometimes they record the quantity of squabs produced in a particular year, but they hardly ever tell us anything about the building. For instance, at Mark in 1301 the dovecote supplied 146 squabs for the abbey, and in 1313 it supplied 377. At Baltonsborough the dovecote produced over 300 squabs a year in the 1450s. Interesting though this is, we long to know more.

At Baltonsborough in the 1450s the only arable crop on the demesne comprised 'beans for the doves'. At Greinton the dovecote supplied 195 squabs but was damaged in 1303, and was not repaired. At Walton in 1315 the dovecote produced 400 squabs, but by 1330 it was in need of repair. At Ashcroft the dovecote produced up to 360 squabs a year at the beginning of the fourteenth century but was leased in 1326; by 1388 it was ruinous and was not repaired.

An understanding of the economic history of the period can suggest why these dovecotes were not repaired. This was a period when many lords of manors were finding it more economic to lease their demesne land to freemen or former serfs for a reliable annual rent than to operate the land themselves. This gradual changeover began before 1300, but was greatly accelerated by the Black Death of 1348. Wages rose steeply while prices for produce remained low. Some dovecotes were left unrepaired because they were less useful to a tenant than they had been to the lord's own household. Naturally the lord was reluctant to repair a dovecote he no longer needed.

In the Middle Ages some priests had the right to keep pigeons. In some places pigeons were kept within the church, as at Compton Martin in 1606 (page 65). By the seventeenth century many rectors and vicars had purpose-built dovecotes; they still exist at Stanton Drew, Horsington and West Camel (pages 72, 104 and 111).

The following references to dovecotes are extracted from the *Victoria County History of Somerset* and other secondary sources. Those at manors are listed separately from those at parsonages. In each case the volume and page are specified in brackets; a footnote on the page identifies the document concerned, so anyone interested in a particular entry may look it up in national or local archives. Items marked (U) are kindly provided from unpublished material. The *Victoria County History* has yet to cover many parts of the county, so more of this evidence will be published eventually. The entries below are arranged in chronological order:

P.S.A.N.H.S.   The Proceedings of the Somerset Archaeological and Natural History Society, now called *Somerset Archaeology and Natural History*.
S.R.S.   Somerset Record Society
V.C.H.   Victoria County History of Somerset

DOVECOTES AT MANORS

1235-52 The customs of Meare mention the garden and dovecote (C. J. Bond, *Somerset Parks and Gardens, a Landscape History*, Tiverton, 1998, 40).

1274   At Newton Plecy a house called Newton Court was recorded with dovecote and gardens (V.C.H. 6, 286).

1276   In East Coker John de Mandeville is recorded in an inquisition post mortem as having held a house, a garden, dovecotes and a vineyard with 105 acres in the park (R. W. Dunning, as note 104, 27-8).

1281   At Charlton Musgrave the site of the manor house included a dovecote and two fishponds (V.C.H. 7, 173).

1286   At North Petherton a house called Newton Court was recorded with a dovecote and gardens (V.C.H. 6, 286).

1294   At the manor of Upton Noble a court, garden and dovecote were mentioned (V.C.H. 7, 61).

1297   The dovecote at Stogursey was let to farm (V.C.H. 6, 207).

1300   At Greinton the dovecote supplied 195 squabs but was broken in 1303, and apparently not repaired (U).

1301   At Mark the dovecote supplied 146 squabs for the abbey, and 377 in 1313 (U).

1303   At Street 200 ploughloads of stone were used to repair the dovecote (U).

1312   At Butleigh the dovecote was repaired and provided with a lock; in that year it produced 74 squabs (U).

1312   At Walton a dovecote was first recorded, producing 312 squabs, and 400 in 1315 (U).

1317   At Stockland Bristol small tithes were payable on hay, reed beds, hemp, flax, wool, milk, apples, calves, foals, swine, geese, and **doves** (V.C.H. 6, 127).

1320   A dovecote was recorded at Chedzoy manor in North Petherton (V.C.H. 6, 247).

1325   At Chilton Trinity the Hunstile demesne included a dovecote with a house, 1 acre of garden, ½ acre meadow, and 6 acres of wood (V.C.H. 6, 255).

1326   At Ashcott the dovecote produced up to 360 squabs a year (U).

1327   At Hinton St. George the household accounts of Bishop Ralph record pigeons consumed from 3rd to 12th November. The account continues to March 1328 but no more pigeons were consumed (S.R.S. 83, 72-107).

1330	At Walton the dovecote needed repair (U).

1338	At Buckland Priory and preceptory in Durston other buildings included a court or manor house, a bakehouse, a dovecote and garden (V.C.H. 6, 261).

1338	At Durston the demesne of Buckland Priory included a manor house, bakehouse, dovecote and gardens. This was a preceptory of the Knights Hospitallers (V.C.H. 6, 261).

1344	At Mark the mill, dovecote and 23 cows were farmed (U).

1347	At Bridgwater Castle detached buildings included stables, a dovecote and a chapel (V.C.H. 6, 207).

1349	At North Cheriton a dovecote was mentioned (V.C.H. 7, 95).

1351	At the manor of Marsh in Wincanton a dovecote was mentioned (V.C.H. 7, 217).

1353	At Kingsdon a dovecote belonging to the lord of the manor was mentioned (V.C.H. 3, 114).

1362	At the capital manor of Henstridge (not Toomer Manor) the dovecote was ruinous (V.C.H. 7, 115).

1381	The estate of Orchardleigh Park was described as 'a capital messuage with a gaden worth yearly 5s, a dovecote worth yearly 7s, 160 acres of arable land worth 53s 4d price 4d per acre', etc. Therefore the rent from the dovecote was equivalent to the rent of 21 acres of arable land) (C.J. Bond, *Somerset Parks and Gardens, a Landscape History*, Tiverton, 1998, 161).

1388	At Ashcott the dovecote was ruinous and was not repaired (U).

1390s	At Bridgwater Castle the detached buildings included stables, a dovecote and the chapel (V.C.H. 6, 207).

1407	At East Quantoxhead a dovecote was mentioned (V.C.H. 5, 121).

1443	At the main manor at Raddington there was a dovecote at the farm (V.C.H. 6, 139).

1446	At Baltonsborough a dovecote is recorded which produced over 300 squabs a year. The only arable crop was beans for the doves (U).

1454	At Stockland Bristol small tithes were payable as noted in 1317 (V.C.H. 6, 127).

1458	At Walton the dovecote was in hand, and produced 200 squabs (U).

1470s	At Butleigh squabs continued to be sold from the dovecote (U).

1511	At Plainsfield manor in Over Stowey the buildings included the chapel house, pigeon house and gatehouse (V.C.H. 6, 163).

1520s	At Brooke's Court, Ilchester, the property included a dovecote (V.C.H. 3, 185).

1531	20d was spent on making a thorn hedge around a close containing a dovecote in the parish of St. Michael's outside the North Gate, Bath (C.J. Bond, *Somerset Parks and Gardens, a Landscape History*, Tiverton, 1998, 41).

1548	At Montacute the revenues of a half-burgage and a dovecote supported a light in the parish church (V.C.H. 3, 222).

1557	A survey of Wookey mentions 'a barton called Culverhey conteyning oon acre oon fayer large culverhowse upon the same' (S.R.S. 83, 4).

1558	A dovecote was mentioned in the manor of Creech in Creech St. Michael (V.C.H. 6, 23).
1573	At Stockland manor the barn and dovecote were in decay (V.C.H. 6, 127).
1574	At the otherwise deserted manorial site of Stoke Beauchamp, Stoke-sub-Hamdon, the medieval dovecote was still present (V.C.H. 3, 242n)
1576	At Chedzoy Manor in North Petherton the dovecote was held with a field called Court Close, which may have been near Court Farm (V.C.H. 6, 247).
1578	Richard Prater died seized of Nunney Glaston and Nunney Castle, two dovecotes and hereditaments called chantry lands (P.S.A.N.H.S. 22, pt. 2, 93).
1584	At Toomer manor in Henstridge there was a great gate, porch, gatehouse, middle chambers, kitchen and pigeon house (V.C.H. 7, 112).
1598	At Kingsdon the dovecote stood in a field named Culverhay (V.C.H. 3, 114).
1604	At Bruton parts of the church were used as a pigeon house (V.C.H. 7, 35).
1604	At the manor of Charlton Horethorne a dovecote was recorded (V.C.H. 7, 88).
1605	At Williton manor in St. Decumans the house was divided between two heirs in 1388 and regarded as two houses. By 1605 the Fulford part was let with a ruined dovecote (V.C.H. 5, 152).
1606	At Milborne Port the vicarage house comprised a hall, buttery, barn, stall and pigeon house (V.C.H. 7, 153).
1612	The Gilberts' house at Charlton Horethorne may have been demolished; a dovecote was recorded (S.R.S. 67, 141).
1623	George Prater of Nunney Glaston died seized of 2 manors, 40 messuages, 40 cottages, 30 lofts, one dovecote, 100 gardens, 1000 acres of land, 300 acres of meadow, with a mill, woods, and other lands in neighbouring parishes (P.S.A.N.H.S. 22, 95).
1632	At Milton Clevedon John Green reserved for his own use the chamber over the kitchen and summer parlour. There was a dovecote (V.C.H. 7, 45).
1634	At the manor of Court Barton in Huish Episcopi there was a court house, which stood in a field adjacent to a dovecote (V.C.H. 3, 4).
Seventeenth century:	At East Quantoxhead a close named Culverhays was mentioned (V.C.H. 5, 121).
1657	At Stockland the dovecote, standing west of the church belonged to the manor (V.C.H. 6, 127).
1668	At Langport a pigeon house was part of the manors of Langport Eastover and Langport Westover (V.C.H. 3, 23).
1692	A survey of Wookey mentions 'dovecotes' (S.R.S. 83, 105).
1695	Charlton House near Kilmerston (south of Radstock) was described as 'a new built mansion house complete with stable, dovecote and other outbuildings (Atthill, R., *Old Mendip*, 29-30).
1703	At Brymore manor in Cannington, the great storm damaged the house and destroyed the dovecote (V.C.H. 6, 78).

Early eighteenth century:　At Maunsel manor at North Petherton four acres around the house included a dovehouse, stables, barns, gardens, orchards, and a large fishpond with an island (V.C.H. 6, 296).

1755　　A dovecote is recorded at Creech St. Michael, apparently not with a capital messuage (V.C.H. 6, 22).

1765　　At Pitney Lorty manor, Pitney, the dovecote was one of the last copyhold properties (V.C.H. 3, 53).

1773　　At Kingsdon the dovecote mentioned in 1353 and 1598 still stood in a field named Culverhay (V.C.H. 3, 114).

DOVECOTES AT PARSONAGES:

Before 1321:　At St. Decumans the vicarage was endowed with four mills and five dovecotes, before the augmentation of 1321 (V.C.H. 5, 166).

1347　　The rectory of Charlton Horethorne received a small income from a dovecote (V.C.H. 7, 89).

1439　　At Stogumber Rectory the buildings included a dovecote (V.C.H. 5, 180).

1547　　At Stockland Bristol the rectory included a dovecote. In 1657 it was recorded as standing west of the church and being in decay (V.C.H. 6, 127).

1548　　At Ilchester the glebe land and dovecote were together worth only 4 pence (V.C.H. 3, 198).

Early seventeenth century:　At Otterhampton the parsonage house had a detached kitchen, barn, pigeon house and stables. The house burned down in 1623 (V.C.H. 6, 108).

1606　　At Milborne Port the vicarage house comprised a hall, buttery, barn, stable, stall and pigeon house (S.R.S. D/D/Rg 248/2).

1615　　The rectory of Charlton Horethorne included a pigeon house; mentioned again in 1638 and 1639/40 (S.R.O. D/D/Rg 240).

1623　　At North Cheriton the rectory pigeon house had fallen down (V.C.H. 7, 99).

1636　　At Kingstone the rectory buildings included a great court with a pigeon house in it (V.C.H. 3, 205).

1638　　At Spaxton the rectory house was described as a mansion, and its outbuildings included a malt-house, pigeon house, stables, etc. (V.C.H. 6, 122).

1716　　Culver Hill was mentioned in a survey of Wookey (S.R.S. 83, 176).

1783-5　At Aller the rectory had a dovecote (V.C.H. 3, 69).

Glebe terriers record the buildings of the parsonage, sometimes with a brief description of their condition or materials. In Somerset they record dovecotes in 85 out of 363 parishes and chapelries, that is, in 23 per cent of them. (In Norfolk Robin Lucas found that glebe terriers mention ten dovecotes in 700 parishes).[186] All the references to dovecotes are quoted below, in alphabetical order. In some cases the entry is so brief that it mentions only a house 'with outhouses pertaining' or some similar phrase. One may reasonably surmise that a dovecote may have been present even if not specified. In a few cases the entry implies that the dovecote was part of another building. or had already ceased to be used for its original purpose. The glebe terrier of Backwell in 1638 mentions a 'double dovehouse', presumably an oblong building partitioned into two cells by a cross-wall, operated as twin dovecotes.

Alverton 1620-30	the parsonage house with one barne, one dovehouse
Ashcott 1638	one vicarage house with dovehouse, a barne, a hay house, a staule, and stable
Backwell 1638	one double dovehouse
Barwick 1635	one pigeon house apertaining and belonging to the dwelling house
Batcombe 1613	the mansion house of the said parsonage with a dovehouse
Bathealton 1613, 1635	a culverhay meadow
Bishop's Lydeard 1635	one dovehouse
Blagdon 1613	a pigeon house
Blagdon 1638	the yard adjoyning to it called the Culverhay
Bleadon 1636	a dovehouse
Bradford on Tone 1638	a dove howse
Brompton Regis 1571	a dovehouse (but not mentioned in terriers of 1606, 1613, 1639)
Brushford 1640	pidgion house
Camerton 1607	a pidgion house
Charlton Horethorne 1615	one pigeon house
Cheddon Fitzpaine 1626	one pigeon house
Chelworth 1613	pigion house
Chew Magna 1638	one dove house
Chiselborough 1638	one dove house
Churchill 1635	a pigeonhouse covered with thatch or helm
Clapton in Gordano 1606	pigion house
Compton Dundon 1636	a pidgeon house
Compton Martin 1606	a pigeon house over the chauncell (but not mentioned in 1637)
Compton Pauncefoot 1606	a dovehouse
Congresbury 1634	dove house
Crocombe 1638	a pigeon house (but not mentioned in 1606)
Cucklington	a pigeon house
Curry Mallet 1635	a peggeon howse
Doulting 1613	a little close in which the pigeon house stands commonly called Culverhay 1 acre
Doulting 1636	then a pigeon house, standing east and west, on the west side of the bake house, containing two field [bays], tiled

East Coker 1626	one other little room adjoining on the south side which was a pigeon house
Frome Selwood (undated)	a pigeon house
Halse 1634	a dove house
Hardington Mandeville 1571	a dove house
Hardington Mandeville 1638	one dove house with one acre of ground called culver hay
Hemington 1634	a dovehouse
Horsington 1613, 1623	a pigeon house
Huish Champflower 1606	one other house called the culver house
Huntspill 1613	pigeon house (but not mentioned in 1606)
Keinton Mandeville 1634	one stable formerly a culver house
Keynsham 1637	and garden and backside and culverhouse feild
Kingstone 1636	with a dovecote standing in the said courte
Kingweston 1613,1638,1666	pigeon house
Limington 1613	there is also a pigeon house
Luccombe 1614	orchard with a dovehouse
Maperton 1606, 1634, 1639	a pigeon house
Marksbury 1606	and pigion house
Middle Chinnock (undated)	one dove house well furnished with doves
Middle Chinnock 1613	the backside wherein standeth a pigeon house
Midsomer Norton 1637	a pigion house
Milborne Port 1606	a backsyde wherein stands a culver house
Minehead 1606	one pigeon house
Mudford 1634	a dove house
Newton St. Loe 1638	a pigeon house
North Barrow 1613	one other old stall with pigeon house
North Barrow 1639	and dovehouse apart from the dwelling house
North Curry 1634	a dovehouse
North Perrott 1606	a dove house
North Stoke 1606	colver house
Norton Philip 1637	one square court between the saide houses with a dove house
Norton-sub-Hamdon 1613	one little rounde dove house standing in the middest of the upper orchard thereto belonginge
Otterhampton (undated)	a pigeon house (not mentioned 1634)
Pilton 1673	one dovehouse
Portishead 1638	culverhouse close
Poyntington 1634	one pigion house with a garden adjoyning
Rowberrow 1623	a dovehouse
Shepton Beauchamp 1613	a dovehouse
Shepton Mallet (undated)	a culverhay and a dove house therein
Sparkford 1639	a pegion house
Spaxton	one pigeon house

Stanton Prior 1606	one pigion house
Stanton Prior 1638	one dove house
Stocklinch Ottersey 1606	a dovehouse
Stocklinch Ottersey 1613	pydgeon house
Sutton Montague 1606	a pigion house
Timberscombe 1571	dovehouse
Walton in Gordano 1616	culver close
Wellington 1638	one barne with a pigeon house in the end of the said barne
West Bagborough 1613	pigeon house
West Coker 1633	one dovehouse at the west side of the said kitchin
West Harptree c.1630	a dovehouse
West Lydford 1635	one dove house
West Monkton 1620	one dove house
West Monkton 1638	pigeon house
Wookey 1634	a dovehouse
Wooton Courtenay 1614	the culverhays orchard
Worle 1635	one dove house
Wrington 1634	with a dove house att the west end of the said barton thatch [sic]
Yeovilton 1613	one pigeon house and a backside called Culverhouse
Yeovilton 1640	a pigeon house.

Chapter 10
The future of Somerset dovecotes

Most of the dovecotes which existed in 1940 are still present. Nearly all of them are redundant for their original purpose, but that is true of most other historic buildings. As they are usually very near a major house the most satisfactory use for them now is general domestic storage. This does not impose extra strains on the buildings, and gives the owners an incentive to keep the roofs in repair. Some owners go one better, and generously maintain historic dovecotes unused. The worst possible use is residential conversion. Experience in Cambridgeshire and elsewhere has shown that this effectively destroys most of what is historic about these historic buildings. In most cases a proposal to 'preserve' the building by converting it into a dwelling proves to be no more than an attempt to form a new house in a place where it would not be permitted otherwise. Only three of Somerset's dovecotes have been converted into dwellings, only one of these at all recently.

On the vexed question of repair or restoration, the principle of minimum intervention propounded by William Morris in 1877 has proved in the long run to be wise; historic buildings are best conserved by keeping the roofs weatherproof, by supporting them against collapse, but not attempting to replace what is not there.[187] Much good repair work has been done in Somerset on these lines. Even so, original features have been altered inappropriately – such as the 'pipe' at Norton-sub-Hamdon. Horne recorded trap-doors closing off the pigeon exits there and at Kelston; both have gone. At Kelston there was also a wooden lattice in one window, and double doors. These have gone too – perhaps because they were incomplete when found, and were not understood by those who undertook the repairs. We can refer those who propose to repair a dovecote to a helpful article in the *Journal of Architectural Conservation* volume 1 no. 2 (July 1995).

Somerset is extraordinarily fortunate in having so many dovecotes open to the public – Dunster, Stoke-sub-Hamdon, West Bradley, Selworthy and Bruton. We would like to see more dovecotes in private possession opened to the public occasionally as private gardens are opened, and suitably advertised. There is a need for explanatory literature and visual displays at most sites. At most dovecotes – even those in public ownership – there is none at all. The display board exhibited at Dunster still carried a misleading text in 2002.

Above all, authors should be prepared to revise their work in the light of increasing knowledge. The endless repetition of historical fallacies first propounded over a century ago by the pioneers of the subject – who freely confessed that their information was incomplete – should be abandoned. Contemporary source material has always been available, some of it in printed form.[188] Careful study of it has illuminated many areas of confusion. Only more historical research in depth, accompanied by detailed surveys of surviving dovecotes, can extend our understanding of these fascinating buildings.

Notes

The following abbreviations are used below:

P.S.A.N.H.S. Somerset Archaeology and Natural History, the Proceedings of the Somerset Archaeological and Natural History Society

S.R.O.   Somerset Record Office

V.C.H.   *Victoria County History of Somerset*

1   E. Horne, 'Manorial Dovecotes and Fishponds', *The Somerset Year-Book* 1923, 85-9.
     H. Grange, 'Dove-cotes in Somerset', *The Somerset Year-Book* 36, 1937, 81-7.

2   Horne's manuscript notebook is in the Library of the Somerset Archaeological and Natural History Society (adjacent to the Somerset Studies Library, Taunton).
     Somerset and Dorset Notes and Queries 24, 1946, 9.

3   R. S. Ferguson, 'Culverhouses', *Archaeological Journal* 44, 1887, 105-16.

4   M. Berkeley, 'The Dovecotes of Worcestershire', *Reports and Papers of the Associated Architectural Societies* 28 Part 1, 1905-6, and *Home Counties Magazine* 8, 1906, 235 - 40.
     A. O. Cooke, *A Book of Dovecotes*, London and Edinburgh, 1920.

5   At the time of writing John and Jane Penoyre are preparing a book to be called *The Building Stones of Somerset*.

6   Chapter 5, book 6, 115.

7   *Oxford English Dictionary*, 1989.

8   E. E. Viollet-le-Duc, *Dictionnaire Raisonne de l'Architecture*, 1858-68, 3, 484-93.

9   R. F. Johnston and M. Janiga, *Feral Pigeons*, Oxford, 1996, 6-12.

10   C. Dyer, 'English Diet in the Later Middle Ages', T. M. Aston *et al* (eds.) *Social Relations and Ideas*, Cambridge, 1983, 191-216.
     T. Gray (ed.), *Devon Household Accounts*, part 1, xxiii. The Reynell accounts of 1627-8 specifically record that sheep or cattle were slaughtered to feed the household in every month of the year.

11   J. McCann, 'An Historical Enquiry into the Design and Use of Dovecotes', *Transactions of the Ancient Monuments Society* 35, 1991, 92-6.

12   U. Robertson, 'Pigeons as a Source of Food in Eighteenth-Century Scotland', *Review of Scottish Culture* 4, 1988, 89-103.

13   J. McCann, 1991 (as note 11), 93-6.
     C. Woolgar, 'Diet and Consumption in Gentry and Noble Households: A Case Study from around the Wash', *Rulers and Ruled in Late Medieval England* (eds. R. E. Archer and S. Walker), London, 1995, 22.

14   J. M. Ridgard (ed.), *The Household Book of Dame Alice de Bryene*, Suffolk Institute of Archaeology and History, 1984.

15   L. Storr-Best, *Varro: On Farming*, 'Rerum rusticarum', London, 1912, 285.

16   L. M. Munby (ed.), *Early Stuart Household Accounts*, Hertfordshire Record Society, 1986, 5-62 (accounts of Hatfield House).

17   R. Willis and J. W. Clark, *The Architectural History of the University of Cambridge*, Cambridge, 1886, II, 441.

18   L. Mascall, *The Husbandlie ordring and government of Poultrie*, London, 1581, unpaginated.
     Anon., *The Dove-Cote, or, the Art of Breeding Pigeons, a Poem*, London, 1740, 12.

19   R. A. Irwin (ed.), *Letters of Charles Waterton*, London, 1955, 59.

20   R. Bradley, *The Country Gentleman and Farmer's Monthly Director*, London, 1726, 29.

21   J. McCann, 'Dovecotes and Pigeons in English Law', *Transactions of the Ancient Monuments Society* 44, 2000, 43, 34-5. For the first time the Statute of 1603 made it a criminal offence to kill pigeons but any cultivator was entitled to drive them off his crops without killing them.

22   J. Worlidge, *Dictionarium Rusticum et Urbanicum*, London, 1717, unpaginated, under alphabetical heading Pigeons and Doves.
     Anon., 1740 (as note 18), 13-4.

23 R. Bradley (as note 20), xvii.
24 For example, E. Pognon (ed), *Les Tres Riches Heures du Duc de Berry*, Chantilly, France, undated, 18.
25 J. McCann, 2000 (as note 21), 40-1.
26 T. Rudge, *General View of the Agriculture of the County of Gloucester*, London, 1807, 326.
27 U. Robertson, 1988 (as note 12), 100-1.
28 In 1941 W. M. Levi, an American commercial breeder, wrote; 'It is a problem to dispose of these old birds . . . The price paid for such birds is so small that it hardly warrants the breeder to figure on an income from them'. *The Pigeon*, Columbia S. C., 1941, 184.
29 T. Tusser, *Five Hundred Pointes of Good Husbandrie*, English Dialect Society edition, London, 1878, 77.
    J. Worlidge, *Systemae Agriculturae*, London, 1669, 67.
    Anon., 1740 (as note 18), 16.
30 M. S. Guiseppi, *Victoria County History of Surrey* 2, 1920, 306-9.
31 J. Moore, *Columbarium: or, the Pigeon-House*, London, 1735, 24.
32 C. Waterton, *Essays on Natural History, chiefly ornithology*, London, 1839, 244.
33 Anon., *The Sportsman's Diary, or the Country Gentleman's Companion in all Rural Recreations*, London, 1735, unpaginated, alphabetical heading - Pigeon-house.
34 St. John Priest, *General View of the Agriculture of Buckinghamshire*, London, 1810, 39.
35 J. McCann, 2000, (as note 21), 25-34.
36 C. Northcote Parkinson, *Parkinson's Law, or the Pursuit of Progress*, London, 1958, 89-100.
37 J. McCann, 2000 (as note 21), 35-6. The case is Dewell v. Sanders.
38 A. Standish, *The Commons Complaint*, London, 1611, 11-14. For this reference we are grateful to Joan Thirsk.
39 J. McCann, 1991 (as note 11), 99-101.
40 G. White, *The Natural History of Selborne*, London, 1788, letter 44 of November 1780.
41 H. Colvin and J. Newman (eds.) *Of Building: Roger North's Writings on Architecture*, Oxford, 1981, 101.
42 Public Record Office, sc6/869/8. For this passage we are grateful to Dr. Mark Bailey of Gonville and Caius College, Cambridge.
43 H. Gill and E. L. Guilford (eds.), *The Rector's Book, Clayworth, Notts.*, Nottingham, 1910, 37. The passage is reproduced in full in J. McCann, 1991 (as note 11), 138. For this reference we are grateful to Dr. David Dymond of Bury St. Edmunds.
44 Colvin and Newman, 1981 (as note 41), 100-3.
45 J. Laurence, *A New System of Agriculture*, London, 1726, 153-4.
46 R. Armitage, B. West and K. Steadman, 'New Evidence of the Black Rat in Roman London', *The London Archaeologist* 4, 1984, 375-83.
    J. Rackham, '*Rattus rattus*; The Introduction of the Black Rat into Britain', *Antiquity* 53, 1979, 112-20.
47 J. McCann, 'The Influence of Rodents on the Design and Construction of Farm Buildings in Britain, to the mid-nineteenth century', *Journal of the Historic Farm Buildings Group* 10, 1996, 1-3 and 24.
48 S.R.O. D/P/Hors. 4/1/1.
49 J. McCann, 1996 (as note 47), 2 and 10-28.
50 J. M. Stratton, *Agricultural Records, 220 - 1968*, London, 1969.
    J. Billingsley, *General View of the Agriculture of the County of Somerset*, London, 1798, 150.
51 J. C. Loudon, *An Encyclopaedia of Agriculture*, London, 1825, 1048.
52 J. McCann, 2000 (as note 21), 40-1.
53 W. Trotter, 'Essay on the Rearing and Management of Poultry', *Journal of the Royal Agricultural Society* 12 (first series), 1855, 196.
54 C. Waterton, 1839 (as note 32), 245-6.
55 R. S. Ferguson, 'Pigeon Houses in Cumberland' *Transactions of the Cumberland and Westmorland Antiquarian and Archaeological Society* 9, 1888, 415n.

57   A. O. Cooke (as note 4), 222-3.
58   Personal communication from M. McGarvie, 20-12-99.
59   W. Gill, 'Some Notes on an Old Building at Witham', *Proceedings of Bath Natural History and Antiquarian Field Club* 10, 1905, 14-6.
60   C. A. Hewett, *English Historic Carpentry*, Chichester, 1980, 263-6.
61   R. A. Croft, *Dunster Dovecot, Archaeological Investigation*, Somerset County Council, 1989.
62   M. McCormick, *The Dunster Dovecote*, undated. Last reprinted 1994.
63   Anon., *A Short Guide to the Parish Church of Saint Julian, Wellow*, 1993, and *Dictionary of National Biography*.
64   V.C.H. 3, 238-9, and the National Trust booklet sold on site.
65   'Established by Abbot Michael of Amesbury, 1235-52; re-furbished by Abbot Adam of Sodbury, 1323-34'; further work by Abbot John Chinnock 1375-1420' (from the Listed Building report).
66   The wing of Birdcombe Court, Wraxall, and no. 20, Vicars' Close, Wells (J. and J. Penoyre, 'Somerset Dendrochronology Project, Phase 3, *P.S.A.N.H.S.* 142, 1999, 311-5). Both examples are in houses of high quality, with more elaborate bracing than this dovecote, but otherwise they exhibit similar carpentry features.
      M. J. Worthington, *Interim Summary of Somerset Tree-ring Dating for 200/3*
67   Report by E. H. D. Williams, February 1977, deposited in S.R.O., and N. Pevsner, *The Buildings of England: South and West Somerset*, London, 1958, 336.
68   N. Pevsner (as note 65), 338.
69   The original is in private ownership in Australia. We are grateful to Derek Maclaren for providing a transcript.
70   G. Marshall, 'The Discovery of a Columbarium in the Tower of Sarnesfield Church, Herefordshire', *Transactions of the Woolhope Society*, 1904, 262-3. His drawing, and a photograph of another at Collingbourne Ducis, Wiltshire, are reproduced in J. McCann, 2000 (as note 21), 28.
71   N. Pevsner, *The Buildings of England: North Somerset and Bristol*, London, 1958, 174.
72   J. McCann, 2000 (as note 21), figure 3.
73   J. McCann, M. McDermott, and F. Pexton, 'A Columbarium at Compton Martin Church', *P.S.A.N.H.S.* 143, 2001, frontispiece.
74   S.R.O. D/D/Rg 32/2.
75   C. Trask, *Norton-sub-Hamdon*, Taunton, 1898, 57-8.
76   *P.S.A.N.H.S.* 67, xliii.
77   S.R.O. as listed on pages 222-5.
78   In the possession of the owner.
79   D. H. Miles and M. J. Worthington, 'Somerset Dendrochronology Project - Phase Four', *Vernacular Architecture* 31, 2000, 108.
80   V.C.H. 3, 135-6.
81   J. Fleming, H. Honour and N. Pevsner, *The Penguin Dictionary of Architecture*, London, 1980, 17.
82   S.R.O. DD/Rg 36. For this reference we are grateful to Colin Brett.
83   From a loose sheet enclosed in Horne's notebook (as note 2).
84   *The Somerset Year-Book* 1937, 85-6.
85   The dovecote at Newton-in-the-Willows is illustrated in J. McCann, 1991 (as note 11), figures 17 and 18. The dovecote at Eriswell is described and illustrated in *The Dovecotes of Suffolk* (as note 119), 100-3, plates 12a and 12b, and figure 39.
86   From 'Cathanger in Fivehead', notes prepared for Mrs. J. Clarke by Robin Bush when he was Deputy County Archivist. The reference of the i.p.m. is C.142/334/63. We are grateful to Mrs. Clarke for this information.
87   V.C.H. 7, 112.
88   S.R.O. T/PH/Ti Henstridge.
89   J. McCann, 2000 (as note 21), 28-9, 34.
90   S.R.O. D/D/Rg. 246/2-3.
91   J. A. Cross, *A History and Guidebook of Horsington*, Wincanton, undated, 19.

92   J. Edgar and R. Iles, 'Kelston Village, Manor House and Garden Remains, *Bristol Archaeology Research Group Review* 2, 1981, and *Dictionary of National Biography*, 1269-71.
     ? N. Pevsner, 1958 (as note 69), 208.
93   S.R.O. DD/Pt H/452.
94   E. D. Foxcroft, 'Notes on Hinton Charterhouse', *P.S.A.N.H.S.* 41, 1895, 92-8.
     N. Pevsner, 1958 (as note 69), 204-6.
97   *The Gentleman's Magazine*, 15 December 1813 (supplement).
98   S.R.O. DD/Rg 138/2.
99   Monuments Protection Programme Dovecote Assessment of English Heritage. Sir Henry Rolle recorded a judgement on dovecotes which has been cited in court in the twentieth century. J. McCann, 2000 (as note 21), 42.
100 S.R.O. DD/SG 41.
101 S.R.O. T/PH/Ti Shapwick and DD/SG 36.
102 *The Somerset Year-Book 1937*, 86.
103 We are grateful to Klara Spandl of the Oxford Archaeological Unit for comparative information.
104 *Country Life*, 1 November 1908, 705.
     J. Collinson, *History of Somerset*, volume I, London, 1791, 81.
     C. J. Bond, *Somerset Parks and Gardens*, Tiverton, 1998, 155.
     R. W. Dunning, *Some Somerset Country Houses*, Wimborne, 1998, 66-71.
105 V.C.H. 3, 160.
106 S.R.O. DD/H/452, box 42.
107 P. and J. Hansell, *Doves and Dovecotes*, Bath, 1988, 126.
     V.C.H. 7, 54.
108 The subject of ritual (or apotropaic) markings has been explored by Timothy Easton. Some comprise geometrical designs of intersecting circles; they were intended to invoke spiritual protection for buildings and stored crops. They occur in buildings of the sixteenth to eighteenth centuries. 'Ritual Marks on Historic Timber', *Weald and Downland Open Air Museum*, Spring 1999, 22-8.
109 P. and J. Hansell, *Doves and Dovecotes*, Bath, 1988, 171.
110 A characteristic of this stone noted by Jenefer Chesher at a workshop of the Somerset Vernacular Building Research Group, 25 May 2002. We are grateful to Jenefer Chesher for the observation.
111 *The Somerset Year-Book 1937*, 85.
112 S.R.O. DD/AL 14.
113 V.C.H. 3, 214.
114 J. C. Loudon, 1825 (as note 51), 1050.
115 V.C.H. 3, 102-3.
116 J. McCann, 1991 (as note 11), 124.
117 Wichenford Court, Worcestershire, which is open to the public. They are illustrated in McCann, 1991 (as note 11), figure 26.
118 Conway Library 687/21 (16), Courtauld Institute, London. For this reference we are grateful to Michael O'Connor.
119 A Lady (J. Austen), *Sense and Sensibility*, London, 1811, vol. II, 140.
120 V.C.H. 4, 233.
121 V.C.H. 4, 158-9, 164.
122 *The Somerset Year-Book 1937*, 84.
123 J. McCann, *The Dovecotes of Suffolk*, Suffolk Institute of Archaeology and History, Ipswich, 1998, plates 12a and 12b, 100-3. A medieval chapel at Old Prebendal House, Crocket Lane, Empingham, was converted into a dovecote in 1619 (dated by inscription).
124 C. R. B. Barrett, *Somersetshire: Highways, Byways and Waterways*, London, 1894, 109.
125 V.C.H. 7, 25.
126 P. Couzens, *Bruton in Selwood*, Sherborne, 1968, 47-9.
127 *P.S.A.N.H.S.* 59, 29.
128 R. Dunning, 1991 (as note 92), 55-60.

129   V.C.H. 6, 147.
130   S.R.O. DD/AH 66/11,12, large-scale plans by Richard Croomer of Bridgwater.
131   R. Dunning, 1991 (as note 92), 59.
132   V.C.H. 7, 171-3.
133   Anon., 1740 (as note 18), 5-8.
134   *The Somerset Year-Book* 1937, 86.
135   V.C.H. 5, 131-5.
136   Queen Victoria's poultry house at Windsor was illustrated in the Journal of the Royal Agricultural Society, volume 12 (first series), 1851, 162, and elsewhere. It includes an octagonal pigeon tower. Ornamental doves are shown in the foreground and perching on the roof.
137   A. O. Cooke (as note 4), 223-4.
138   S.R.O. T/PH/Ti Stogursey.
139   Personal communication from Penelope Walker, 7 September 2001. The other winter bee-house in Somerset is at Lower Cockhill Farm, Castle Cary.
140   J. Fearnley-Whittingstall, *Historic Gardens*, 1990, 63-4.
141   J. McCann, 1998 (as note 121).
142   J. McCann, 1998 (as note 121), 42-6, 76-8.
      J. McCann, 'Two More Dovecotes in Suffolk', *Proceedings of the Suffolk Institute of Archaeology and History*, forthcoming (in 2002).
143   Anon., 1740 (as note 18), 6.
144   Colvin and Newman, 1981 (as note 41), 101.
145   A useful rule of thumb is that the age of a deciduous tree in years is roughly equal to the girth in inches, measured at chest height.
146   Colvin and Newman, 1981 (as note 41), 103.
      J. McCann, 1991 (as note 11), 143-5.
147   Colvin and Newman, 1981 (as note 41), 102.
148   In Essex and Suffolk, where there is little building stone, there is a continuous native tradition from the fifteenth century of using brick for prestigious buildings. (There are a few twelfth-century brick buildings too, but these may be by imported craftsmen). The bricks used at Fairfield were probably brought from Bridgwater, still a town mainly of brick.
149   R. F. Taylor, 'A cob dovecote at Durleigh (near Bridgwater)', *P.S.A.N.H.S.* 112, 1968, 101-3.
150   J. Laurence, 1726 (as note 45), 153. Earthen buildings in Northamptonshire are not described as cob, a West Country word. The local word is mud. J. McCann, *Clay and Cob Buildings*, Princes Risborough, 1995, 17-20.
151   L. Keefe, *The Cob Buildings of Devon: 2 Repair and Maintenance*, Devon Historic Buildings Trust, 1993, 2-3.
152   *The Dovecotes of Suffolk* (as note 119), 110.
      D. C. Bailey and M. C. Tindall, 'Dovecotes of East Lothian', *Transactions of the Ancient Monuments Society* 11, 1963, 27.
153   Colvin and Newman, 1981 (as note 41), 101.
154   *The Sportsman's Diary* (as note 33).
155   D. Girton, *The New and Complete Pigeon Fancier*, London, 1785, 33-4.
156   Others are described in *The Dovecotes of Suffolk*, and in J. McCann, 'Two More Dovecotes in Suffolk', forthcoming (as note 140).
157   J. McCann, 1991 (as note 11), 101-7.
158   We are grateful to Barbara Bowes for this example.
159   J. McCann, 1991 (as note 11), figure 26, 139.
160   *The Sportsman's Diary* (as note 33).
161   A. Standish, 1611 (as note 38), 12.
162   J. McCann, 'The Dovecote Turret of Hadleigh Deanery', *Proceedings of the Suffolk Institute of Archaeology and History* 40, 2001, Part 1, 27, 29.
161   R. S. Ferguson, 1888 (as note 55), 421.
164   Observed at volcanic cliffs on the south-east coast of Madeira, Spring 1993.

165 Colvin and Newman, 1981 (as note 41), 103.

166 Bailey and Tindall, 1963 (as note 150), 27, 30, 36.

167 J. McCann, 1996 (as note 47), 2-3, 10.

168 W. Johnson (ed.), *The Journals of Gilbert White*, London, 1931, 300.

169 L. S. V. Venables and P. H. Leslie, 'The Rat and Mouse Population of Corn Ricks, *Journal of Animal Ecology* I, 1942, 67.
     R. A. Davis, *Control of Rats and Mice*, H.M.S.O., 1970, 22-3.

170 See Note 110.

172 J. Hillam, *Dendrochronology; Guidelines on producing and interpreting dendrochronological dates*, English Heritage, undated, 8, 10-2 (available from English Heritage, free).

173 A. Standish, 1611 (as note 38), 14.

174 S.R.O. DD/SAS c.549 and V.C.H. 3, 23 (see page —).

175 S.R.O. DD/SAS c.844.

176 J. Kip and L. Knyff, *Britannia Illustrata*, London, 1720, I, 76.

177 From Horne's notebook (as note 2), the National Buildings Record Centre, *P.S.A.N.H.S.* 71, 1925, 34, and S.R.O. T/PH/Ti Fivehead.

178 W. H. P. Greswell, *The Forests and Parks of the County of Somerset*, Taunton, 1903, 46-7.

179 *Somerset and Dorset Notes and Queries* 18, 25.

180 J. Webb, 'Notes upon a Preceptory of the Templars at Garway', *Archaeologia* 31, 1846, 182-7. His measured drawings are reproduced in J. McCann, 1991 (as note 11), figure 6, 113.

181 *Medieval Archaeology* 1, 1957, 169.

182 M. Aston, 'Gardens and Earthworks at Hardington and Low Ham, Somerset', *P.S.A.N.H.S.* 122, 1978, 23.

183 H. Riley and R. Wilson-North, *The Field Archaeology of Exmoor*, London, 2001, 109-11. For this and the previous reference we are grateful to Stephen Croad.

184 R. F. Taylor, 1968 (as note 141).

185 V.C.H. 6, 286.

186 Personal communication, 5 October 1994. '**Rectory** or **Vicarage** . . . are both misleading terms which are better applied to the whole living. For that reason, the equally venerable and less troublesome word **parsonage** is preferred'. David Dymond, 'The Suffolk Parsonage: a Documentary Study', *Eavesdropper* no 24, Summer 2003.

187 From the Manifesto with which William Morris founded the Society for the Protection of Ancient Buildings in 1877.

188 For instance, Ferguson disregarded Bishop Swinfield's detailed household accounts of 1291-2, published by the Reverend J. Webb in 1855 (as note 167). They would have made clear to him that fresh meat was eaten (by the wealthy) all the year round. Similarly, he disregarded the only couplet in Thomas Tusser's farming calendar of 1577 which mentioned a dove-house – although he quoted a less relevant couplet about dried fish – and Varro's statement (page 22, note 15). Among more recent work, see U. Robertson, 1988 (as note 12), J. McCann, 1991 (as note 11), and C. Woolgar, 1995 (as note 13). These studies were undertaken separately and without knowledge of each other, but came to similar conclusions.